I KNOW
My Way
MEMOIR

⠠⠊ ⠠⠅⠝⠕⠺ ⠍⠽ ⠺⠁⠽

Always Remember
to Color the Sky Blue

Theresa Marafito
with Linda Odubayo Thompson

Publisher: Linda Odubayo Thompson, 3-6 Steven Drive, Ossining, NY 10562
Editor: Pedro Odubayo Thompson, CCE, CTP, Revayo36@gmail.com

Author/Publisher: Linda Odubayo Thompson, 3-6 Steven Drive, Ossining, NY 10562

E-Mail: linda@ghostbookwritergoldilocks.com
Author Website: www.ghostbookwritergoldilocks.com

Editor: Pedro Odubayo Thompson, CCE, CTP, Revayo36@gmail.com
Cover/Interior Design by: Fusion Creative Works, fusioncw.com

For information about special discounts available for bulk purchases, sales promotions, fund-raising and educational needs, contact Linda Odubayo Thompson, linda@ghostbookwritergoldilocks.com

First Edition

Hard cover laminate ISBN: 978-1-7322096-2-6
Hard cover dust jacket ISBN: 978-1-7322096-1-9
Soft cover ISBN: 978-1-7322096-0-2

Dedication

This memoir is dedicated to our Mother, Theresa (Terry) Marafito, and all the lives she has touched; family, friends and her beloved commuters for over fifty years.

To those who are partially-sighted or totally blind, she shows by example that with a little humor and a lot of "guts" nothing in life is impossible.

Contents

Foreword   7

Part 1: My Early Years 1933–1945   9

Part 2: Coming of Age 1945–1948   33

Part 3: The Apron Strings Become Untied! 1949–1953   53

Part 4: Love and Marriage 1954–1956   77

Part 5: Soon the Stork Will Make a Delivery!   101

Part 6: "There's No Place like Home!"   119

Part 7: Memories of an Unusual Play Time Activity!   143

Part 8: Our "Coming Out" Party in the Community   159

Part 9: One Moment in Time Changed My Life Forever!   173

Part 10: Two Weeks Spent at a Special Summer Camp   203

Part 11: Stand by Your Man! It Happened in the Spring of 1966   217

Part 12: Hurrah for Us, My Jerry Had the Midas Touch!   235
         The Golden Years Began in 1967

Part 13: Would My Faith in God See Me Through, Yet Again?   261
         The Year of Our Lord, 1970

Part 14: The Four Day Squeeze!   283

Part 15: Where There Is Death There Are New Beginnings!   303

Part 16: 1986, the Year My Perfect World Crashed and Burned!   321
         Would I Ever Recover from This Terrible Loss?

Part 17: Look! There's a Ray of Sunshine Peeking   341
         Through the Storm Clouds! 1987–2002

Part 18: Ashes to Ashes, Dust to Dust March 18, 2008   371

Afterword   383

Recognitions   389

Acknowledgements   391

About the Co-Author   393

Foreword

It was Shakespeare who penned, "What's in a name?" In my case, not much. Check though, you might with the American Society of Composers, Authors, and Publishers (ASCAP) or the latest listing of Who's Who in a given genre, I guarantee you won't find it listed. My name has never appeared on any sports pages, nor has a disc of mine been played on any of the rock radio stations out there. So, you might ask, "Where does this broad get off writing a funky narrative about herself, there's got to be something about her..." there is. I'm blind right now, and I was born partially sighted. In the following pages, you will learn how my world went dark. Here is another thing, unless you live next door to one of my kind, you don't really understand our disability.

All the men you've seen on the movie or television screen, who were they? Beggars? Musicians? Geniuses? What about athletes? There are tens of millions of visually impaired or totally blind men across this land who aren't any of these.

Now, let's look at the typical blind woman as portrayed on the screen. Primarily, they look pretty, and they act intermittently helpless and prissy. You see blind women sitting on a couch with their trusted white cane by their side, and when they actually get up to go to another room in their house or apartment, they can't manage without their white helper. The one place that visually impaired or blind people know the best is every inch of their home, and they certainly don't need that crutch.

Just test this assumption by gathering a group of sighted and visually impaired or blind individuals and turn out the lights. Who would manage better in their surroundings, the sighted or visually impaired people? Those who were sighted would probably feel very lost and disoriented, right? Try it out for yourself and see how you fare!

Although I would not presume to speak for all the rest, I hope that through meeting me, my family, and my friends, you'll come to know all of us just a little better.

PART 1

My Early Years 1933—1945

Chapter 1

"What Is This Thing Called Love?"
Cole Porter, musical "Wake Up and Dream"

Convex lenses, oversized pencils and crayons, thick-ruled oaktag, a green medical clinic card, and a radio, these were the tokens that propelled me across the game board of life during my first eleven years. Along the way, there would be a few free rides on the "Reading Railroad," innumerable orange "Chance" cards, and my own fair share of forfeits in the real-world Monopoly game of life.

Yet, I was rich, not with the sort of wealth that could be folded away in a wallet, but with an inheritance that was nonetheless very real. My parents seemed to have an everlasting fountain of love, which would gush forth daily for our family and those who would grace our humble apartment in the Bronx, New York. As for me, the very special friendship that I had with my Sister Helen would endure for a lifetime.

At a time when our country was digging its way out of a crippling depression, I laid claim to the richest legacy of all, for I was loved! My parents accepted my visual handicap, as they did my Sister Margaret's mental illness. They saw it as the "will of God," and to their simple way of looking at it, they had been chosen (not cursed) because they would, with the help of God, have the strength and courage to do what was best for both of us.

Aside from this, I am sure they felt that my suffering and theirs would be short-lived. After all, the doctor had assured them that two simple surgical procedures on my eyes would leave me as good as new. In fact, it took a lot more than were predicted, but with each of the thirteen that followed, my parents felt that surely this last one would totally restore my sight.

This period of their lives must have been devastating, for by the time I was four years old, they had come to the slow realization that one of my eyes would be left in total darkness while the other would only be blessedly equipped with precious-little usable vision. Aside from this, they had made the heart-breaking decision to commit my Sister Margaret to a state-run institution for the intellectually disabled. Never again would she return home to live a normal life with those who loved her. My parents were strong and hearty immigrants from Ireland, but we wondered how much they could absorb before completely breaking down under the continued strain.

Caught in the midst of all this was my Sister Helen, who was five years older and outwardly and inwardly completely normal. That she grew to be a happy, adjusted child now seems incredible, since in those early years, she surely must have felt lost in the shuffle.

To my recollection, Helen never complained when she could not have a pair of roller skates like her friends who frequented the local roller rink. Helen would say that she would be happy just watching them, and they wanted to have her by their side. So they would say, "Come on Helen, you can borrow our skates, and we'll have races!" Instead the money for roller skates was used to buy a piano for me. "All those type of children," advised our neighbor, Mrs. Murphy, "are blessed with musical talent. You'll see. You just prop her up there on that stool, and someday she'll be playing to an enthusiastic audience in Carnegie Hall." God must not have been in a very "giving" mood in my case, and our neighbors must have had second thoughts as the sound of sour notes and failed attempts to play a five-fingered chord boomed through their apartment walls.

By most economic standards, my family would have been considered poor, and yet, I never thought of it that way, perhaps because everyone in our neighborhood seemed to be too. If there were families receiving Home Relief checks, no one was the wiser, for work was sacred and indolence, intolerable. But there was no fear in our ranks, and seldom were any of the doors locked against intruders in apartment houses in the Bronx.

No one had to be alone, and they couldn't be if they tried, since life revolved around an open air shaft and a shared telephone in the building. My Mother Mary would yell down the air shaft, "Does anyone have any extra sugar?" and another tenant would yell back, "Will a cup do?" Mom would reply with her cute Irish brogue, "Ah that would be a fine thing!"

Another day the air shaft chatter would center around that poor blind girl, "She's a bright little thing," we would hear them say of me, "but so very shy." And I suppose my Mother strained to believe on both scores, while within our own four walls she was surely praying for a blessed moment of silence. Our five-room railroad flat on the third floor, so called because all the rooms from front to back were lined up behind each other, was my castle. In these familiar surroundings, the docile lamb turned into a precocious, hell-raising monster whose sole aim in life was doing all that was in her power to ensure that "her will" would be done.

The attention that I received from my Sister Helen was a real thing called "love." She would say, "Come on, pest. I'm gonna take you to the movies, but you'd better swear to button it up and be quiet 'cause it's Mrs. Miniver!" this was the hot new flick at that time. Right away I stated, "You know me, Helen, I'm always good. Just get me some bubble gum and…" and Helen countered, "Nothin' doing. You know what Mama said about that."

Once inside the theatre, after subjecting Helen to several changes in our seating arrangement, my wails of "Can't see over that lady's hat," and six trips to the bathroom, I finally slumped back in my seat, acknowledging temporary defeat. Three hours later, Helen nudged me and asked, "Hey, how come you're so quiet?" impishly, I replied, "Well, maybe I'm just trying to be good, as promised." But as the last words were spoken, a huge wad of gum spurted out of my mouth. She screamed, "Where did you get that?" to this day, I can recall the look on her face: it was priceless! My response was, "Not giving it up and you can't make me, since it took the better part of three hours to scrape it off the bottom of my seat!" you are probably saying "yuk" at this revelation.

Stubbornness was always a part of my persona despite the odds that were against me moving forward in my life. The following Christmas I was the reluctant recipient of a lovely doll from Cousin Katie. This was not just any doll, and certainly unusual in our part of town, for it had real hair, moving eyes, and individually set plastic teeth. I didn't care. I hated dolls and had little patience trying to imagine they were sucking on their bottles or loudly crying because they needed to be changed. Helen, on the other hand, adored them all, so after dutifully thanking my Cousin, I surrendered it to "Mother" Helen.

My new dentist kit was much more to my liking. What I wanted was action and games similar to those that my next-door neighbor Billy had, complete with squadrons of battleships pumping torpedoes into the heart of ships manned with those sneaks from the "Land of the Rising Sun." Those were more my speed! Although Helen condescended to humor me by subjecting herself and "Susie" to several cleanings and drillings, she soon tired of it and I was alone in my fully equipped dental laboratory. Eventually I asked myself, why not? No one will ever notice. The fact that they did notice is an understatement! You see, I had to lock myself in the bathroom, the nearest room of refuge at the moment. The whole apartment building heard Helen scream, "What's wrong with that kid?" she found her beloved doll Susie, surrounded by twelve of the neatest extractions in the history of dental surgery. It is a wonder that she decided to let me live to see another day.

This stunning green/white "Irish Blessing" plate graced the parlor wall of Theresa's family apartment in the Bronx, New York. Similar plates were displayed in the homes of other Irish families.

Chapter 2

"I See Your Face Before Me"
Guy Lombardo

One day on the many trips across town via two trolleys to the clinic, my Mother asked the eye doctor, "Is she going to be able to see better?" sighing he answered, "Not very much of an improvement can be expected, frankly, Mrs. McDonald." One look at my Mother's face made me want to cry out, "He's wrong, Mama, I can see a lot and I'll prove it." In those days, the big "E" chart with its fuzzy numbers and swimming lines was very much a part of my life, as were the ugly machines with their ice-cold chin rests and their creepy purple lights. These doctors didn't know what they were talking about with their numbers and measurements. Who cared if I couldn't see that dumb letter up there without getting practically on top of it? The ball that I bounced in the playground or on the city streets wasn't twenty feet away, nor was the food in my dish or the dial on my radio. I could see all of them "just as well" as anyone else.

One hot afternoon in July when I was about six, after we sat for four hours in a stuffy waiting room, my Mother looked particularly haggard and drawn, and I vowed that I would find some way to cheer her up. Since that stupid chart seemed to mean so much to everyone, I decided that I'd fool them at their own game. There might be something that I could do to make her smile and look happy again.

So, while she was detained with the trio of doctors pondering my case, I sneaked over to the chart, and committed each line of letters to memory. When, finally, I was asked to step up to the line, the performance I gave should have won me an Oscar. I had decided beforehand that to carry it off, my recovery of sight could not be too sudden. The docs would be sure to catch on. Slowly and haltingly, I went through the motions each time we went to this clinic. A few months later, I could be heard saying, "Oh, yeah, now I see that bottom line—uh, I think it says PQRNWVT. How's that?"

My Mother's reaction was quite unexpected. She started to bawl and then kissed me and hugged me until I thought my ribs would break! "She'll make out all right," one doctor explained. Another continued, "You don't have to worry about her."

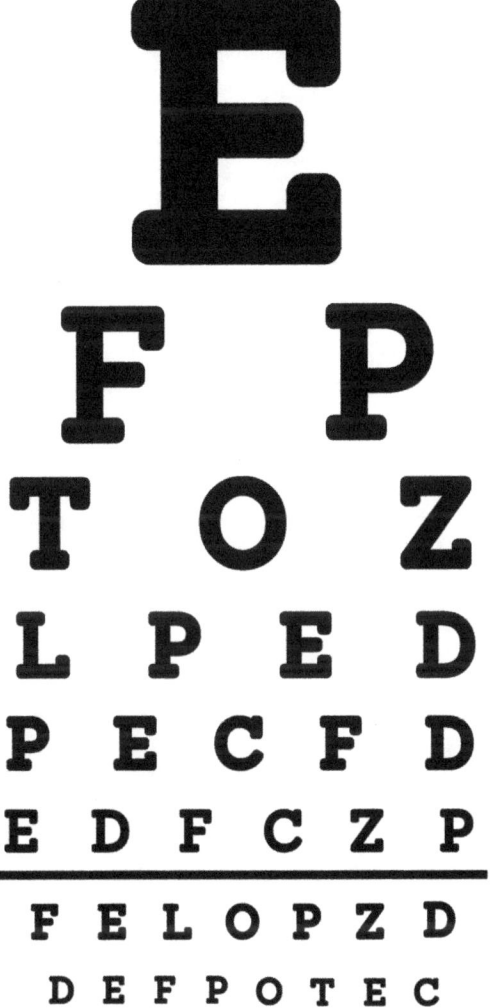

We all recognize this diagnostic tool that's supposed to measure what a patient can see at a distance of 20 feet. In the last two decades or so, this chart went high-tech. A camera now flashes one line at a time on a blank white wall. With a tap of a button and the images gone waiting for its next patient.

Chapter 3

"Little Lady Make Believe"
Eddie Cantor

The time had come when decisions had to be made about my schooling, and long were the hours when I could hear my parents mulling over the options. My Mother was heard saying, "The man from that residential school told me that if we didn't send her away, we'd be doing her the greatest injustice of her life." "Send me away?" I would scream inwardly. "You can't do that to me!" "Yet," continued my Mother. "There she would be a blind child, and might forget how to use the vision she has." "That a girl, Ma. You're on my side," I muttered, and hugged my pillow with joy.

If one is to believe in miracles, and my folks were among that number, the answer came in the form of a notice from a program known as the Sight Conservation Teaching Service of New York. My parents explained to me, "Theresa, you can go to school right nearby at P.S. 43. You'll be in a special class for a few periods a day. The teacher will help you to learn how to type and read from books with larger type." I wasn't sure whether this different type of class would work for me because it wasn't necessary to have those ugly books and fat pencils. Didn't they know that, if anything, those tools made it harder to focus because the eye had to move up and down those thick letters and numbers instead of zeroing in on small block letters! Still it was better than being sent away.

Besides, I had just about completed a self-imposed crash course in the gentle art of "bluffing." As far as I was concerned, no one had to know I couldn't see just like anyone else, and I decided that the only remedy was to do my very best to try to fool all of the people all of the time. Since early childhood, I had never permitted myself the luxury of falling, since I was sure that it would be said that it was because I could not see. I therefore became an observer and never plunged forward without first sizing up the battleground.

Also, I tried never to stare at anything for more than a second, primarily because said action was physically impossible. A lateral movement of the eye back and forth is called Nystagmus, and that was my issue. So, the net result was that when I focused on one person's face, I actually saw the features of a person next to them. This made things complicated for me, and rather than have people wondering what was wrong with me, I decided never to give them that much chance to question what was happening.

I did try to take part in neighborhood games, principally because Helen dragged me downstairs with her. But with sunlight and shadows darting across my visual spectrum, I never could run fast enough or play hide and seek. I was always the first one out! One day, Helen decided that it was time I learned how to jump rope. After I missed a few times, she appeared beside me and whispered, "Listen to when you hear the rope hit the ground; then just jump in." It worked! It sure did, although it took about an hour to make it happen. Somewhere along the way we must have had some unwelcome observers, for to this day I recall Mary Walsh, who towered over the rest of the kids, confronting Billy and Buddy, crossing her arms and bellowing, "Ya see anything funny here, boys? Just try and flap your gums again and I'll flatten ya one by one!" they stuck out their tongues in unison and beat it down the street. But by now, I didn't even care if they were laughing at the way I was squinting in the noonday sun. I could jump rope, and now I wouldn't have to sit upstairs and listen to other kids singing, "Strawberry shortcake, huckleberry pie" the current ditty sung while jumping rope.

Chapter 4

"School Days, School Days,
Dear Old Golden Rule Days..."
Will Cobb and Gus Edward

Once I started first grade, being a member of a "special class" did have certain advantages such as accessibility to highly individualized attention, but it had its drawbacks, too. There were always questions from the other kids as to why blind and partially sighted kids left the classroom at certain times during the day, where we went, upon return to our normal classroom, why we had to sit up front? This was particularly embarrassing for visually impaired kids who happened to be tall for their age, as seating arrangements were usually made according to height. As far as I was able to judge, there were no valid reasons for being placed in the first row, since most of the time I couldn't see the blackboard anyway. It was true that on a cloudy day I could make out numbers and words, provided they were large enough, but the instances of overcast days were less than you might think. Besides, having to shade my eyes from the glare of the overhead light defeated the original purpose. Then, too, I was usually supplied with a copy of whatever material the teacher had written on the board. Or, I could get up with my pencil and paper in hand, move closer, and copy what I saw in front of me.

To my own way of thinking, even from the beginning, too much attention from the teacher was far worse than none at all. I hated being singled out and if a teacher seemed to lean toward being over solicitous, I counterattacked by throwing her completely off guard. If she was going over an arithmetic lesson or using small groups of words on the blackboard, I just followed the movement of her chalk as she formed the letters and numbers. I promptly raised my hand when she called for an answer. Stunned by my performance, more than once she put me to the test, which I again passed with flying colors. I felt great and never permitted myself to realize that I wasn't fooling anyone that I could really see stuff on the blackboard. Those precious moments of triumph were the sweetest kind of victory, and I felt good all over. Okay, baby boomers, your classrooms had a green board; millennials and the little tots today have a whiteboard.

There is no doubt in my mind that attendance at a regular public school was not the easiest path available to me. There were constant pressures, keeping up, seeing enough, and trying to act like the rest. But overall, I was being prepared to accept life as it was, and being able to live by the norms established by the world was essential. I grew up knowing that every bit of special treatment, adaptation, or favor granted on my behalf only served to mark me off as "different" or "deserving" and this, not in my wildest nightmares, could I accept.

Traveling back and forth to school was a challenge in itself even though Mom and Helen walked with me to school for months. The other kids were allowed to go it alone, and I was confident that I could do it, too. But it took months of pleading to convince my parents, and even then, I knew they followed behind me at a safe distance. There was only one small street that I had to cross, and I learned from the outset that watching the cars was far easier than trying to see a traffic light, obscured by glare or sunlight.

Going into and out of buildings was the hardest obstacle to overcome, since my eyes couldn't adapt to sudden changes in light. My solution was simple, when in doubt, bluff. Exiting from the vestibule of our apartment building, I would find some reason, any reason, to pause for a few seconds to make the necessary adjustments to my surroundings. As if by magic, the multicolored blur was momentarily transformed into a gigantic panorama, resplendent with color, shape, and movement. The brownish-red blob across the street became the familiar row of apartment houses, with windows, doors, fire escapes, and people looking out. Emerging from the sheet of white below were the contoured outlines of streets, with gutters and byways for passing vehicles and pushcarts. It only took a few moments. I could adjust my eyeglasses, pull up my socks, push back my pigtails, and look around, as if in search of someone, anything that afforded a pinch of borrowed time.

There were occasions that I intensely dreaded, fire drills, going in and out of church, or, in fact, any movement that had to be made spontaneously. Still, I found some reason for stopping, and even that was better than having to admit that I was in trouble. It was amazing how many ways I found to explain away whatever goofs I happened to make. If I wasn't able to see something, I would say that it had been because the sun had gotten in my eyes or that I just wasn't paying attention. If I was approaching someone I thought might be familiar, I deliberately glanced away or fumbled with whatever I was holding. In this way, I could be quite casual saying, "Oh, I didn't see you!" and hope that the person would think nothing more than that. The reality was that I really couldn't distinguish who a person was with a quick glance.

Pride can be the most expensive commodity in the world, paid for at too high a cost, and spent before it can ever be enjoyed. If only I had known that we all don masks at one time or another in our lives, hide behind them, and endlessly search for inner strength to bring us through. Not even my closest friends, or the members of my immediate family knew, for sure, how much I could see. I worked hard at fooling them, and in the long run, I learned to use every bit of vision I had to its fullest potential.

Probably because I did not have many diversions outside of school to distract my attention, I was almost compulsively hungry for any challenge that came along, including education. Unfortunately, my teacher must have noticed this eagerness and decided that I was wasting my time going over and over material I had already mastered. The result was that I was "cycloned" through elementary school in five years instead of eight and found myself, ready or not at the age of eleven, on the threshold of an accelerated high school career. I have often wondered in later years how my social life might have been different had I been permitted to advance through school at a normal pace, for at the time, one friend would have been worth more to me than a dozen stars on my report card.

Chapter 5

"Kumbaya, My Lord, Kumbaya.
Oh Lord, Kumbaya..."
The Seekers

My parents found out about a place known as the Lighthouse for the Blind and Visually Impaired located on Lexington Avenue and 59th Street in Manhattan. It was only a subway ride away from where I lived in the Bronx. This Agency offered a recreation program for kids with poor vision, and it was there, on Saturday afternoons, that I had finally learned how to roller skate. An indoor auditorium had been used as a makeshift rink, and the beauty of it all was that there was no one watching, or so I thought, and there was nothing to bump into. After all, I reasoned, if totally blind girls could whiz around, completely uninhibited and free, then so could I.

Based on my joy at the Lighthouse, my folks must have realized that I needed another outlet, a time to unwind, and just be myself and so enrolled me in a camp run by the New York Institute for the Education of the Blind. This special camp was located in the north-western corner of Vermont just this side of the Canadian border. Most of the girls who attended Camp Wapanacki came from residential schools for the blind, and I had met a few of them previously at the Lighthouse. If I had harbored any illusions of grandeur when comparing myself with those who saw less than I could, I was due for a very rude awakening both at the Lighthouse and later at camp.

To my amazement, I didn't learn to swim, row a boat, or run races faster than they did. Yet, to my way of thinking, I had to have more going for me. I found myself pitted against kids who could not see where they were going and others who had to use a rope for a guide. And yet, I was coming in third, fourth, and even last!

For the first time in my life, I felt a very deep sense of admiration for a group of kids who represented, in my eyes, the end of the road, and the direct opposite of what I wanted to be. Even as young children, they accepted people for who they were, not what they looked like or pretended to be. As long as those of us who had partial vision knew enough not to use it as a crutch, we were accepted. Our camp director, Pop Downs, made sure we didn't forget it for one minute!

One night, he announced that we were all going on a "lantern hike." The hills of Vermont had some pretty rough terrain, but I was not especially worried. After all, I could see pretty well, and even offered to act as a guide for two totally blind kids. "Don't worry," I told them, "with this high-powered flashlight of mine, we'll be right up there in front of the pack." God, was I in for a shock! Just as we were about to embark on our hike, Pop Downs announced, "Leave all flashlights back at the camp." He had to be nuts if he thought that I was about to grope my way around in the dark, and in a shaky voice I asked, "Hey, Pops, I thought this was supposed to be a lantern hike!" "That's right, Red," he grinned, "But I'm the one who gets to hold the lantern!"

Sometime during the ordeal, Pops came back to the three of us, ostensibly for giving us a hand, but his kind of help, we soon realized, we could have done without. In dead earnest, he had stationed himself several yards in front of us, had beamed the huge spotlight straight at me and had said, "Come on Red; straight ahead!" a minute later, the three of us were on our hands and knees in a foot of mud, trying to wedge our way out of the mesh of knotted underbrush. With one swift motion, for he was built like a bull, Pops swooped down and fetched us up like a trio of drowning kittens, all the time singing and taunting, "poor blind, poor, poor blind!"

Three hours later, I really was a sight to behold. Slumped on my bed, I was covered from head to toe with scratches, bumps, and bruises; my clothes lay heaped beside me, tangled in a maze of twigs, leaves, and acorns. It took two days to get the debris out of my shoulder-length red braids, and even longer than that to forgive Pops for what he had done. We hated his guts for the moment, and yet, all of us loved him for what he was trying to do. Pops knew that his charges were soft and he was determined to make us tough and insulated against the hurts and disappointments that he knew, only too well, would plague us later in life. If we had gotten mad or had dared to cuss him out, he could have understood and accepted, since this would have been indicative of a certain amount of spunk, but tears were something else again. Crying and whimpering were signs of weakness, even in girls, and Pops would not permit us to indulge ourselves in a pool of defeating pity.

He had his own way of getting a message across to each of us. One morning, as I passed him on the path, Pops deliberately brushed against my arm, knocking the letter I had received from home out of my hand. Without knowing what I was doing (for I was unaware of any precedent), I leaned over and started groping around the ground until I was able to retrieve it. "What the hell is wrong with you, Red?" he boomed, and I was stunned at so volatile a show of anger. "Don't tell me you couldn't see that letter on the ground," he roared. Stunned, I stammered, "I—ah—I—ah…." "I, nothing! Drop it. That's right," he said, "Drop it!" I obeyed quickly for I had never seen him behave quite like this before. He went on with his scolding, saying, "Now this time, pick it up without feeling around like a damned fool. Use the vision you've got and stop acting like a helpless blind person. I know a lot of kids around here who would gladly trade places with you, if you don't want to use your eyes." I would have liked to punch him in the kisser or kick his shin, and he probably wouldn't have minded because Pops was hell bent on teaching me a lesson, one that would stick with me later in life. The message came over like a ton of bricks. Being around a bunch of kids with little or no vision, I had slipped unknowingly into a pattern of "blindisms," which could only be misinterpreted by the sighted world in which I would have to function.

I have no doubt that were it not for Camp Wapanacki, some of us might have gone through life without knowing what it was like to be tossed back and forth atop a hayloft or sink a bucket into a well by means of a crank. Certainly, back in the city, even given the right sort of opportunity, there were few sighted people who would think of letting blind or partially sighted children build a bonfire, much less cook their own food over it. But, by the end of the season, I, and others like me, had been transformed from a bunch of tender-footed city slickers into a cohesive, solid unit, able to meet and commune with nature.

Meet my birth family! From left to right, there's Chubby little me, next is my Sister Helen; followed by Dad Michael, and finally, my dearly beloved Mother Mary.

PART 2

Coming of Age 1945—1948

Chapter 6

"I'm Beginning to See the Light"
Harry James

Summer 1945 was a confusing time for adults and children alike. The nation had lost a president, we dropped bombs, and at last there was an end to a long war. Phrases like "concentration camp," then there was "suffering from shell shock," along with "purple heart," and "missing in action (MIA)," had become a part of our vernacular. The baseball Giants were still on the bottom, the Yankees were still on top, and as for "dah bums from Brooklyn," who ever heard of them anyway? A plane crash over the English Channel had taken the life of a man who became a legend, and whose music would live on, keeping us forever "In the Mood" a skinny young man, with "baby blues" latched on to a microphone larger than his hand, and was knocking them dead at the Paramount.

In our world there were changes, too. Our old haunt, Bronx Beach, would never be the same. True, there was still the long ride on the steaming subway, the sandy towels, and who could forget the leaky sandwiches, and the twenty-pound "portable" radio we lugged along the way. The minute we arrived at the lockers outside the pool area, Helen and her friend Ruthie broke out in smiles and exclaimed, "Hey, look. They're back!" "Who's back, Helen?" I asked. "Why the boys; they're home from the war." At age eleven, I hadn't really noticed that they had been missing, but Ruthie and Helen were almost seventeen, and they seemed very impressed, even awestruck.

Impatiently, I tugged at Helen's sleeve as she stared off dreamily in the distance. "Helen, I heard that the family moved out on the top floor of 459." Helen answered me, but she was smitten with the handsome soldiers in their dress uniforms bedecked with shiny medals. "Oh, yeah, so what?" "Well, aren't we gonna do it? You know, go up on the roof, climb down the fire escape, jimmy the window, and check the place out." Helen laughed and remarked, "Nah, that's kids' stuff." Getting aggravated, I countered, "kids' stuff? Helen, I heard the people even left behind a piano, pots and pans, we could play hide and seek in the closets and…" Getting impatient with her younger Sister, Helen continued, "No dice, squirt. Besides, we might get hurt." I insisted saying, "We never did before." Finally, Helen said, "Well, we could now, and besides, we're too old for that kind of stuff." "Fudge," I said disgustedly. "If that's what growing old all is about, then you can keep it." But grow, I would, and if it is possible for an eleven-year-old girl to be old, then the gray hair should have been showing by mid-September.

Chapter 7

"Going My Way"
Bing Crosby

"Evander Childs is the only high school in the Bronx where there is a special class that can help you adjust since you are so young," my Mother told me. "But you needn't worry about getting to that school! I'll be right there with you all the way. The walking will do me good." "Nice try, Mama," I said, "But this time I'm going to have to go it alone. If the powers that be think that at age 11 I'm old enough to attend high school, then I'm going to get there on my own, just like Helen does!" Helen took this opportunity to throw in her own two cents. "How are you going to know what station to get off at?" "The same way you do. I'll read the signs!" "You will, huh?" laughed Helen. "Yes, I will!" I stuck my tongue out at her. "Even if I don't see the sign, there'll be other ways to know the Gun Hill Road stop. There is a curve in the tracks, followed by the screech of brakes, a blurred sign with three short words, and a pack of kids pushing to get off."

The first day, after passing through the turnstile, I silently congratulated myself saying, "You're not just okay, kid. You're sensational!"

Gun Hill Road, and the three blocks leading to Evander Childs High School proved, most certainly, to be my own Mt. Everest. I knew I would have to face the ordeal alone and for the first time in my life, I was not one hundred percent sure that I would be equal to the task. One wrong move or mistake in judgment could leave me standing stranded somewhere in the middle of a four-lane thoroughfare amidst honking horns, rattling trucks, and a stream of traffic coming at me from three side streets. Whenever possible, I reverted to my old habit of crossing at the same time as other pedestrians, but even this was easier said than done in the glare of the morning sun, unbroken by any tall buildings to serve as temporary respites.

In those days, before the advent of the high-rise buildings, there were just four blocks of empty lots and even the sidewalks, jagged and broken, seemed to have been lost and forgotten in the passage of time. In the springtime, the few trees and bushes growing wild along the path proved to be an even more formidable menace since they were apt to cast zigzag shadows along the walk. In the fall, I had weird visions of clusters of leaves, laughing up at me. Until I was able to memorize the location of every niche in the road, a puddle of water or piece of stray debris from the lots could rekindle the same kind of lurid nightmare.

Crossing under the elevated trains caused me to move forward, relying on sheer guts. If the sun had been too bright on the streets leading back to the Third Avenue Line (also known as the Third Avenue El), the opposite was true crossing under it. The roar of trains from above and traffic below, all in an atmosphere of complete darkness, sent chills down my spine. There was no defense for it, nor any possible chance for me to try to bluff my way through.

All I could do was dawdle at the corner, waiting for people to come along so that I could follow their footsteps.

I could never say, for certain, which unnerved me more, the sun, the rain, or the wind; each proved to be equally debilitating, since it rendered one of my senses virtually useless. I had never admitted, even to myself, how much I depended on hearing, preferring instead, to believe that my eyes could take me wherever I wanted to go. But the cold air beating against my face, cut off those telltale sounds that could have alerted me to imminent danger. I had once read that people who see with only one eye are lacking in true depth perception, but I had always discounted this as nothing more than medical double-talk. A few solo trips on Gun Hill Road, in the midst of piled-high snowbanks and stretches of partially cleared ice, proved how wrong I could be. Curbs and sidewalks were lost in a collage of pink and purple bubbles, and more than once I found myself veering off into the depths of even more treacherous terrain.

Chapter 8

Pink Is the Color of Venus

If I was outclassed, out-dressed, and outraged at Evander, it was not solely because I came from a different part of town or even that I was much younger than my fellow students. I didn't look like an Evander Girl. I was at least twenty pounds overweight, and sported a pair of thick ugly glasses. In addition, I had to squint a lot to make use of whatever lighting prevailed at the moment, and in so doing, my face at times must have taken on a strange, contorted look. I didn't like what I saw in the mirror but wasn't sure that I could ever effect a change that would make any real difference. No one seemed to notice me, anyway.

It wasn't that I didn't have friends. A few months into my freshman year, I had met Dottie, who lived only one block away from me, and who, for reasons of her own, seemed almost as much in need of companionship as I did. It was amazing to me that I could talk to her as with no other sighted girl I had ever known, and soon we were traveling back and forth on the long trek together, laughing and clowning around as we went. It was so weird that our friendship was limited to our trek back and forth to school. Dottie and I established a regular meeting place, rather than depending on a chance rendezvous, but I was careful not to become irritated if our signals got crossed and we failed to meet. The last thing in the world I wanted was to abuse our new friendship by expecting too much from her. Making her feel that she had to jump at my every command was the last thing that I expected. It was important to me that Dottie knew that she owed me nothing, save whatever friendship I might have earned.

During the first months at Evander, I ate alone in the cafeteria, since everyone seemed to have been paired off before the first day of school. Imagine my delight, then, when Gertrude and Toby, two of the most popular and well-dressed girls in my homeroom class, asked me if I would like to join them at their table. All sorts of channels seemed to be opening for me.

Day after day the two girls would talk of boys, dates, and occasionally, when they seemed genuinely interested in coming down to my level, would ask me about the cartoons that I watched or which episode of "I Love Lucy" I found the funniest. After all, people were starting to view these shows on a gadget we called a television. When we were finished eating, I would always offer to dump their trash, this being my small way of repaying them for bothering with me.

One day, out of the clear blue sky, Toby asked me, "Do you have a boyfriend?" I blushed and shrugged my shoulders. "Not yet," I said. Gertrude asked, "Don't you like boys?" "Yes," I replied, but I was lying, of course. They never even entered my mind, I was only eleven-years-old. If we were to move the clock forward several decades, it might certainly be possible that a girl of my age would have had a boyfriend!

"Well, then," said Gertrude, "If you like boys, why don't you wear lipstick?" again, I shrugged my shoulders while silently chuckling over what they would have to say back at the old homestead about that. Here is what my Mother might say, "Theresa is only eleven and she wants to wear lipstick so that she can go out with boys, sit on the beach, and get pregnant." This was the way it always happened in the movies, wasn't it?

Soon, the grin on my face was reduced to a gape. Before I could say another word, I felt something wet and rubbery press against my lips. "There now," said Toby, "how does she look in red?" another dab. "No," said Gertrude "orange is better!"

"How about blue?" now the pressure of fingers pinching my lips was sharp and cold, and soon, as I struggled to pull away, the dabs missed their mark and landed on my cheek, nose, and chin. First red, orange, and then blue. The baby in me wanted to cry. The mule in me wanted to lash out and hurt as I was being hurt. But in the end, I did nothing but sit there trying desperately to cover my face with my hands and push off my attackers.

Mercifully, the bell rang at just this point. I dashed out of the cafeteria into the bathroom and used soap and several paper towels to remove the gunk off my face. Feeling humiliated, I ran down the stairs and out past the hall monitors to the street. Breathlessly, I tore across the avenue, mindless of traffic or glare until a red sports car stopped smack in front of me. "Want a ride?" said a male voice from within. Without stopping to consider the options, I flung open the door and fell headlong onto the front seat, throwing my books on the floor. Only after having gone a block or so did the words of my mother come thundering into my consciousness, "Never accept a ride from a stranger! You know what will happen to you if you do." Peering out the window at the oncoming subway station, I asked tearfully, "You are going to let me out over there, aren't you?" "Sure, I am," said the man, stretching his hand over until it touched my thigh. "But you're not really in that much of a hurry, are you? We could take a nice long ride out to the country and…" At this moment, we slowed down to round a corner, and with one tremendous thrust I swept up my books and lunged out of the car to safety. "What a baby you are," I told myself. "What a real stupid baby!"

Next morning, no sooner had I taken off my jacket than Toby and Gertrude appeared out of nowhere. How much more torment could I stand after what they did to me yesterday? As I was turning away from them with tears starting to form in my eyes, Toby grabbed my arm and said, "We're sorry." Gertrude continued, "That was a rotten trick we pulled on you yesterday, and you didn't deserve it 'cause you're a good kid." "That's okay," I stammered, trying to look as if I meant it. What I wanted to do was inflict some kind of pain on them in retaliation. "Look," said Gertrude, "We bought something for you. It's a tube of light pink lipstick. It'll be just perfect for you. Can you read the name of it?" "Sure, I can," I said, but this was a lie. I would have had to hold it up to my nose, and that was closer than I wanted it to come to my face just yet. "The name of it is Pink is the Color of Venus," said Toby finally. "Can you dig that? Venus is the Goddess of Love, you know, so you put just a little of this on and the boys will come begging for a date." They never did, of course, but still, there was within me a romantic tingle, ever so slight and enhanced in no small measure by the fact that it was our secret and my parents would never be the wiser!

Chapter 9

"All Through the Day"
Perry Como

If my social life had its ups and downs, so too did my academic career. In elementary school, by virtue of my placement in the Sight Conservation class for all periods in the school day, the assumption had been that I was not legally blind but merely one who had some "small issues" in seeing. In Evander, there was quite a different approach to my visual difficulties, one that would turn out to be a pain in the neck to say the least.

You see, at Evander, all students that had some level of visual impairment, and regardless of the extent of their loss of sight, spent only a few periods in a special class which was centered on the use of Braille. For me, it was almost as if I were being abruptly asked to deny the precious vision I had. But rules were rules, and the previous summer I had been placed in a Braille training program downtown. I had quickly discovered that learning this elusive system of raised dots and all those shortcuts was quite another thing from using it as my sole means of communication. Anyone can master the basics in a matter of weeks, but it takes years of concentrated practice before Braille can be read with any degree of speed or ease.

But with no other options open, I halfheartedly decided to give it at least a fighting chance. So, the first day at school, after I returned from the special class to join my assigned fellow perfectly sighted students in room 331, not wishing to make a spectacle of myself, I deliberately chose a seat in the back row. Slowly, I slid the braille stylus, board, and slate onto the desk and for a few minutes laboriously attempted to punch out notes on material that the teacher considered to be a comprehensive outline of the work ahead during the semester. To my dismay, it only took me a few minutes to realize that I was falling hopelessly behind, and then too, there was that awful noise of the stylus hitting against the steel guide. I just knew that every eye in the room had to be on me, and I dared not look up, lest I face head-on the curiosity of a dozen inquisitive glances.

I had done my duty! I had tried and failed! Almost gleefully, I opened my book bag and dumped the cumbersome equipment, instead dragging out an ordinary pencil and paper. Before long I was able to scribble down notes along with the rest of them, even though I knew that six months or even six days later I might not be able to read them. Come on, those of you reading this memoir, admit it, how many times did you take notes in school, only to look at them a week later and have no idea what you wrote!

How could I expect anyone to understand that I could hardly read my own handwriting, and yet could see with comparative ease, any material set down in print? Sure, this might sound confusing to you, it is because the printed letters in the books are darker and easier to identify than my own personal handwriting. There was only one solution to my problem and that was, each night, to type all that I had learned during the day, referring back to my notes only for certain key words, which with luck would rekindle instant recall. At least in the privacy of my own home I could read my notes with a jeweler's loupe my father had bought me, but it soon became abundantly clear that I had damned well learn after the first reading or go blind for real from overstrain. Fortunately, I found that my memory was almost letter perfect and if ever there was a trait that helped to carry me through, most assuredly that was it.

Let me explain more about this Braille class, we had an exceptionally fine teacher. If ever a person came fully equipped to fulfill the requirements of the job, Myron Lesowitz was surely that man. Proficiency in one subject was not enough. His role as coordinator, counselor, and advisor demanded that he be master of all. A brilliant mathematician in his own right, he made geometry, algebra, and trig come to life on the board in front of me. It was his function to supplement that which was being taught in the regular class sessions, and the two periods a day spent under his tutelage proved more meaningful than any other single experience to date.

I was about to meet a girl named Josephine who would become a lifelong friend. Here is what happened. The second day of my sophomore year, I was the first to arrive at Room 344, the official homeroom of the Braille class. The door opened, and in strolled Mr. Lesowitz, arm in arm with a good-looking, olive-skinned girl with dark hair and eyes that suited her well. "Theresa, this is Josephine. I'm going to be busy for a while, but I was hoping you could show her around, maybe see that she gets to her first class, you know, that sort of thing." "Sure thing, Mr. Lesowitz. Come on," I said, motioning her toward the back of the room. "I'll show you where we hang our coats. Did old Lessie give you a schedule yet?" "Yeah, I've got it right here in my pocket." She drew out a small card and handed it to me. I took one look at it and grinned. "Aw, come on, he's not going to pull the same kind of jazz with you, too!" I drew closer, about to share a very special kind of confidence. "Now, look, Josephine. If you're really smart, you'll just tell him straight off that you don't need Braille. They try to force it down your throat at the beginning, but if you stand your ground, no one can make you use it." Josephine thought for a moment, "Well, if I don't use Braille, then what else is there?" getting exasperated, I continued, "Look, I'm telling you, you can use what everybody else uses, a pen and paper." Josephine shot back, "Maybe you can, but I can't."

I gaped at her incredulously. The light was beginning to break through the foggy dawn, but there had been nothing to forewarn me. When she looked at me, her gaze had been right on the money. Josephine had moved down the aisle with the agility of a deer in flight. How was I to know that she was totally blind? "Boy! I really blew that one, didn't I?" Josephine laughed and said, "Yeah, but don't feel bad. That's the nicest thing that's happened to me today. Now, how about it? Want to walk me to my first class? Independent, I'm not, well—at least for the moment!" with that, she slipped her arm into mine, and although I was careful to warn her about oncoming student traffic and turns in the hallway, it was soon obvious that if anyone needed to relax, it was me and not her. As we reached our destination, she waved, turned on her heels, and slipped into a seat. "Thanks a lot. I'll see you at lunch." "Yeah," I repeated. "See ya!"

From that point on, there developed a sort of mutual admiration society between us, she, respecting my casual approach to school work, and I envying her savoir faire. She knew how to talk and joke with people, and what was even more impressive, she got along well with boys, something I had never been able to do. We often said as time went on, that if only each could borrow a little from the other, the sky would be the limit.

Now, here is another oddity that I faced during my years at Evander. Most certainly, I missed being included in the extra courses taken by the members of my regular class. In those days, anyone who attended that Braille class was barred from taking home economics, art, and music. Gym was one period I could well do without since I was hardly equipped to participate in competitive sports, but didn't they think I should learn how to cook, sew, and iron? I was, in fact, not permitted to use the school swimming pool even though I had a Junior Life Saving Certificate from summer camp. This enraged me, but I suppose they had their reasons.

It would take a few decades before this situation would be quite the reverse. Partially sighted and totally blind children would be assimilated into the normal curriculum, and in many schools, there wouldn't be a dedicated program such as a Sight Conservation or Braille class. The regular grade teacher would be faced with the responsibility for educating these special students and could no longer shuffle them off whenever a difficult situation presented itself. They would have an administrative teacher provided by the Board of Education to guide classroom teachers and to make available textbooks and tests in large print or Braille, if needed. This singular advance in education would make it possible for children to attend neighborhood schools, rather than being shuttled off to those for the blind, far out of their district, maybe in a different state altogether. In the long run, it has been proven that kids who play together and share nonacademic interludes make a decidedly better adjustment socially. This concept was too premature in the 1940s to have helped me.

It was understandably difficult for any of my teachers to try to guess just how much I could see on any given day, but there were times when one or another of them would assume that to have partial vision meant that I was only one step away from darkness. One well-meaning biology teacher, for instance, seemed genuinely elated when she presented me with a huge piece of oak tag on which she had reproduced a human cell complete with wall, nucleus, and oh yes, gobs of bloody protoplasm. "You see, dear, I splashed that in with some finger paint and catsup dotted with bits of sand to remind you about the molecules. Now, if you'd like to, you can feel it...." "Ah, no thanks. Seeing it is enough ... I mean I can see it just fine!"

Chapter 10

"Yes, I'm the Great Pretender"
The Platters

With the passing of time, I have been exposed to studies that claim to prove behavioral patterns of blind and partially sighted adolescents; but as I read, there is something about them that doesn't ring true. Here is an example of what they state, in general, Handicapped children, are the dreamers, those who fantasize, the social hermits who run from the reality and make of their existence a safe cocoon wherein they cannot be hurt. After each encounter with this sort of psychological babble, I assured myself that the clinical rubbish contained therein did not apply to me, or did it? You decide!

To be sure, I did have more than the normal share of spare time on my hands since I never really had to work hard on homework assignments. Also, Josephine lived way up in the East Bronx, and Dottie withdrew into virtual isolation at three o'clock each day. Helen and I still went to the movies once a week, but our interests were veering off in different directions. She and her friends got their kicks out of going to stag dances for Irish-Americans at the old Star and Munster Halls. Although none of them had ever made it seem so, I didn't want to become a leech. Besides, eight-handed reels had never caught my fancy.

Here's what was important to me. For hours I would sprawl out on the couch, radio in hand, listening to the latest play-by-play description of games played by my beloved New York Giants. Most girls in those days were not caught up in baseball, but I didn't care what anybody thought. There were times, of course, when there was a break in the action and the teletype machine being used to relay every ball and strike from the ball field to the local radio station, would break down and I would drift dreamily off into my own private world where I alone played the starring role. I had been elected president of my class, amid cheers and verbal salutes, or I was being lassoed into the waiting arms of my fearless cowboy lover, or I might have been dying of some exotic disease, with my loyal subjects gathered around me. These long lapses into dreamland never bothered me, certainly not to the point where I thought that my actions weren't "normal!"

Regardless, I was certainly not about to ask Josephine or Dottie, or for that matter anyone, whether they, too, had the same sorts of fantasies. To my way of thinking I was acting normal in at least one aspect of my life. Down through the ages, every teenaged girl at one time or another, develops a crush on an older man. For me it was my Cousin Walter, my shining knight in uniform, quite tall, very muscular, and certainly ingratiating. On several occasions when he was on furlough, he asked if I wouldn't enjoy going up to the Polo Grounds to see a Giants game in person. I never got any sleep the night before, and oh, how I wished that it was I, and not my Cousin Kay, who held the key to his heart. There were other terrific men in my life, namely my history teacher, Mr. Klein, and Bernie, who was going with my Cousin, Mary, but alas, the trouble with my heart-throbs was that they were all betrothed to someone else.

Besides, by this time, there was something new in my life, something that psychiatrists might have regarded as more "normal." It was amazing what a stupendous impact a twelve-inch television screen could have on my days. From the moment it was brought into the house, I silently claimed it to be mine alone. My God! It was like the world as sighted people saw it! No matter how close I had been to the screen at the movies, there had been so much I had missed. What was the man holding in his hand? Who was he looking at off in the distance? What did the letter that was held up for the audience say? Helen always filled in these details very willingly, but it wasn't the same as seeing it for myself. I couldn't explain why it was that images were far clearer on a screen that was much smaller than that used at the picture show. Perhaps it was that the TV camera zoomed in on the action, and there was no need to scan across a large area in the hope of catching what movement was relevant at the moment. My Mother and Helen bawled me out for sitting so close. "You'll strain your eyes," they would say, and I would mutter under my breath, "So what! It's worth it!"

503-Form 11-3500-7-48

Evander Childs High School

Gun Hill Road and Barnes Avenue
City of New York

HONORABLE MENTION FOR OUTSTANDING CITIZENSHIP

Name___Theresa___McDonald___ Class___251-7

Is hereby rated superior by the faculty in one or more of the following characteristics:— Courtesy, Health Habits, Dependability and Cooperation.

HYMEN ALPERN
Principal

PART 3

The Apron Strings Become Untied! 1949—1953

Chapter 11

"When in the Course of Human Events, It Becomes Necessary..." U.S. Declaration of Independence

"Well, young lady, what do you think you would like to do with your future?" an astute-looking gentleman peered at me over a stack of applications. The State of New York, under its Rehabilitation Program was contemplating spending thousands of dollars on my education and the least I could do was to try to come up with something mature and professional. But for a chubby, freckled-faced kid of fifteen, sophistication was out of reach, so I decided that a touch of humility might be my only trump card. "I don't really know for sure, but I had thought about teaching." Did I just say that? Oh my! Once uttered, the words seemed to dangle on the end of my tongue, and I wished that there was some way of sucking them back in. My response had been nothing more than an echo of a conversation overheard between two other applicants not ten minutes before in the waiting room.

The first one, said confidently, "Tell them you want to be a social worker or a teacher, and they'll love you to pieces!" and the other applicant added, "After all, there's very little room for innovation when it comes to blind people, even those with a college degree." I supposed that they had been referring to the fact that there weren't any blind doctors or rocket scientists floating around in that cold world outside, but whatever the implications, I didn't have time to do anything more than take their word as gospel truth.

Let me see, their first suggestion, I knew, was completely out of the question for me. I could picture myself across the table from some poor soul pouring his heart out. I had always been a softy and would probably finish bawling my insides out right in front of my client, and this would do neither of us any good. On the other hand, was teaching a better alternative? Why had I suddenly deduced that this bit of strategy wasn't as faulty as the first? Maybe my memory was too muddled up at the moment, but there was no way that I could have overlooked the one overriding flaw in my personality that was bound to sabotage my thoughts about leaning in this direction. They were sure to find out about it sooner or later.

How often in the past had I become miserably immobilized when having to present an oral report on a given subject in front of a classful of eager students poised and ready to take notes? It was tolerable only if I had something like a lectern to lean on, or failing that, had a report, anything to hold in my hand! Without these manual props, the event would leave me quivering like a bowl of jelly. Quite a dilemma I was facing!

The die was cast, and the thing to do now was to remain calm while within a war was breaking out between the hotdog and chocolate milkshake I had gulped down earlier. The interviewer was going to tell me that I was out of my mind to think that the State of New York would even think of sponsoring me, of all people, through four years of college, to be a teacher, what a dream! Some freshman

"MissPopularity" I'd make! I was too fat to even sway gracefully! But I was too young to work and ready to graduate from high school. I felt inwardly reassured that they would have to do something with me, and perhaps packing me off to some cozy suburban college might prove to be the lesser of the two evils.

Chapter 12

"The Best Is Yet to Come"
Frank Sinatra

After much soul searching and having taken a monumental battery of psychological tests and several trips to institutions of higher learning, I chose a rather small college out on Long Island, Adelphi, and I was never sorry. Even though the college I had selected was only two hours travel time from the Bronx, as summer 1949 flew by, it could as well have been two thousand miles away as far as I was concerned. What sort of starry-eyed insanity was it that moved me to even think of severing the umbilical cord forever and setting out completely on my own? Damned if I knew.

While both of my parents were looking at me as though my goodbyes would be forever, Helen seemed genuinely jubilant. "Wow. At long last, a whole room all to myself!" I was quick to reply, "Aren't ya gonna miss me at all, Sis?" Helen thought for a long moment. "Well, come to think of it, yes. There'll be about two minutes every night when I'll think of you." "Really?" I said with tears forming in my eyes. Laughing, Helen continued, "Yeah, 'cause that's just about how long it'll take me to miss the gum wrappers under the pillow and the pretzel crumbs all over the sheets."

Despite her assurance that the best thing that could ever happen to her was getting rid of me, every extra cent she had was put toward decking me out in proper style. After trying on the latest dress she bought me, I asked, "Is this a bribe, all these clothes and everything?" with a smile on her face, she replied, "No, just the first installment on a loan with double interest paid in advance!"

For Helen, love and sacrifice was the backbone of her commitment to our family. At the age of eighteen she had taken on sole support for the four of us. My Father had been forced into early retirement, and although none of us knew it at the time, he was slowly dying. Therefore, so many of the things that most young people take for granted, dates, travel, and independence, were willingly surrendered in the name of mature responsibility, and the best that I could do was to get out of her hair and leave it all to her. Helen's final words were, "Are you kidding? The quiet and neatness around here will probably kill me. Go out there, squirt, and knock 'em dead. Show ''em what brains are all about. In the meantime, we'll always be here cheering you on."

Adelphi proved to be a renaissance for me, if one were to concede that I had ever lived at all until then. My roommate in my freshman year was a godsend, a mother, sister, and guardian angel all rolled up in one neat package. Before a month had passed, it was clear that she knew me better than I understood myself, and Gloria was not one to hold back when there was something to be said.

One afternoon in late October she found me searching book-by-book for one volume in our college library. "What do you think you're doing?" I glanced back over my shoulder at her. "Oh hi! What does it look like I'm doing? I've got a research chapter to read on Contemporary Man, and this is the 'C' section." Shaking her head, Gloria continued, "Sure it is, but at the rate you're going, you will be here until midnight. Did you ever think of asking someone to help you locate what you want?" I replied very strongly, saying, "Yeah, but I like to do things on my own." Putting her hands on her hips she exclaimed, "You call it being independent. I call it being down-right stubborn." I turned on my heels, exasperated, and glared at her. "Look if someone offers help, I accept it." Gloria was now in full battle mode as she retorted, "Well, isn't that just peachy. And how, I ask, is someone supposed to know that you need help in the first place? Last time I looked you didn't have a sign on your back that said, 'Sorry folks, I am legally blind, but let's keep it a big secret.' You don't carry a cane or walk with a dog. For heaven's sake, you don't even wear glasses anymore, and yet, by some miracle, the whole world is supposed to know when you need help, and when you're going to be in the mood to accept it."

In a louder voice I shot back, "Boy, you don't pull any punches, do you?" Just as forcefully, she replied, "No, not when I see someone who's supposed to be so damned smart wasting away an afternoon 'cause she's too proud to open her mouth and ask for help. Wake up, kiddo. There's another book in this library that's got a line written just for you, 'No man is an island.' You think about it!"

At this point the librarian sidled over in our direction to see what all the fuss was about. "Can I help you?" with a sigh, I reluctantly replied, "Yes, I am looking for the correct volume that discusses this subject." As I handed over the paper I was carrying, the last thing I saw was Gloria nodding and smiling as she left the library.

Later while hanging out in our dorm room, Gloria said, "You know, you're not going to believe this, kiddo, but there are a few tiny things about you, not much mind you, that people might actually find kind of nice. So, do like the song says, baby, 'let your hair down' and give it a try." I will always remember Gloria. She knocked some sense into me and helped me to take the first step on my journey toward womanhood.

In my own dark hours, I had been unable to reach out and cement lasting relationships. This disappeared now with the realization that I would only be as "special" as I chose to be. No longer was there the compelling, nerve-wrenching drive to prove that I could go it alone that had so isolated me from others up until now.

Chapter 13

"I'm Searching for My Place in the Sun..."
Stevie Wonder

Gloria had to leave Adelphi, just as I was at the point when I had come to depend on her for my mere existence, in the same way I had back home with Helen. I was devastated. What would I do without her? I had begun to make it on my own socially, but Gloria was very much my personal crutch, and I was sure that no one could ever take her place.

Guess I was wrong! Someone did. Her name was Rita and after one week, I was sure that she was as worldly as any girl could be. Why, she even read dirty books with nude women on the cover. Once Rita caught me in the act of perusing one with a magnifying glass. I was not about to miss any of it even though I could sense twelve sets of beady apostolic eyes from the altar at St. Jerome's Church in the Bronx glaring at me with disapproval.

"You don't know what it's all about, do you?" asked Rita. "Says who? I know more than you think." The last thing in the world I was about to admit was that I had reached the tender age of sixteen and still did not know the score. "Well," Rita began, "Just in case you missed a few details along the way, let me fill you in." As I sat there drinking in every sizzling morsel of information, I could feel my ears expanding and my brain leaping as it raced to gather me up from the playpen and drop-kick me onto the merry-go-round of young womanhood.

Just as with sex, certain other age-old institutions that I had been taught never to question were to be placed on the firing line. I had, according to my Mother and Father, been properly raised as a child of God and a member in good standing of the chosen flock as were the Jews. But Protestants were renegades who had broken with the "real church." There was virtue and sin, and black and white, and we, the Catholics of the world, had been lucky enough to be born on the right side of the street called "truth." It was quite a wakeup call that there were people who just didn't see it that way, and what was more, were willing to argue the point. This was shocking to me, but now at least, I was not alone on the religious chopping block.

Rita graduated, and into my life entered my new roommate Barbara Pulese. We were as good as a matched set, both in appearance and temperament. I suppose that the reason we got along so well was that neither demanded more than the other was able to give. We both enjoyed moments of solitude when it wasn't necessary to gab about anything. What was more, Barbara and I were both Roman Catholics in a world of "pagan nonbelievers."

"Here they come," they would say. "The knee-bending, fish-eating idol worshippers." I don't know how, but we actually learned to laugh and walk away all the stronger for it. When the day arrived when I could grin back with equal sincerity when one or another said, "Hey, why don't you look where you're going?" I knew for sure that at long last, I had found my very own "place in the sun" and that nevermore would I be the one to be burned.

*I'm in college now and will graduate next year at the tender age of 19.
Is that really me decked out in an evening gown? Who would have thought!*

Chapter 14

"Take a Walk on the Wild Side..."
Lou Reed

On my urging and after she graduated from Evander Childs High School, Josephine had enrolled in Adelphi, and I will never forget her first night on campus. Apparently, someone had clued in our waiter as to Josephine's blindness, for when he approached the table he took all our orders first, and then pointing to Josephine asked, "What is she going to have?" everyone sat there numb until I broke the silence. "Tell you what you do, Jim. Just ask her yourself. You know, she really can speak very well." Josephine looked up, fluttered her eyelashes provocatively, and said, "Okay, Jim, what have you got in mind?" he grinned. "You'd be surprised, honey! Oh, you mean what can I recommend for supper? Let's see, we have." As he started to laugh, "You got me so shook up, I can't even read the menu." "Now, there, that makes two of us, doesn't it?" Josephine said, and the whole table broke out laughing.

Josephine's adjustment to college life was far less painful than mine, but as the months passed, her inherently restless nature began to get the best of her. It was around this time in my life when people started calling me "Terry" rather than the more formal "Theresa," and this was just fine by me. "I'm getting bored," she said one particularly quiet Friday afternoon. "Hey, Terry, why don't we go to Manhattan tonight to see the old gang at the Lighthouse, you know, just for old times' sake?" laughing, I retorted, "You've got rocks in your head!" Josephine came right back with, "No, I'm serious. We've got enough money for the train and subway and a mouth to ask for directions, so what else is there?"

Edie, Josephine's roommate, had been standing in front of the dresser combing her hair and stopped midstroke, listening to Josephine's latest flight into delirium. Getting into the conversation, she added, "Hey that sounds like a great idea. The two of you would probably have a ball!" I protested, shaking my head furiously and added, "All this studying has gone to your head." Taking a breath, I continued, "Take the train, she says just like that! As if I really know my way!" "Aw come on, Terry," said Josephine. "Where's your sense of adventure?" I retorted, "I cashed it in with my last insurance premium. Barbara, Edie, somebody, tell this totally blind crazy girl that she's nuts!" but instead of them backing me on my objections to this ridiculous plan, the two of them dashed toward the closet and started pulling out one hanger after the other. "Now, let's see, this blue skirt with the gold shirt would be good for Terry, while the white skirt and that pretty pink blouse would go well for Josephine." Nodding, the conspirators turned around and presented their selections to us.

In an hour or so, as our college dorm faded into the late afternoon sun, there stood poor Barbara, having second thoughts, but smiling and waving just the same, and Edie, with just a tinge of apprehension showing through as she screamed a warning for us to duck out of the path of a car that had appeared seemingly out of nowhere. "My God!" I said. "We'll get killed even before we get off campus!" Josephine just laughed, and I told her it was a good thing she hadn't been able to see how close we had come to being sliced into instant mincemeat.

As the train lumbered into Penn Station, a surge of untamed excitement raced through me at the same time as the naked fact that neither of us knew where the hell we were going projected itself into the sober light of consciousness. "Let's see," I said, struggling to recollect some of the instructions given us by one of the janitors back at school. "I think he said, take the IRT 7th Avenue uptown to Times Square, then the shuttle to Grand Central, and finally the IRT No. 4 uptown to 59th Street." "Sounds right to me," said Josephine. She continued saying, "A real snap!" from what I could recall from previous trips, it would have taken a real escape artist to navigate through the confusing jungle of passageways leading out of the Long Island Railroad section of Penn Station, but who cared? We had lots of time.

The train ground to a halt, and instinctively I shaded by eyes, and peered out to catch a glimpse of the platform in semi-darkness. "Our folks should see us now!" Josephine remarked as we made our way up the ramp and into the waiting room of Penn Station. laughing, I said, "Bite your tongue, kid. If they had any notion what we were up to, they'd skin us alive. On second thought, they'd start on me first. I'm supposed to be the sober, studious type, and they know you're something of a renegade, anyway." Our Fathers, we agreed, would greet the news with their usual characteristic sense of quiet compassion. But our Mothers, they were something else again! "Can you hear them now?" Josephine giggled as she continued. "Yeah, my Mother would say, you could get run over by a train. You should be studying and not running off to dances." I laughed and said, "This is what my Mother would ask, 'How will you get back to your dorm on time? Don't they lock the doors at a certain hour?' and she would continue, 'If you would have let one of us know, we would have taken you there!'"

As luck would have it, Josephine and I found ourselves in the midst of a theatre crowd and no one seemed to be headed in the same direction as we were. Once, while waiting in line for tokens, Josephine slipped her arm out of mine to blow her nose. "For God's sake, hold on," I said. The mere thought of being separated made my blood freeze, but before I had time to reflect on that prospect, I spotted the first shoulder-high sign, which I was sure I could see up close. They certainly didn't make things easy for our kind of people in subways, I thought. Signs were placed too high in the air, and I had always felt ridiculous squinting up at them.

"Here we go, 'Shuttle Straight Ahead. Follow the Green Lights.'" Good thing that I am not Color-Blind, or just this little issue would be a game changer as most people who have this problem can't tell the difference between green and red. I peered up at the ceiling, then to my left, straight ahead, and to my right. If indeed there were any colored lights, they were managing quite well to elude my searches.

I broke with one of my longtime hang-ups and decided to ask someone. "That's easy," said a typical Wall Street executive type in answer to my query. "Just follow the crowd," he said, making a sweeping gesture with his hand toward a flock of humanity stampeding down a nearby corridor. It was only after a few minutes of walking that I spotted the elusive green lights.

Once we arrived at Grand Central via the shuttle, I did think it might be expedient to check with someone before plunging down a narrow hallway that did not seem to allow for any abrupt U-turns. This time, I selected a rotund man who seemed to be deriving no small sense of vicarious pleasure in being squeezed between a 36-26-

36 and a 58-42-60. I asked, "This is the way to the Uptown Local, isn't it?" "That's what the big sign says, goily. Can't you read?" too bad, I thought, I had never learned how to give a dirty look, or I was too polite to give this jerk the finger! Surprisingly enough, the advice given me by the janitor back at school paid off, and the rest of the trip was relatively uneventful, since I was already quite familiar with the East Side subway system.

When we reached 59th Street, finally, we had a surprise waiting for us. The skies had opened in a torrential downpour. Just what we needed. Rain did peculiar things to people. It caused them to walk up the down side of the sidewalk to avoid getting soaked. It made them loiter under awnings and canopies, creating a human obstacle course, or caused them to run through traffic, amidst screeching vehicles and honking horns. As if all this wasn't bad enough, there were the multicolored lights that skirted in and out of the puddles, distorting every inch of sidewalk. Usually nighttime was my favorite part of the day, since taxi cabs, stop signs, and oncoming vehicles were silhouetted against a background of black. But when you added the element of rain to the mix, the entire scene was transformed into a conglomeration of schizoid shapes and images, changing, and re-flecting from one moment to the next.

"We're going to get our hair all wet!" Josephine groaned. That was all that was bothering her! If only I could be that cool. "Let's make a run for it." I said. Luckily, we made it with very few outward signs of damage, but as we approached the entrance to the Lighthouse I couldn't help breathing a sigh of relief followed by a silent big "Amen." Our mission had been accomplished, and yet another page had been added to our personal declaration of independence.

Chapter 15

"That Old Gang of Mine"
Mitch Miller

As time went by and our trips to the city came to be almost matter of fact occurrences, we even flirted with the idea of staying a little later than was our custom. It was still possible to make it back by one A.M., and besides, the fun really started after the dances. There was a rundown pizza joint on the corner of 60th and Second Avenue with rustic old tables in the back adjoining the bar. And there, for a few hours each night, a little guy with a mustache played his heart out on an old Italian accordion.

One night we managed to wrangle an invitation from a fellow named Frankie, who considered himself to be every girl's matchmaker and Lord Protector. "Hi, Red," he would say. "Gee, don't you look really nice tonight!" I wondered how he would know, since it was obvious he could see very little, but still I began to think pretty, and this was a step in the right direction.

There was a certain aura of nostalgia about that old back room, with its chairs huddled around tables bedecked with steaming trays of lasagna, ravioli, baked ziti, and don't forget their specialty,

Neapolitan style pizza with all the toppings imaginable. But more than this, there was music. Blind people, I had found, needed only the downbeat of a chord to light a spark within them that could burn on as long as anyone was there willing to play. There was something about singing together, whether it was the need to unwind and release pent-up frustrations or merely the warmth of genuine companionship. No matter what it was, Josephine and I both loved being part of it.

Almost invariably during the noisy intermissions, the conversation among the others would drift aimlessly toward the one subject that even music could not help them forget for any length of time. Only now, in retrospect, is it possible to see what should have been all too obvious then for anyone who dared to look. Was it hope or despair, bitterness or resignation, anticipation, or fear of what might have been in store for them? In all fairness, it would have been hard to guess since there was little in their manner that gave a clue to their inner struggles. Most of the others were older than Josephine and me, and perhaps they had become immune to the disappointments life had dealt them. They knew already that it was no use dreaming, as most people do, of a better life. Certainly, each could have been doing so much more with the working part of their daily existence, and yet, somehow, the great American dream had passed them by and had denied to each the opportunity to build his own better "mousetrap."

At the time when racial and ethnic consciousness was threatening to split our great nation apart, there sat a group of people who would have considered third-class citizenship to be three steps up from where they had been for years. Yet, among their ranks there was no bombing or rioting and never any demonstrations to appeal for equal rights. They were stuck in dead-end jobs where their salaries would continue to lag below the "poverty level." This was a boom time for most American youth and yet, in the largest city in the nation, there were very few opportunities for gainful employment. Most visually impaired and totally blind people took what they could get, work in sheltered programs under the direction of the New York State Commission for the Blind, in factories run by various agencies or at home, turning out piecework for next to nothing.

Pizza time was also "tall tale" time, although no one could say for certain whether the intake of beer didn't add a few bubbles of exaggeration, just to sprinkle some spice to complement a story being told. If there was strain and tension in our day-to-day existence, then this was as good a place as any to let their hair down in a cathartic outpouring, the like of which no "outsider" could even begin to comprehend.

Would a fully sighted person laugh as we did at a tale told by Frankie D., of his drunken promenade down a skinny subway platform, during which he sought to enter a train that was not there, and after hauling himself back up to safety, tore across the platform and pitched himself off the other side? After all, as drunk and as lovable as he was, he still could have gotten killed. Somehow, at the time, this never entered our minds.

Once started, the stories began to pour out in bunches, each more laughable than the other. How's this for an encore? Anthony who had a beautiful tenor voice that was really sweet when we all sang together would start. "Last week, Rich and I were walking up the stairs of a swanky hotel, when suddenly I spotted two other guys coming down toward us. So, being two nice polite fellows, we stepped aside. The trouble was, so did they. After going at it a second and then a third time, I decided what the hell, this was getting us nowhere, and so up we went, smack into a wall-to-wall mirror."

Each one of us mapped out our daily trot to the subway, using physical props whenever possible to guide us along. What happened, when by chance, one or two of these props were taken away? Mario recounted how he had lost his way in a snowstorm and was searching frantically for a fence that adjoined his property. When he asked someone to help him find it, he was told that he had just walked over it! "Yeah, but when you're blind, you get all kinds of help along the way," commented Anna who was as round and fully packed as she was good looking. "I mean it's crazy how a little vision can play tricks on you. On my street, I'm always having to walk around a million little kids, but last week, it got to be too much when I said, 'excuse me, Sonny,' and Sonny turned out to be a Johnny pump (fire hydrant) and not a boy wearing a football helmet!"

Harry agreed. "I know what you mean about partial vision. Once when I was doing the grocery shopping, I picked up this package of steak from the refrigerated case. There I was with my nose practically on top of it, squinting to see the price and the weight of the meat, and this guy walks up to me and says, 'Gee, Mac, if it smells that bad, throw it back in!'"

"Well, getting back to the subway platforms…." This was Jerry, who had on this and earlier occasions caught my eye. He was slim, muscular, had a broad smile, and seemed to sport a year-round Caribbean tan. Taking a sip of his beer, he started telling us a story, "I started to play in a semi-pro band after high school, and every time we had a job I would stay in the city with one of the guys. They pull in the buses and trains at seven o'clock up where

I come from. That meant carrying my trumpet case and an overnight bag. Anyway, one night this totally blind guy, Angelo, asked if he couldn't tag along. 'Okay with me,' I said, 'but since you can't hang onto my arm, you'd better just trot along behind me, and I'll whistle so you can hear where I'm going.'" All the others around Jerry groaned in expectation.

They knew what was coming. "Well, okay, there we were inching along the platform at Brooklyn Bridge Station, and I'm whistling and yelling, 'Angelo ya still back there?' 'Yep sure thing,' he tells me. We walk a little further and I say, 'Angelo, you still okay?' and he answers, 'Yep, just keep on goin'!' then, we're almost to the stairs leading up and out of the station, and I say, 'Angelo we're almost home free.' There was no answer from him. I turn around, now I am getting concerned! Once again I yell, 'Angelo,' but he's nowhere in sight. Well, you all know what happened. He's down on the tracks, sure enough, but that's not all of it. When I reach down my hand to help him, would you believe that he wouldn't come up! Can you just imagine it?"

In total astonishment Frankie said, "Sure, he's not coming up without his saxophone. Right?" "that's it. There he is down there feeling around for his horn, third rail and all, and me screaming, 'you're going to kill yourself,' and him telling me 'shit, I'm not coming up without it.'" "Did he get hurt?" we all asked in unison. "Not a scratch. I was worse off than him by long shot, but I'll tell you that'll be the last time you'll find this kid playing guide dog to a nutty musician."

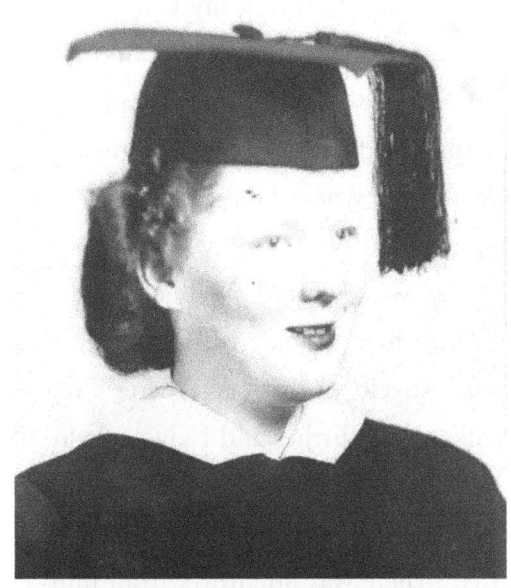

Wow! College graduation at age 19?

Theresa graduates magna cum laude from Adelphi College and is presented her BA degree. Within a short time, she would add two Master's degrees in Special Education and History.

PART 4

Love and Marriage 1954—1956

Chapter 16

"Matchmaker, Matchmaker, Make Me a Match"
Musical, *Fiddler on the Roof*

There was something about this Jerry, easy with the dollar and very self-confident. It was this last quality that fascinated, yet irritated, me the most. He was so damned cocksure, seemed to know just where he was going, and I thought as we talked that it was almost as if sorrow and disappointment had never touched his life, as it had for the others in our pizza parlor gang. How wrong I was! With a good bit of prodding, I learned that after graduating from high school and turning down a scholarship to college, he had roamed the streets of New York in search of work, any work. Although he did manage to get himself hired three or four times, as soon as his employers found out that he had only partial vision, Jerry had been told the same old dribble, "Sorry, we'd like to keep you on, but it's just too risky, accidents, you, know! Sorry!" finally, after a year or two on the waiting list, he had been placed in one of the vending operations sponsored by the government in the General Post Office on 33rd Street in Manhattan.

What was it then with this fellow? Even after three or four dates, I still couldn't figure it out. Jerry shoveled money and gifts at me like he had his own private minting machine, and yet I knew from the others that he couldn't be earning more than sixty dollars a week. Only as time went on and I began to get a peek at the face behind the mask did I come to know that for Jerry it could be boiled down to his stubborn, pigheaded pride. It had brought him through it all, that dogged determination never to admit to being licked, but there were many nights out on the town before I could convince him that he didn't have to buy my affection. I certainly wasn't about to let him know I liked him more than I was willing to admit even to myself.

"Play the field," was the advice I had gotten back at school from a number of students. "Don't get tied down with one of the first guys you like," echoed Josephine's roommate Edie. Maybe they were right, but as I wrestled my way out of one backseat clinch or another, his name kept pricking its way back into my consciousness. Helen was no help either, since she considered herself to be my personal matchmaker. More than once, though, I took serious issue with her choice of suitors. Listen to this, see what she did to me!

There was one evening when the two of us boarded the same subway. She was headed down toward 86th Street, and I was bound for school. No sooner had we entered the subway car than Helen spotted a rather slow-witted guy whom she had seen at the Lighthouse several years before. Sam was sweet and lovable, but a complete boob, and yet, it was impossible to hate such a fellow, and most of us had simply done our best to avoid him. Before I could dissuade Helen, she had called him over and nudging me in the ribs said, "You remember Sam, don't you?"

As if I ever could have forgotten him! Oh, well, the damage was done, and I supposed the least I could do was to be gracious. "Of course," I said. "How have you been?" definitely not really caring about what he was about to say. "Fantastic!" he boomed. When I say he boomed, I am not kidding. People could hear this guy in the next car. I wanted to slide under the seat and be rid of him. Perhaps he was deaf on top of being nearly blind! "I've been so busy, I haven't had a chance to tell the gang what I've been up to." Without any encouragement on my part, he launched into a long discussion of psychotherapy and physical fitness and their effect on his whole existence. "You're not going to believe this, but my vision has doubled within a matter of months. Soon I'll probably see well enough to drive a car."

God help us, I thought! This most certainly had to be the wildest pipe dream of all, for despite his claims to the contrary, we all knew that he was almost as blind as a bat. With that, he took out a book and in a voice that was even embarrassingly louder, proceeded to read aloud, pausing to wipe his glasses and glance at us from time to time in search of some sign of approval. God, how I wished he would shut up or at least lower his voice. "Well now," said Helen. "This is my stop, so I'll leave you two alone to chat." Sticking out my tongue at her, thinking, "That dirty rat, that lowdown snake-in-the-grass, how could she?" there was nothing to do but resign myself to fifteen minutes more of dribble, and now I could sense many other eyes focused on us. Much to my chagrin, Sam continued, "You see, Terry! It's not just psychotherapy alone that has worked this miracle. It's the ability to use my reflexes to the fullest extent, so I can better respond to my environment. This is where the exercise comes in, and I'm proud to say that I'm ready at all times to act on a moment's notice, and of course, my increased vision makes it that much easier." I mumbled, "That's swell, Sam!"

Thank God, the subway was pulling into Grand Central Station. In a few minutes, after one short stop on the local, I would be rid of him. "Look, Sam," I said, peering through the throng of people on the opposite side of the station, "our train is in. Let's make a run for it!" without thinking, and sure that he was at my heels, I darted across and in through the doors of the Downtown Local. Then suddenly remembering tagalong Sam, I turned on my heels only to find that he wasn't behind me. Neither was he sitting down nor pushing his way toward the middle of the car. My God, I thought, he is probably still out on the platform, fumbling to find the door.

Much as I would have liked to, I couldn't just leave him there. I would have to go and haul him in. Edging my way out of the train and onto the platform, I scanned the entire area. Sam was nowhere in sight. He was not back on the express, which was about to close its doors. Where the devil was this goofball? There was no reason why he would have gone upstairs, but Sam just couldn't disappear off the face of the earth; that just isn't possible!

I decided to give it one more try before boarding the local once again. By now it should have been easy to spot him on the platform since most of the people were already jammed inside the open doors of the Local. There was no one; not a soul except a guy in an open acoustical phone booth. Oh, no. It couldn't be! Why didn't Sam tell me he had to make a call? Thoroughly annoyed, I dashed over to the phone booth only to find Sam just standing there with that same dumb grin on his face and not making a call at all. "Sam!" I screamed, moving closer to determine what I thought that I was seeing. He called out, "For God sake, get in; you'll miss the train!"

That night I wrote a note to Helen, relating the final chapter of this fiasco and concluded with the phrase, "So much for miracles, therapy, and reflexes, and by the way, Yenta, you're fired!"

Chapter 17

"The Bells Are Ringing for Me and My Gal"
Dean Martin

Throughout my entire school career, I had never been a joiner, and therefore, when Edie and Barbara urged me to try out for the Glee Club, I was characteristically reluctant. I genuinely liked all the music majors but knew that most of them could sight-read five part harmony with little or no effort. Since I had never been able to read print music easily, and certainly not at a distance, I knew I would have to memorize the words and listen to the harmony very closely during our practice sessions. "Come on," said my roommate Barbara. "We're singing the Messiah, and there will be very few lines in each chorus to learn, since there is so much repetition." Fortunately for me, Edie had a fine, cultured alto voice, and it really didn't take long before I stopped faking it and started participating. The night of the concert arrived, and Mom, Helen, and Jerry made the two-hour trip to share it with me. Few moments in my life have been as exhilarating and … emotional as standing there in my choir robe belting out "Alleluia, Alleluia," backed up by a full orchestra and knowing that those who meant the most to me were sitting right there in the audience enjoying it all. I had gone on a long, self imposed diet and had shed thirty pounds at that point, and what was more, I wore an air of self-confidence and poise that surprised even me. Wow! I was really feeling my oats! A slim size eleven, a nouveau coiffeur, and a boyfriend to boot!

My dates with Jerry took us everywhere, legitimate theatre, the opera, Broadway shows, and when funds were low, the Lowe's National or RKO Royal on 19th Street. Finding a seat in a darkened theatre was, for us, a major undertaking until we fell on a scheme that was really quite foolproof. Once in the theatre, we would hesitate until the light from the screen shone especially bright on the backrests of the seats below. Those that were shiny were obviously unoccupied. The others that were in shadow were not. One evening making our way down the aisle, we decided that a pair of seats were empty. I proceeded to set my weary bottom down only to find it planted firmly on the lunch of a man sitting next to me. I don't know to this day who was more irate, he, because I squashed his tomato, or I, because it left a circle of red droplets on the back of my dress, in the worst possible place!

"When are we going to talk to your folks?" Jerry asked six months after my college graduation. I supposed that it was inevitable, as was the showdown which was sure to be forthcoming, when I announced my intention to marry an Italian. That was the sort of thing that good, clean Irish-American girls just didn't think of doing. A Jew could marry a Gentile, an American Indian could tie the knot with another tribe member, but for a McDonald to marry a Marafito, why, as Old Mrs. Fitzgerald put it, that was "as bad as bedding down with a Chinese person!" no one in my family should have been surprised, for I was, after all, the black sheep of the household, untouched, it seemed, by the precepts of Irish tradition that should have counted for something. What made matters worse was that Helen was steeped in ethnic heritage, had made a trip back to the "old sod" a few years before, and was even now going with a spectacular fellow named Dan, straight from Tipperary no less. Boy, I was really in for it! This little "rebel" had come home and had promised her heart to, of all people, an Italian!

To my shock, once the initial storm had passed, it was my Father who took to Jerry first. After all, anyone who distrusted the English and thought living in the world of FDR had been great, couldn't be all that bad! Helen was no problem either, since she and Jerry were buddies right from the start. My Mother was going to take a little longer, but even she relented finally when we announced that we would wait a year before tying the knot. I suppose that by this time they all knew that Italian or not, he was ambitious, thoughtful, outgoing, and what was more important, we were in love!

It's Theresa's wedding day 04/18/1954.

Theresa and Jerry were just pronounced husband and wife,
their love will last forever.

Portrait of Theresa and Jerry as husband and wife.

Unfortunately there were not many photos of Jerry's parents. This portrait shows them celebrating their 50th wedding anniversary, which took place several years after Theresa and Jerry's marriage.

This was probably the last photo Theresa would have of her parents, since her Father was quite ill at the time.

Chapter 18

"Just Picture a Penthouse"
Nat King Cole

"What's a matta for you? You people musta be craze!" Mrs. Taglerini, a diminutive, olive-skinned lady, meticulously attired in a housedress and checkered apron, stood in the doorway of her ground-floor apartment, frantically waving a large wooden spoon in our direction. There was no sense trying to sneak up the stairs quietly! We knew what was coming and even worse, that her wrath was fully justified. "You know, when I firsta meta you," she zeroed in on Jerry, "I say to myselfa, that's a niza Italian boy." For a moment, her voice mellowed and seemed almost reverent, but her mood quickly changed, and now her spoon was sweeping just like an orchestra conductor getting ready for the final bars of a classical piece. It would move from the tip of Jerry's nose across the living room and toward the door of what was obviously her kitchen. "When you geta marry and move a upastairsa, I says, thatsa niza. You fixa upa the apartmenta, puta ina the new pips, that's a niza, too, buta," grabbing Jerry's jacket and motioning him to follow her. "Three daysa now, I washa my husband'sa shirtsa a, they no comea cleana, I cooka the spaghette and the water, she's all a reda and browna, and now, I says to myselfa, that'sa no niza. Wadda ya thinka you do?"

The time was ripe to jump in and offer some plea in self-defense. We limply attempted to explain that in the process of installing a new sink, my Brother-in-law, Norman, had found it necessary to replace copper tubing, since the original fixtures had been so clogged with grit and grime, and that in the process of connecting the maze of elbows, nuts, and joints, Norman must have unwittingly sent fifty years of rust plummeting down the drain and into the water supply of the apartments just below. What we had frankly not counted on was that it would take so much time for all the residue to work its way down through the jungle of pipes and into the sewage system below. There was nothing any of us could do now but wait and pray that Mrs. Taglerini's patience would withstand the telltale gray in her wash and multicolored ziti in her pot, for just a little longer. Indeed, if the antiquated plumbing in our newfound Shangri-la had been our only problem, we might have considered ourselves fortunate, since we had been able to lasso this three-room apartment, three flights up, for a mere fifty dollars a month.

Chapter 19

"On Top of Spaghetti, All Covered with Cheese..." Parody of "On Top of Old Smokey"

Coming as I did from a small family, my initiation into the Marafito clan was nothing less than staggering. There seemed to be kids, carriages, food, and people everywhere. Jerry's oldest Sister, Rose, was working on her eighth bambino; Brother Sal had three and Sister Kay had two.

Once a year, during the feast of Our Lady of Mount Carmel, all the Marafito clan gathered in the family home backyard on 8th Street in Verplanck, New York. No excuse would be tolerated for missing this celebration, so dead or alive you were there! I spent the better part of several hours sorting out names and faces and was genuinely satisfied with my performance until Sister-in-law Teresa, married to, uh, I think to, Jerry's Brother Sal announced, "Now wait until you meet the rest of the family!" my mouth fell open. "You mean there are more?"

Laughing she continued, "Sure, there's the 'gumbahs' and 'gumares.'" I breathed a sigh of relief. My college Italian taught me that these were just corruptions of the Italian equivalents of Godfather and Godmother. "Well," I said with a shrug, "that's only two people, right?" everyone around me roared. Soon I would learn why.

"Terry meet Gumbah Antonio." "This is Gumbah Vincenzo." "Now you must meet Gumbah Ernesto." Finally, I made it through the crowd finding my dearly beloved. "How many times were you baptized anyway?" not sure why I was asking, Jerry replied, "Just once, as far as I know." "I am totally confused," I said with a great big sigh! "I was just introduced to several gumbas." Jerry was smiling from one ear to the other. He continued, "Oh, you mean them?" as he swept his arm around the deepening crowd. "Oh, hell, they're all good friends; we just call them that. After all, chances are they really are somebody's godfathers and godmothers."

After each of these introductions, there was the same comment—"Che pulita!" now my dictionary translation of "pulita" was "how clean she is!" had they thought I was going to be dirty? Finally, I learned that what they were actually saying was "how cute she is." Well, that was loads better than being labeled Mrs. Clean.

At the end of each trip up to the "Point," as Verplanck was known, we were loaded down with all sorts of goodies. I was never quite sure whether this was their way of helping us out or an overt attempt by Jerry's Mother to ensure that her dear little boy would not starve.

*Jerry and Theresa are standing outside Jerry's family
home in Verplanck, New York.*

Chapter 20

"From the Sublime to the Ridiculous!"
Thomas Paine in *The Age of Reason*

One Monday morning, college diploma in hand, I headed toward the downtown business area in Manhattan. There was a general employment recruiting office, and after noting some of my vital statistics, the lady at the front desk directed me to an advertising firm on 5th Avenue. A receptionist greeted me at the door, handed me a tiny card to fill out, and disappeared. Wow, what luck! I could complete the required information on my own with the help of some extraordinary new low-vision lenses I had purchased from the Lighthouse, and there was no one around to notice how closely I had to look to carry it off.

The girl returned presently and ushered me into a swanky inner chamber. The gentleman sitting in this huge padded leather chair reminded me of a little dwarf in the "Wizard of Oz." He was so pleasant and unquestioning; I couldn't believe my good fortune. He explained that his last girl had gone and gotten married, leaving him high and dry, and that as far as he was concerned I could start immediately.

Holy dollar bills! No qualifying test, no need to show him my creds, nothing! He must be really desperate, I thought, and then the torpedo struck with all its force, killing my short-lived bubble of enthusiasm. Well, you can guess why I could not get this job! I launched a defense and stated that there is evidence that shows that handicapped people had much lower accident rates and higher records of efficiency. My words seemed to fall on deaf ears. A few other potential employers refused to hire me on the basis that the job in question involved the typing of outgoing letters, and they would have to have someone proofread material I had turned out. Remember this was too early for the invention of a word processor and even an electric typewriter!

I found it increasingly difficult to think of any rebuttal that would satisfy all their doubts. At night, I would toss and turn, mulling over how I could have handled an interview question differently, and by the end of the week I was thoroughly disheartened and doubtful that I would ever find an open door, ready to swing at least once behind me before it closed. Surely, I was not the first, nor would I be the last handicapped person to find herself at the short end of the economic stick.

Down through the years I had heard episodes recounted that were certainly more deflating than any I had experienced. I recalled a story about a young couple who had been refused rental of an apartment on the third floor because the landlord insisted that they might fall down the stairs and sue him. Another woman had been denied occupancy because it was felt that her presence in the building would be too depressing for the other tenants, and then, too, she might start a fire in her kitchen. Yes, these things did happen and how crazy to think that people could really react that way!

Not willing to give up, I had a bright idea, one that should have been obvious since I had a Master's degree in Special Education. Right away I contacted the Institute for the Blind, the very school where Jerry had graduated from several years ago. Listen to this story about my two-year stint when I was subjected to some really twisted ideas about teaching blind children.

Initially I was appalled to see kids with as much sight as I had groping their way around dimly lit halls and being forced to read Braille even though they had enough vision to read print. Remembering what Pop Downs taught me back in camp, to always use my vision to the fullest, I mounted a campaign to help the children I was teaching to do the same. Again and again I pleaded with the school administrators: if the students don't have progressive eye conditions, shouldn't they be encouraged to use what percentage of vision they have?

One child who seemed unusually bright and had extremely good partial vision became a source of concern for me. She looked skyward to the light instead of focusing on the person she was talking to. "Hey, Barbara!" I would say, "I'm down here, look at me. I want to see your face, not your chin!" I was reprimanded by my supervisor saying that I was wasting my time working with Barbara in this way. My job was to teach only arithmetic and reading, not to be concerned showing these children the social graces.

After a nature trip when we returned to the classroom, I encouraged some of the totally blind children to mold in clay what they had felt outside, and we would use different colors for leaves, branches, and stones. Those who had some useful vision were encouraged to draw what they had seen with crayons I bought. They were not part of standard equipment in this school for the blind. Immediately my supervisor had something to say about this situation.

"What do blind children know about color, and as for the others, you're expecting too much of them, getting them to remember what they saw on the field trip, good heavens!" blind children, I agreed, had no concept of color, but still it was important for them to understand that a leaf in autumn was first green, then gold, and finally brown. This was part of life and for them to be closed off from a world of color simply because they could not see seemed to be the height of absurdity.

At this point, it was time to move on and I could no longer condone the backward thinking of a school that was supposed to help blind and visually impaired students prepare for the real world out there. I knew other blind women who had procured good civil service jobs typing case records for the Department of Welfare. Now was the time to look into this opportunity a little further.

Upon investigation, however, I learned that people could only take the civil service test if they passed the course given by the Lighthouse. The training, I was told, could last anywhere from one to three years. This sounded really ridiculous to me! Jerry was the sounding board for my screams and protests. "You mean to say it's going to take three years to learn how to operate a simple machine and brush up on my typing skills?" he replied, "Of course not, toots! But don't forget, the longer they keep you there, the more money they get from the State of New York, and they'll argue that without government and private contributions they wouldn't exist at all." My anger meter was slowly rising into the red zone. "Well," I said slamming a typing manual down on the table, "they're not going to make me part of their numbers game. I found a course that's absolutely free and it's right near Grand Central Terminal." It was a do-it-yourself deal where students could progress at their own speed, take a test and if qualified, receive something resembling an official certificate. It took me exactly ten days to get this coveted piece of paper.

So, off to the Department of Welfare I went and was not sorry! Miss McCabe turned out to be one of the warmest human beings I had ever met. I tried to tell her how much I appreciated this chance, including my pledge to do everything in my power to justify the confidence this Agency was placing in me. "Nonsense!" she said. "You don't have to prove anything. We have a vacancy available, and apparently you're qualified. We need no other criteria. Now just try and relax and know that I'll always be here if you need to talk to me."

I could have hugged her but instead followed her down the hall. We arrived at a large room containing ten desks, all but one of which were occupied by girls busily typing. Eleanor was my immediate supervisor, and after introducing me to all the typists, she handed me a disc and suggested trying a short report first. Since it was only about a half hour from quitting time, I set to work on my first big assignment, and there on the instruction sheet in big, bold letters was the guideline, "Five carbon copies." I swallowed hard, remembering that if I made a mistake I would have to insert a mini-sheet five times and erase each error individually. No problem. I would just go slower than usual and try to continue thinking positive.

When I was about three lines from the bottom, it happened; the voice on the other end of the Dictaphone calmly stated, "Operator, please delete the last line!" oh, no, she couldn't do that to me! I hadn't listened far enough in advance, and there had been no indication of the correction on the markup sheet. I was dead in the water, and I knew it. To attempt to eradicate two words so close to the bottom of the page would have been an impossible task in itself, but a whole line, no way! There was nothing to do but give it the old college try, and to my delight, I was actually able to wade through three of the copies. Alas, the fourth proved to be my Waterloo. To remove one whole line, an eraser was needed but I pressed it too hard, and there, smack in the middle of the page, was a deep gash.

Can you see how far technology has brought us forward today, with the ease of simply hitting the "delete" key on a laptop or desktop keyboard, and voila, presto, the error gets fixed! And as for copies needed, the print option gives you that also, how simple! I felt a tap on my shoulder. It was Eleanor again. "Say, everyone's ready to go home. You don't have to stay here all night, you know." In my preoccupation, I had failed to notice the flurry of activity around me and lamely I tried to explain that I had wanted to get the report finished before leaving.

Looking down at the cause of my obvious distress, she said, "Tomorrow's another day, Terry, and anyway, I shouldn't have started you off with a ringer." I looked her way and gratefully mumbled something about hoping I would do better tomorrow. Eleanor continued, "I'm not worried about that," she said. "Now go home and get a good night's sleep." I couldn't wait to do just that, although I knew full well that I'd never close my eyes for fear that I would wake up and find that it had all been a wonderful, impossible dream.

Although there were a few moments before nine o'clock in the first two weeks when I was able to exchange casual chit chat with my new coworkers, the truth was that ninety-nine percent of my concentration was centered on trying to keep pace, or so I thought, with a seasoned group of semi-professional typists. At lunchtime, I would run downstairs, grab a sandwich, a bottle of Coke, and would be back in my seat well before I should have been. Coffee breaks and spontaneous lapses for bits of girl talk were luxuries I felt I could not afford, since I realized that if I blew this opportunity, I might well be ruining it for any future handicapped employees.

As time passed and the quality of my work improved, I gradually started to relax. One afternoon when I had cut my lunch break in half, as usual, a slim, dark-haired girl tapped me on the shoulder and asked, "Hey, eager beaver, are you trying to show up the rest of us?" my God, that was the last thing I wanted to do, I told her, and hastened to explain that since I had been so green, I was afraid of being fired if I didn't produce my share of the workload. Her reaction was immediate and unexpected. "If you keep on going at this breakneck speed, it will be you who manage to get the rest of us canned!" what a relief! Even though Eleanor had assured me that my work was adequate, I had always supposed that she had been leaning over backward to bolster my morale.

"I noticed you wear a pair of pretty thick glasses when you're proofreading your material," said another typist, Laura. She continued, "Are you nearsighted?" thinking a minute on how to answer this question, I replied, "No," I explained. "It's a bit more than that," and when I finally leveled with her, she was flabbergasted. "So, that's it," she mumbled, almost inaudibly. "I guess I shouldn't be telling you about something," and she paused not sure whether to continue. "But they don't call me, big mouth Laura for nothing." I urged her to continue, "Oh, come on, please tell me. I'm not made of glass. I don't shatter or crumble, and besides I've always admired people who tell it like it is."

Laura took a deep breath and explained, "Well, okay, you remember when Eleanor was introducing you to the rest of us?" she didn't pause for an answer from me. She proceeded, "Well, when you said, hello, you never looked directly at any one of us and I thought to myself, boy is she stuck up!" we both laughed, and she was relieved to see that my feelings hadn't been hurt. Yeah, that's one of the problems some of us have. It's hard to keep our eyes still in the first place and trying to focus on the face of someone six or seven feet away is even more of a challenge." She sighed and asked me, "Now that we cleared that up, why don't you join the rest of us when we go out to lunch? That way, we can all get fired together!" we were both laughing as she uttered these last words.

I was delighted. Another wall had come crashing down, and with it, the lingering fears that my best would never be good enough. From that moment on, all of us gabbed about something or nothing, ate together, shopped, and went on various fad diets. The feeling of really belonging made me warm all over.

PART 5

Soon the Stork Will Make a Delivery!
April 1955—January 3, 1956

Chapter 21

"Don't Worry, Be Happy"
Bobby McFerrin

These were some of the happiest years of my life. I felt totally fulfilled, both as a woman and a wife. Then early in April of 1955 I found myself skyrocketing into another role I was definitely not prepared to undertake. You see, I was pregnant. When entering the office one day, I pointed to my stomach, made some baby noises and asked my coworkers, "How could it be possible?" after the laughing quieted down, the girls reminded me that it took two to tango. Nevertheless, I couldn't help worrying. I wasn't ready. Jerry and I had so many plans for the future. So how was it possible that a tiny baby was about to upset the whole applecart, and it hadn't even been born yet!

In a fit of despair, I called Helen to tell her the news, silently wishing that it was she who was pregnant. Helen wanted children so desperately, had miscarried more than once, and had lost a baby in her fifth month of pregnancy. In the end, she would pop out five children, and the first tried to be born in the hospital elevator.

"How could you possibly not want a baby?" she asked completely dismayed. "It's not that I don't want one," I protested. "It's just that I don't want one now. My thoughts right now are around Jerry who is like a caged lion living in our three small rooms in the city, and he longs to get back to the suburbs where he can spread his wings without clobbering himself on clutter and furniture that is difficult to navigate around." "So, what's that got to do with being pregnant?" Helen was getting exasperated with me. I could see I was getting nowhere. "What's it got to do with it? Everything! We went up to a fast-growing small town, Croton-on-Hudson, a Northern Westchester Community about ten miles from Verplanck, and we bought a parcel of land. Jerry and I figured that in a year or two, we would have enough for a good down payment on a new house." "Great, that's really fantastic!" she was smiling and clapping her hands with joy for her baby Sister. Helen continued, "Then you can get your little girl out of the steaming city tenements and she can ride her bike in the wide open spaces. What could be better?" it was a losing cause to think that I would change her mind with my barrage of protests. I should have known that in the first place. Shaking my head, I continued, "How could we possibly save money with a new baby coming? I won't be able to keep on working, and without my salary our dream of living in the suburbs would be just that, a fantasy!"

Later, it was Jerry who finally hit on the solution to our seemingly insurmountable dilemma. "What's to stop you from going back to work? Your Mother will be living with us in our new home, and you couldn't find a better babysitter than her, could you?" what he said made sense. My Father was still hanging on to life, but who knows how long he would be with us. It had already been arranged that my Mother would live with us. Leaving her alone in a five room apartment in a neighborhood whose whole character had started to decay made no sense at all, and Jerry had not forgotten his death bed promise to Dad that we would take care of Mom as long as she lived.

"Then you really want the baby?" I asked still feeling uncertain. "Of course, I do," he said with enthusiasm while smiling from ear to ear! He hugged me and made me believe his words, "Everything will be all right. Whatever we face in our life as a couple, we will make it all happen together!" his words were reassuring but deep down there were silent, foreboding reservations I didn't even dare to share with him. I'd make a heck of a Mother. I didn't even like children, especially babies, and they didn't like me either. Every time relatives would ask me to hold their infant, as soon as it was in my arms, it would howl so loud that even a deaf person could hear the little one. In the end, though, I decided that since we were going to be stuck with one another, maybe, just maybe, we could grow up together. It was a good thing, I thought, that unborn babies didn't get to pick and choose their mommies; even on bargain day any self-respecting tot would have passed me up as a born loser.

"You won't be unhappy if it's a girl?" I asked Jerry, suddenly remembering my Sister's reference to its sex only weeks after it was conceived. "You're crazy. First you don't want a baby at all, and now you're telling me it's going to be a girl. No, just for the record, I don't care what it is, and besides, I can remember enough biology to know that my little XY chromosome was the gizmo that determined its sex in the first place."

Blissfully, we passed through the heat of the summer in our tiny bird's nest, and as our chief source of entertainment we would lie awake at night with the windows open, listening to the various domestic battles emanating from above and below us. At times, when the plot really thickened, dishes, glasses, and an occasional pot of macaroni and beans went crashing down to the bottom of the airshaft. Smacking my lips, as I was finishing my latest carton of butter pecan ice cream, I turned to Jerry and asked, "Think we're going to turn out that way?" "We'd better not," said Jerry laughing. "We don't have that many dishes to spare." "Ah, good point," I responded as I dug into my other pregnancy favorite, coconut custard pie, yum yum! Years later, my soon-to-be born daughter Linda would tell me that it was my fault that she cringed each time she was presented with either that dreadful pie or ice cream dessert choice!

Come Christmas when my baby was due, my bundle of joy decided that it would hang around in my tummy for a little more time, and besides it was cold outside anyway. The days passed and, here it was New Year's Eve and no cramps, no water breaking, nothing at all! "Should I be worried?" I asked myself. Not long ago, a Cousin of mine died in childbirth, and Jerry and I decided that whatever it cost, we would err on the side of caution and so chose a very nice obstetrician. Keep in mind, in those days this was rare, not the norm. "It is New Year's Day," announced Jerry. "I'm taking you on the Third Avenue El to see if we can shake things up a little."

Chapter 22

"For Unto Us a Child Is Born"
Isaiah 9:6
Popularized in Handel's *Messiah*

The clatter of steel against steel jolted me into a state of semiconsciousness. Not that I was about to leap to my feet, eager for the challenge of a bright new day that was definitely not my style. Far back in childhood I had developed a case of chronic morning syndrome, at least that is what I called it anyway. It wasn't that I was cranky or miserable when first waking up. Maybe numb, immobile, uncoordinated, but never nasty! "You'd make some hell of a whore," Jerry had once teased. "You'd never be able to stay awake long enough to make any money!" he was probably right, but who cared? No howling horny tom cat or clanking squeaking garbage truck was going to rob me of my beauty rest. For sure, I needed all I could possibly get!

I pulled the covers up over my head and was just about to let Dr. Freud have another "go at my dream cycle," when suddenly I remembered the alarm clock waiting for its moment of sadistic triumph. I had always felt that in some devious way Jerry had attached the wires of that mechanical time-bomb to the springs of our bed, for when it unleashed its siren, it sent electrical charges through every cell in my body. Then after the initial sound blast, it was replaced with a bunch of girls tap dancing their way across my brain! This would not happen this morning. I would silence the demon forever.

I reached out in the direction of our night table, but to my surprise my hand got jammed against something metallic. "What in the name of…?" I thought, struggling to pry open my eyes, I found myself staring into the beam of a beacon-light spotlight no more than three inches from my face. None of this is making any sense, I thought, starting to panic! My first impulse was to scream, but a hand came firmly down against my lips. And the howl died in my throat.

"Ah, you're awake!" a grizzled voice said from above. I breathed a sigh of relief. Burglars didn't go around waking up their intended victims before ripping them off. I squinted and tried to move, but every bone in my body seemed to ache. Once again, feeling a lot more scared with every moment that passed, my left hand reached out. Where the hell was Jerry? My hand was firmly grabbed and pressed downward and back under the covers.

Ah, now I know. I was in a concentration camp and a band of little North Koreans had been waiting for me to awaken. Soon they would take my poor broken body and toss it onto a rack of nails, and they'd pound and squeeze until I screamed for mercy. I wouldn't tell them anything! No way! I'd die first…tell what? What did I know any way?

Should I pretend to sleep so maybe I could buy a little more time before the torture would begin? With great trepidation, I dared to open my eyes and glared up at the light. "Oh, does the light bother you?" now there was a switch. A torturer with a heart, and a

woman to boot. At least it sounded like a female. "They told me …
I mean, it says right here!" she said as she waved what looked like
a clipboard in my direction. "That you're … oh, never mind!" with
that, the voice and the light were gone in a flash.

I grinned and almost laughed aloud. Dummy, I told myself.
All this was just a bad dream… see what happens when you watch
too many late-night horror films. That was all this was! But was it?
The metal bars were real as were the pains shooting up from under
the sheets. The pulsating sensation seemed to travel up and down
my body in slow agonizing waves. Suddenly, there was a tiny wail
off in the distance, and my waves of sleepiness cleared and brought
me back to reality. This was the maternity ward in the Westchester
Square Hospital, and sometime last night I had given birth to a
lovely eight-pound baby girl. Now the smile on my face was one of
satisfaction. I had really gone and done it. The freckle-faced tomboy
who had preserved her virginity the way a miser guards his money
had stepped up to the plate and hit a "grand slam," and had brought
forth a bouncing baby girl!

Again, there was a fretful cry, and for one lingering moment, I
toyed with the notion of summoning that woman who sounded like
Nurse Ratched from "One Flew Over the Cuckoo's Nest" back to
my bedside. Frantically, I thought of a dozen questions starting with:
Was my little girl all right? Were they taking good care of her? What
if … What if …! Even if they weren't, could I have done better?

The whole nightmare of the night before came bounding back
into conscious memory and left me very fearful. You see my little
girl decided that it was time to come into the world but apparently
didn't know which way was out of its warm cozy environment. The
end result is that she tried to come out sideways and had everyone

in the delivery room scurrying around to deal with this disturbing situation. Finally Linda was born, but there was so much blood that they packed me so tight with gauze, and I was told firmly, "Don't move a muscle or even blink an eye until the bleeding stops."

Later, I would find out that when Jerry was given the news about the birth of our daughter, and when he asked how we were doing, the answer he received was that your baby is fine, and then "... Your wife has lost a lot of blood...and...and...,ah, only time will tell. Well let's see." Jerry later told me that he had almost fainted on the spot. My poor Jerry!

I'd wait awhile to find out how my little girl was doing. It still appeared to be late night or early morning, and by this time it was obvious that I was not alone. In the glimmer of light ribboning in from the hallway, I was able to make out several beds. There were two snores, one groan, and a whistle, as far as I could judge, and all were very much asleep.

I suddenly realized that I was dying of thirst. I tried to muster up some little bit of saliva, but even that was nonexistent. "All day I faced the barren waste, without the taste of water...cool, clear, water!" the words of an old country western song sang by Sons of the Pioneers vibrated through my head. Then followed a rather spirited discourse between my brain and my right arm. "Hey, down there, the little Mama's thirsty. Do something. There's got to be a button attached to that metal bar you can beep to summon help." "I already tried that," said my arm, "but the clip snapped off and as of this moment, it's sitting down there in your slipper." "Okay, then reach up and turn on the overhead light. You know there's got to be one." "Not me. I hurt too much. Besides, I work on union scale and I don't budge until 9 am sharp!" I had tried and lost, and the best I could do now was to settle back until my jailer made her next appearance.

It was a lead-pipe cinch that I wouldn't be going anywhere before then, since there appeared to be a double set of guardrails all around my bed. Doggedly, I tried to concentrate on something other than my parched throat. Poor Jerry. I wondered if he'd had a chance to really see our baby. The nurse had hooked up a special light right outside the nursery viewing window, but how was she to know that too much light was as bad for "our kind of folk" as no light at all!

"Nurse! Water!" the gasp came from across the way. Help was on its way. The rustle of a crisp uniform whisked past my bed. "Me, too!" I whimpered. "Well, of course, little Mother. How are you feeling?" "Wow!" she had called me "Mother." I didn't feel very much like one. There was no surge of maternal radiance, no inner glow. I was just an overgrown kid ready to sell her soul or even her body for just one drink.

"Are we feeling better?" she asked, replacing the empty cup on the night table. "Yes, we are," I said. "But why do we need these bars up now?" "We don't want to be falling out of bed, now do we?" before I could plead my case further, the bars were up once again, and the starched water carrier was gone.

A bell somewhere struck 5 and an instant chain reaction rocked the entire floor. Wagons rolled, doors slammed, bottles jangled out their own version of the "Anvil Chorus" as they struggled to maintain balance on the carts whizzing by. I heard the Nurse Ratched–like person, who seemed to oversee the tactical ground patrol, announce for all to hear that the first order of the day was the infernal mouthwash. The most ridiculous part of this fiasco was that one could not simply take a slug of the atomic potion and dispose of it in one container. There had to be a huge beach towel to support the mini bathtub, which in turn, cradled yet another set of pans. I grinned as I tried to methodically divide equal shares of the remains of the brew into each receptacle.

By this time, too, I was aware that I was not alone in my misgivings about our 5 am cocktail. There were four other women in the room. Since I was apparently the latest arrival, conversation centered around how much my baby weighed, my doctor's name, and how long I had been in labor. One woman had just given birth to the last member of a full baseball team. For two of the others, this was the third and fourth time around, and this left two novices, including me.

Before we could pursue our conversation further, we were bombarded by the earsplitting crash of bedpans being liberated from their nocturnal resting place. The rails of my bed screeched to a lower position, and a friendly voice inquired, "Did you void during the night?" I was dumbfounded. "Did I what?" "Look dearie," she said, her voice slightly less patient. "I can go look at your chart, but surely you must know if you were able to void during the night." Suffering sardines! I had hemorrhaged, screamed, been stitched and unstitched, knocked out and tossed from one stretcher to another, but apparently even all that had not been enough. My only association with the word "void" was the legal terminology that referred to the process of declaring a law defunct. If there was a connection between that sort of judicial mumbo-jumbo and my present predicament, I failed to see it.

I wondered briefly if I was supposed to have "voided" all alone, with the help of others, or by means of some abstract mechanical device unknown to me. I would be vague in my answer. I would just tell her that I couldn't remember whether I had or not. At any rate, a refrigerated bedpan was shoved under me and at once whatever might have been forthcoming froze in its tracks. Apparently, my performance did not meet with the approval of the maître d, for I was promptly informed that unless I could void before long, I would have to be catheterized. So, that was it! For crying out loud, why couldn't she have just asked me if I had made a tinkle or was it a stinky they were after? It didn't matter now, and I would find out eventually, but I did think that the threat of catheterization was a bit severe.

I wondered what it was about my excretory system, of all things, which led me from one embarrassing situation to another. Just last year, I had gone for a regular checkup to the tiny office of a recently arrived Hungarian refugee doctor. Sizing me up in one anatomical glance, he proclaimed, "Ve vill haf to haf a urine zample, you know." "Oh, why sure." He had caught me off guard for a minute. "Well, tomorrow, I'll..." "Tomorrow, nonzense! Ve vill do it now!" "Ve vill, huh!" I thought, glancing around in search of a bathroom. "Zertainly," he continued. "Nudding like de present, eh?" before I knew what was happening, he had slipped a three-ounce Dixie cup into my hand and was aiming me in the direction of a small anteroom no bigger than a large telephone booth.

Disposing of my jacket on the floor, since there didn't appear to be any hooks in sight, I soberly set to the task of unleashing myself from the rubber girdle I had donned for the first time that morning. Whether it was the stomach cramp, which froze me in a paralytic bow toward Allah, or the blood that was by now rushing toward my head, I couldn't say, but one thing was sure: I had passed the point of no return, and that last desperate tug had not succeeded in freeing me from my elastic bondage. That urine "zample" that he had wanted might be forthcoming sooner than either of us expected. What a shot for "Candid Camera," I mused. There I was, girdle hunched over at half-mast and, of all things, trying to empty the contents of my kidneys into a three ounce cup. Assuming I could aim my deposit in the right general direction (and this was not certain), what then? What, for instance was I supposed to do with the overflow? Alas, no use crying over spilled urine now.

The memory of that incident brought a smile to my face as I said, "You know, nurse, I really don't need those bars anymore. I'm not under anesthesia now, and the bed is much too big to fall off." A simple pat on the head was all I got and a casual, "We'll talk about it later, dear. It's just a safety precaution." I began to get a sneaky suspicion regarding the real reason for her rebuttal but decided not to jump to hasty conclusions.

I muttered something about hospital rules and Mrs. Baseball in the next bed solemnly assured me that no regulations were made without good reason. The younger set rebelled as one girl recounted her experience of the night before, when she had been forced to give her complete family history while in the throes of two-minute labor pains. The rest of us agreed that some rules were just meant to be broken.

It was at this point that Nurse Ratched made her appearance once again. She stormed into the room, stationing herself directly in the center, and announced the next battle maneuver. "You know, as I explained yesterday, and as I will repeat for all of those nonbelievers, exercise is the healthiest way to recover from childbirth. If you stay glued to those beds, your stitches are going to kill you, and in the end, when you finally go home, you'll be too weak to take care of yourself, much less a newborn baby. Therefore,…" she paused, and I almost expected to hear a drum roll and the blare of a trumpet. "Therefore, when the breakfast trays are brought in, I want you all out of your beds and out here at the center table to be served." A groan arose from all corners of the room, and during the ensuing rumble, Ratched slipped over to my bed and whispered, "This does not apply to you; just sit tight and we'll take care of everything."

She darted off, leaving the strongest words of protest still forming in my larynx. Was I somehow immune to all the agonies and miseries resulting from lack of exercise? "Hey, Terry, come join the rest of us stitch bitches. You'll love gliding along inch by inch, and we've got a bouncy new cushion over here to soften your fall." They all roared while I struggled to find a way to explain why I wasn't allowed to eat at the table with them. Finally, I told them I had been confined to home base, orders of Nurse Ratched.

"Why the red-carpet treatment, honey?" it was the novice across the room. "I haven't the foggiest notion why I'm not up there suffering with the rest of you, but I assure you that it's not my own choice."

From the doorway came a voice proclaiming, "Here come the goodies, girls." A chubby black woman appeared at the door with a cart full of delicious smelling food, but instead of serving the others first, she headed straight in my direction. "Don't you worry, Lambie, I'll take care of you personally. I know all about your problem, and you got nothin' to worry about. You see, I got a Brother who's just the same as you are, and I've had lots of practice knowing just what to do."

My face turned scarlet. My secret was about to come undone, and all that I could do was lie there. It had been inevitable, I suppose, but a gnawing feeling deep within me told me that the worst was yet to come. I knew that I had met a well-meaning "do-gooder" who was about to butter my toast, pour my coffee, and tell me that my eggs were at 12 o'clock. God, how could I stop her! I reached for the cream and carefully poured it into the steaming cup of java, even though I detested the taste of coffee, especially in the morning. Unfortunately, her reaction rubbed salt further into the wound. "Well, will you look at that? She can pour the cream without spilling a drop!" bully for me! It hadn't been hard not to miss since there hadn't been much cream in the pitcher, and I was not about to blow this scene, not while I was on center stage. My plump friend, however, was not to be dissuaded from her intended mission. "Your eggs are at 12 o'clock; your roll is at 6; see, I know how to do it! You should see how well my Brother does. He's even learned to play with those braille checkers and read stories on those talking book things." Oh, God, now I was in real trouble. Not only was I being publicly exposed but also likened to a rather slow-witted type, probably in his late seventies. "Thanks, but that really isn't necessary. I'll be just fine, and besides, you have four starving women over there who need you more than I do."

"Oh, I haven't forgotten about my other mamas. I want you all to look out for my little friend, here. We don't want anything to happen to her, do we?" that did it! The time had come to rise to the occasion. "Look, I appreciate your help, but I really do see quite a bit, and there isn't anything special that I need."

Thank God, the other novice came to the rescue. "Come on, Jennie; we're starving, and it's a cinch that she'll do okay on her own." "Okay," she said, "But I'll be back later to help you brush your teeth." She retreated to the hallway with her cart and didn't hear me mutter to my collection of mamas, "Well, I wonder if she'll let me hold the toothpaste, if I'm really a good girl!"

This seemed to break the ice. Mrs. Baseball was laughing so hard she snorted coffee up her nose, and soon all of them were giggling and moaning because it hurt their stitches to laugh. By the time the rest of the women had finished their breakfast, the color began to fade from my face, and I apologized for all the pomp and circumstance surrounding my confinement. "It is so hard," I explained, "to put down people who are sincere without hurting their feelings."

Taking a sip of water, I continued, "I'm sure they all mean well, but I somehow get the feeling that to their way of thinking, if I were allowed to venture forth, I would be sure to step into some unnatural disaster. Watching me would take a full-time nurse, so it's safer and cheaper to keep me here in bed where I can't get into any trouble." "What could possibly happen?" a small Chinese woman who had been setting the breakfast trays back on the rolling cart stood erect, making an impatient gesture with one hand. Seeing that I had gained an unexpected champion, I whimsied, "Well, I could fall out of the window or down the elevator shaft or sail into that tray of juice glasses over there." My little Chinese friend exploded in laughter, broken by a comment from the gal on my right. "Well, if you can see all that, then what's the big fuss about?" I shrugged my shoulders, and continued, "Search me. I certainly wasn't in any shape last night to even think about it, but my guess is that somewhere out on that chart of mine, my good doctor had made mention of the fact that 'the patient is partially blind.'"

"Yeah, I can see that. They just figure you can't see anything at all, right?" Mrs. Baseball asked with interest. "That's it, and to tell the truth, they're not alone. It's easy to understand total blindness.

You need only close your eyes, and there you are! But when you tell someone you can only see a little, that's another ball game."

"Well," asked another. "Don't glasses help? I know when I watch television, I need them myself." I thought for a minute. "In some cases, glasses help a little, but there are probably tens of thousands of us walking around who find them more confusing than helpful. My husband Jerry can't see out of the sides of his eyes. They call it 'telescopic vision.' Now, there's no pair of glasses that's going to correct that. He confuses people every time when he can call 'double wood' at the end of the bowling alley and yet can't see his own hand in front of his face. I'm just the opposite. I'm nearsighted. Weird, that's what we are, just plain weird." "Not so weird," commented Mrs. Baseball. "You still figured out how to have babies, didn't you?" good Lord, I thought that I was starting to help these fine women understand the various levels of vision different people could have, but I was tired and my mind was on what would surely be coming next.

During this conversation, deep down I was slowly slipping into a state of quiet, compelling terror, for the moment of truth would arrive in a few minutes. Soon, I knew, the babies would be brought in and then all my talk of self-reliance was sure to go to pot. I had dreaded this even more than the labor pains. How could I tell them that I had never held a baby in my arms that didn't howl and try to get away from me? How could I explain that even now I didn't want to hold my own child? With my luck, she would probably throw up all over the place, scream her head off, or scowl up at me and pull away as all the other babies in my life had done. God, what was I going to do? I surely had to be the only Mother in the world scared of her own newborn.

Eventually, the dreaded moment arrived, and to my relief, my chubby-faced, pink-cheeked little girl was placed in my arms by one of the sweetest, most compassionate nurses I had ever met. I guess my anxiety was written all over my face, for she paused for an inordinate amount of time to make sure that I was in complete control before going on to her next station. "She probably won't drink more than an ounce," she warned, "but we don't expect anything more than that for the first day." To my delight, Linda guzzled down four ounces almost without stopping. She even burped when she was supposed to, and as I leaned over to kiss her pudgy face, I knew that somehow, we would muddle through together.

PART 6

Chapter 23

A-G-I-T-A!

When you eat pickles and ice cream or spaghetti and peanut butter together, not to mention wolfing down pizza with a chaser of whipped cream, the dictionary would call the result Heartburn, the man on the street would call it a bellyache, and a good old fashioned country doctor would term it Gastroenteritis. Mr. Webster, Mr. And Ms. John Q. Public, and Dr. Marcus Welby, you've got it all wrong. Heartburn is buying a house you can't afford. A bellyache is deciding to build it yourself to save money you don't have. Meanwhile, acute gastroenteritis is taking on five loans in addition to a mortgage and keeping two steps ahead of the sheriff each time the first of the month rolls around. You can call it what you like, but I feel the Italians have said it all when they boil it down to one all-inclusive word, agita. Agita is going into a hair salon for a strawberry blonde rinse and coming out with orange hair! Agita is when your favorite big-league baseball team is losing 3-2 with the bases loaded in the bottom of the ninth, your big slugger is at the plate, the count is 3 balls 2 strikes, and then it happens, your giant picture screen goes dim because one satellite or another wasn't beaming in your direction! And, finally, agita is what we had in the year of our Lord, 1956, as we stood hand in hand on a sandy lot full of wrecked cars, broken mattresses, and a year's worth of relics, discarded thereon by those who didn't understand that someday this was to be our very own Shangri-la.

"We don't even know what kind of house we want to build here," said Jerry as he settled himself down on the jagged remains of a Beauty Rest. "Sure, we do, honey. I've got it all up here." I pointed to my head and continued, "We can build one of those precut homes that we saw last week and save all kinds of money subcontracting the work out ourselves." Jerry grinned. "You know what they say about precut homes, don't you? They're guaranteed to burn oil like crazy, fall apart at the joists and if we're lucky, wait for about ten years before it starts caving in on us completely."

"Aw, Jerry, what do they know anyway? The company we talked to last week has been in business for years. It'll be such fun mapping out our own dream house, just the way we want it, and drawing up our own blueprints." Jerry laughed and asked, "Doing what?" right away I answered him, "Sure, we can draw up our own blueprints. Remember, I took a course in college. I can do it! I know I can! Look at all the money we'll save!" Jerry quickly replied, "Oh, that's pretty good, a visually impaired lady with her nose to the drawing board. One sneeze and you could wipe out an entire laundry room." Confidently I countered, "Okay, go ahead and laugh. So, I must look close to see. The finished product is all that counts, and what you need is a little more confidence in me. Besides, they'll have their own experts to look it over and catch any mistakes."

Jerry pulled me close as a startled couple walked by and gaped at us sitting there among all the rubble. One of them said to us, "Don't you two have a home?" "We sure do," said Jerry. "And this is it, or at least it will be in six months from now." "Maybe we're really crazy," I said with a big sigh. "So much depends on my staying healthy and being able to work off all those loans. You know, our fancy financing scheme was slightly illegal, and if we ever fall behind, well Sing Sing prison is in the next town." Jerry replied with great conviction, "Don't worry about it! We've got your Mom to take care of our little Linda, six hundred dollars in the bank, and the big guy upstairs on our side. What else do we need?" "How about a little luck with a capital L thrown in, just in case?" I remarked in a tremulous voice.

As we rose to leave, I dug one of the innerspring coils out of my rear end, threw it down on the mattress, and said, "Well we made our own bed, so I suppose we might as well make up our minds to lie in it." Jerry said laughing, "If this is the kind of bed we're going to end up in, we'd better learn to make love standing up." My final remark for the moment was, "Let's go meet our parents, and I am sure they are going to say that we have rocks in our heads to even think about this venture."

Hours later, in front of both sets of parents, Diamond Jerry and his new roommate exuded nothing but unequivocal optimism. We had made our bed, and we were sure as hell prepared to see our project through to the end, even if everything else we possessed belonged to one finance company or another. But before meeting them, we had made some firm resolutions. Jerry and I were not about to ask our folks for help. It would only be a matter of time now for my Father, and never would he live to see any of his grandchildren. He wouldn't walk a second time down the aisle of St. Jerome's with

Helen, who so much more than I had borne the brunt of carrying the financial load for our family. Jerry's Mother and Father weren't in a position to help either! True, they owned their own home in the small town of Verplanck in Westchester County, but this and a ten-year-old Chrysler were their only claims of affluence. "Whena you own a homea," Jerry's Father had explained in his broken English, "That's a gooda and whether you worka or you no worka, you canna no get a helpa. Alla they tella...you...isa sella your housa!"

Chapter 24

"Our House, Is a Very, Very Fine House"
Crosby, Stills, Nash, and Young

The next few months were spent frantically lining up subcontractors, surveying, and having our lot "dejunked." Now, acid attacks the human digestive system in varying degrees. When we received the first estimates for labor and cost of material, the mildest symptoms appeared in the form of one prolonged stomach cramp. When the carpenter foreman broke his leg after tangling it in a bicycle chain hidden in the sand on our lot, heartburn set in. And when I learned from Youngstown, Ohio, that I had placed an order for ten feet of cabinet space when only nine and a half actually existed, the tears began and threatened to kill my excitement. I thought I had done so well! "How could you have forgotten to figure the thickness of the outside wall?" Jerry asked incredulously! "Because I thought it might look cute to have cabinets hanging both inside and outside the house, why else?" I said half in tears and half laughing!

But the worst was yet to come. "They're going to excavate our property tomorrow," Jerry announced with great excitement in early August. "And I'm going up there to see it firsthand. I will remind myself to take movies so we can show our grandchildren every step of the excavation process, shovel by shovel." The next night I anxiously awaited his call, but when it came, there was an aura of doom and gloom in Jerry's voice. "Did they dig out the lot?" I asked with growing concern. After a prolonged moment of silence, Jerry replied, "They sure did!" "Well, why do you sound so sad then?" I couldn't imagine why he was sighing and his words were laden with recognizable signs of doom and gloom! "They dug it out all right, but would you believe it was the wrong piece of property!" Jerry said sounding quite exasperated. "What? How could that be?" I couldn't figure out why this screwup happened. Were we doomed before we even got started?

Taking a deep breath, Jerry continued, "Search me, 'cause the surveyor was blinder than us, I guess! Mr. Keller sold us two lots and kept one for himself. We just dug out the wrong two, that's all." "That's all, you say. What do you mean?" I asked now really concerned and trying to envision just how in hell we were going to pay to have it redug! Finally, after yet another prolonged moment of silence, Jerry asked, "What do you think, babe? Should we forget the whole stupid idea?" Were my ears actually hearing right? Was this my devil-may-care cockeyed optimist at the other end of the line? "Jerry," I said pleadingly, "we can't quit now. There's got to be something you can work out with the excavator. After all, it was his fault as much as ours!" Jerry said laughing, "It's all taken care of, toots. I just wanted to make sure you were with me all the way." "That's what it said in the original contract, didn't it, for better or worse? I just didn't think we were going to get so much of the 'worse' all at once." I sighed with resolution!

The first day on the job it became abundantly clear that for every shovel of sand displaced, ten more cascaded down to take its place. By noon, my Brothers-in-law Sal and Normie together with Jerry found themselves buried shoulder deep in good Croton sand. As Sal later described it, and as only he could, "Shit with all that son-of-a-bitchen' sand piling up on top of us, I yell to Brother Jerry to throw me a shovel. Then I take one good look at him and damned if he isn't out cold, just standing there with his eyes poppin' out of his son-of-a-bitchen' head, just a God damned statue in the sand." Jerry quickly replied, "You got it all wrong, Brother, I didn't pass out. I was just resting my eyes."

"That may be so," said Normie, laughing so hard that the can of beer he had in his hand spilled all over his shirt. "But that's the first time I ever saw a guy taking five with a shovel poking into his gut."

If our Sahara "dig out" had been slightly off mark in August, by mid-October, its course was very much on target. The foundation had been dug out and the delivery date for the house had been set and all that now remained was for Sal and Normie to tie in the pipes. Several days later we were to learn that our newly poured basement floor was being put to another use. "Hey, Jerry, someone's been shackin' up in your cellar." Sal announced, with a vicarious note of glee in his voice. "How come?" Jerry asked not sure what Sal was talking about. "Well, every night before we leave we stack up the rolls of insulation in neat piles. Then each morning when we come back, there they are all laid out in the middle of the floor. There're even a few marks that look like the bastards were trying to carve their initials in the cement. Jerry, what are you runnin' here, a goddamned whore house?" Jerry held his chin in his hand, thought for a moment, and said, "Well, figure it this way, Sal. Someone's been baptizing our house only it ain't with holy water!"

If the preliminaries had been chaotic, the main event proved downright anticlimactic. There were no snags, few delays, and contrary to all predictions, my blueprints had not produced a bay window in the middle of the fireplace. Each time we came up to Croton it was like seeing one gigantic jigsaw puzzle with its many pieces being fitted into place, and we could hardly contain ourselves until the day would arrive when we could turn the key in the front door.

Finally, that long-awaited magical moment had come, and we found to our consternation that the key did not fit! For the first three days, therefore, until a new set could be made, every time the block of wood holding the door open was accidentally kicked aside, you guessed it, the door would slam shut. The alternate means of entry was up a ladder and through a window, and I got some rather strange glances from occasional passersby not to mention our new neighbors, who certainly had every reason to think it peculiar that we had to break into our home at least four times a day.

Jerry and I knew from the very beginning that with five bank loans plus a mortgage and a new baby, we would have to run a tight ship, and so I contented myself to wait before adding any extra frills. So much of the interior work had been done on our own, such as sanding and varnishing woodwork. We both felt as though we knew every nail that was sunk and each spackled crack on a very personal basis. In our own small way, we had created something from nothing, and it would be ours to enjoy forever and ever.

If agita could be said to have a color, then ours assuredly was to be green. All the experts and financial counselors had warned us in advance about the extras, closing fees, insurance and liability policies, property clearances, and carrying charges. What they didn't mention was the one thing shown so exquisitely in vivid color in all the real estate brochures that I saw, but was missing from our own small place in the sun. There wasn't a blade of grass, a shrub, or even a twig to be found anywhere on our property, and what was more, we didn't even have the soil to grow anything. Sand we had, with excellent drainage, but not even a spoonful of plantable, mineral-enriched dirt!

Chapter 25

"It's Good to Touch the Green, Green Grass of Home"
Porter Wagoner

"That'll be $150 ma'am," said the tall man in the green overalls. "The second and third loads will come tomorrow." "What's all that bumpy stuff in this load?" I asked, still in shock! "Oh, that, just a few rocks, stones, you know, that sort of thing. Your husband got a choice: good, better, or best; and he chose better, so here it is." As I pointed in dismay toward the pile of rock laden dirt, Jerry said, "No sweat." I couldn't imagine what plan Jerry could conjure up to deal with this mess! Finally, I asked, "What are we going to do, spoon 'em out one by one?" Jerry laughed and replied, "No, dummy, I've got an old piece of screen we can use." "That's swell," I replied feeling very disgusted. "How much you want to bet, we finish with a bigger pile of rocks than we do soil, and for over 400 bucks, no less!"

I was right, almost. At any rate, a couple of kids mistook it for Mt. Everest, started climbing and promptly disappeared somewhere in the rock pile. Several days later, after raking, hoeing, and over-working assorted muscles, we were ready to plant.

It took a bit of persuading to get Jerry to come inside that first night. Turning off the faucet, I yelled out the kitchen window, "What are you going to do?" Jerry was sitting contently in a rickety chair amid our soon-to-be-thriving, luscious lawn. "Sit there and watch the seeds sprout?" maybe he should have, who knew? The next morning, I awoke to see him dashing out the door, red towel in hand, like a matador out for the kill! I yawned and looked out the window and there on our lawn it looked as if the swallows had come back to Capistrano. "Those goddamned birds are eating up our lawn!" he screamed.

"You shouldn't have planted the seed so shallow" advised a growing band of experts congregating on our sidewalk. "Okay," said Jerry, digging, and raking once again. "This time, those little bastards won't get to my seeds!" they didn't, but neither did the sun or the rain apparently, for weeks later our lawn was still a lovely shade of brown!

"How about sods?" asked those same experts. "You know the kind they use on golf courses. They're exposed to heat, wind, and rain, just like here. You can't miss." By now all three of us, Jerry, Nannie (that's what our little Linda liked to call my Mother), and I had permanent grooves in the palms of our hands and a circular indentation each in the shape of a handle. But alas, even the blasted sods were to have their growth ups and downs. "I know the sods are supposed to be bumpy at the start," I commented a week later. Jerry added, "Eventually they will grow and fill in so that the surface will be even and lush." Still feeling apprehensive, I sighed and said, "But I never thought it'd be quite this bad at the start." As I waved my hand from left to right over our pathetic-looking lawn, well, "bad," was an understatement at that moment. Jerry and I thought that we were on our way toward finally having some sort of nice grass, and my thoughts were dreaming of possible picnics in the future.

My plans would have to wait a little longer because, on arising another morning, we were greeted to yet another horror! My finger was pointing at a million little mounds, the work of an army of industrious moles. A little later, Jerry returned from the hardware store with a sack of pellets in hand and declared, "I've got something that'll blast their little bellies clear off the face of the earth!" "Begosh and begorra, that's not nice," commented Nannie, shaking her head in disapproval. "I read in the paper that they're blind!" "I don't care if they're deaf and dumb and retarded," snorted Jerry. "They've got to go!"

As I recollect this incident, I am smiling remembering the famous movie "Caddy Shack!" you are probably nodding your head at this moment and laughing about the poor golf course caretaker who resorted to dynamiting the whole place to get rid of gophers! Finally, after a great deal of painstaking labor, weeding out crabgrass, sprinkling nightly, and providing the right kind of plant food, we knew we were halfway home and that our carpet of grass was on its way.

Chapter 26

Our First Christmas in Our New Home
1956

Christmas had always been a very special season for us. "This year," I reminded Jerry, "we'd better start acting like the natives. You've been a country boy long enough to know how everyone has their lawns decked out with flashing lights, wreaths, and mechanical figures." Though the will was there, the money wasn't, but Sears offered, for very little money, a set of Wise Men and a polyethylene wedge on which was painted a very good reproduction of the Nativity scene. "It isn't much," Jerry sighed. "But I'll hook up some floodlights and place the three Wise Men diagonally across the lawn, so it will appear as though they're going toward the stable." "That sounds great," I agreed, "and in the meantime, I'll go down to Siberia and put that cardboard dollhouse together."

The room at the extreme end of our basement that Jerry was using as a darkroom for some subcontracting work, was my logical choice. A perfect spot for a workshop for Santa's helper, I thought. I won't even have to pretend that it's the North Pole down here, damnation: it is freezing. I had always enjoyed putting things together, especially when the skills involved were leaning toward more "think power" than manual dexterity. I opened the carton. My God, there must have been hundreds of pieces, but they all looked so appealing, and I had plenty of time to figure out which of them went where.

After folding tab E over fold R, connecting slot M to V/W, stapling corners XYZ/DEF, and wedging points OQ and T through flanges PFT, I began to feel a numbness in my hands and a shiver running down my spine. That was it, I thought, frostbite is setting in. I'd better quit and see how the other half of our great team is doing with his Nativity project.

Once back upstairs, I whipped up a vat of steaming cocoa and summoned Jerry in from outside. But between the howl of the subfreezing wind and the pounding of his hammer as he drove the supporting stakes into place, it was several moments before he heard me. A quick exchange of progress reports indicated that we were both on our way toward completing a fulfilling afternoon of work.

"Ah, what in the name of God! That's the strangest thing," said Nannie, coming in from the living room to put up a pot of tea for herself. Placing her hands on her hips, she continued, "I can't understand it." After taking a long sip of the steaming cocoa, I asked her, "What's strange, Nannie?" "Well, while I was sitting there reading Ann Landers in the paper, I looked up and a car came around the corner and almost landed up on our sidewalk. The first time it happened, I thought it had skidded on the ice, but then, just a few minutes ago, the exact same thing happened again!" while sipping our nice hot drinks, we concluded that people were merely admiring our Nativity scene. What else could it be?

Jerry grabbed his gloves off the radiator where they had been defrosting, adjusted his earflaps, and again was on his way, explaining that even though it was bitter cold, the snow was acting as a terrific anchor for the figurines outside. The day before, he had purchased a few animals to add to our Nativity scene and so said, "You know, those donkeys have so many points and curves, and the sun reflecting off the snow is so bright, I hardly know where to place them." "Donkeys?" I asked putting down my mug and feeling more human now that I could feel my fingers once more. "I thought the wise men traveled on camels." "Well, who knows or cares, these boys are saddled up now and like it or not, they're stuck with their mounts."

Another hour passed before the finished product was ready for inspection. As I made my way through the maze of wires in the snow, I tried to get far enough away from the scene to get a good perspective. Oh, no! He didn't, he wouldn't, and he couldn't have! I couldn't believe my eyes, for there, majestically sprinting toward the Christ child were the three wise men, decked out on donkeys but with the donkey's noses pointed in the wrong direction. Now I realized why cars were practically crashing into our lawn! I broke into hysterical fits of laughter. I couldn't help it. I knew that Jerry had worked so hard to make our first Christmas special, but I just couldn't stop laughing! "What the hell's so funny?" Jerry asked, really getting exasperated. As the tears rolled down my cheeks, and between my spurts of laughter, he let forth with a few well-chosen curse words. "Shhh!" I said. "You shouldn't swear in front of the Christ Child!" "No, hah! Some Messiah he is, laying there laughing his insides out at me. Hey kid, you're some pal! Let's see," he said suddenly, after expounding for a time on his miseries. "Can't we pretend that the three Wise Men have already seen the child and are going home now?" "Either that," I replied, "or you'd better get them straightened out and headed in the right direction tomorrow.

We don't want those folks across the street to think that those poor blind people don't know the front of a jackass from the back!"

After straightening out our three "Wrong Way Corrigans" the following week, Jerry returned from work carrying a huge, mini fire truck that he had bought at Korvette's in the city and had carried home on his back from the station. Obviously quite pleased with himself, he said, "Hey, look what I have! The guys I ride home with thought I was nuts, but there it is. Isn't it a beauty?" I didn't dare dampen his spirits by telling him that little girls didn't usually run around in fire trucks, and besides, I was sure Linda would love it anyway. After the accessories were assembled, it really looked slim and trim, even I had to admit that. "I just have to put the steering wheel in place, and then I'll have it made," said Jerry, but as the minutes passed into hours, it was apparent that he was in trouble, even though he was not one to give up quite easily. I'd been married long enough to him to know that.

"Never mind," he said, finally, pushing it aside. "I'll go into Korvette's tomorrow morning and see how the wheel shaft is put together on the floor model they have on display." "You're going to go and feel around inside the fire truck?" I exclaimed incredulously. "Why not?" he whipped. "That's why the model is there in the first place." In spite of his self-assurance, the next evening he admitted that he had felt just a bit foolish stepping over the rope at the exhibit, bending over the truck, and feeling his way from the shaft to the wheel, even more so when the salesman asked me, "Did you lose something sir?" I answered chuckling, "No, just checking the transmission!" the salesman wasn't sure what to do at this point, so he turned away shaking his head, and Jerry thought that this guy would have a great tale to relate to his colleagues.

Christmas morning that year was a smashing success. The home-made dollhouse went over big, and if we hadn't promised to take the fire truck downstairs, I think Linda would have driven it straight up the Christmas tree. And so, we had it all, a home, a tree, and yes we will look forward to our beautiful lawn in the spring. Our day of happiness was complete, and yet all of it, house, garden, furnishings, we would have willingly traded one month later if in some way, we could have prevented the tragedy that was about to touch us all.

Chapter 27

In the Blink of an Eye!

As the three of us stood there looking down at our little Linda, almost hidden under the weight of a pressure bandage, we all wondered how it could have happened. Linda had been a happy, healthy baby in every respect, but by the time she celebrated her first birthday, it was obvious that something was not quite right with her eyes. Perhaps we should have expected this, being legally blind ourselves, but in truth, ninety percent of children born to visually handicapped parents do not carry any inherited factor. Such was the case with Linda. She had Congenital Cataracts in both eyes, not passed on through genes but rather because of a mild case of German Measles during my pregnancy.

It could have been much worse, we were told by one specialist after another. She could have been deformed or intellectually challenged. This was small consolation now when the surgeon in New Jersey was about to put her tiny eye to the knife, just after her first birthday. A simple procedure, we were told and assured that in a little while she'd be fine.

For several months, it seemed as though their predictions had been correct, until one day one of Linda's eyes became noticeably bloodshot and swollen. So much for the surgeon's prediction that her vision would be one hundred percent going forward! But now we felt another opinion was in order before that eye became more infected, possibly affecting her other good eye. Jerry and I were beginning to panic knowing other friends who had one issue or another with one eye and how rapidly the problem passed over to their other good eye.

We took Linda to another specialist and his verdict left us stunned and impotent. The retina in the swollen eye had been detached for many, many weeks, probably since Linda's initial surgery. We were told now, "There is a danger that the infection will spread to the other eye. The only recourse is to remove that one immediately. Please don't take my word for it. By all means go elsewhere, but for God's sake hurry. She still has one eye left that can be partially saved."

After getting over the initial shock of hearing this devastating news, of course, we were crushed with should have, would have, could have scenarios! Jerry and I were sick with guilt and remorse. Why were we so gullible? Had Jerry and I wanted to hear and believe too much that Linda's initial operation was just a simple procedure and rushed headlong into surgery, sure that a speedy removal of the cataracts would cure all? This latest eye specialist continued by saying, in so many words, that no surgeon should have operated on Linda's eye at so early an age.

So many people echoed our thoughts. They would say, "Sue the bastard. Make that money-grabbing, so-called surgeon pay! If not for operating too soon, or detaching the retina during the procedure, then surely for not telling you!" but what was the use of trying to sue a member in good standing of the prestigious American Medical Association? Others had traveled down the same road, and had come up empty- handed. So, what chance would there be for us with only the word of one man against another? Besides, no amount of financial remuneration could restore the light of life into the bad eye of the tiny baby in our arms, and the best we could do now was to go through the motions of living, always with the gnawing guilt that somehow, some way, we could have done more for her.

"We'll make it up to you sweetheart," we all assured her. At this, she looked up, squinted through her remaining eye, and tugged at Jerry's shirt. "Why is Mommy crying?" choking back tears threatening to gush forth, Jerry declared, "She's not going to anymore, baby. We're all going to be happy from this point on. You just wait and see and maybe next year, you'll have a little brother or sister to play with." Linda thought about it and asked, "Will she talk and cry and see just like me?" the tears poured freely once again from both of us. "There'll never be anyone else just like you, sweetheart. Never again." As the weeks and months flew by, the hurt and anguish of our ordeal slowly dwindled, although it was never erased by the passing of time.

"Why are you going away?" Linda asked me one day in October 1958, as she saw me gathering a few nightgowns and some toiletries and placing them in a small overnight bag. "Because very soon now, Linda, I'm going to be bringing home a brand-new little baby just for you." I had been right about one thing. The bundle of fluff delivered by Caesarian Section was little, slightly over five pounds, and completely unconcerned with the world around her.

"What color are her eyes?" I asked the nurse the second day, when our new daughter was permitted out of the incubator for a few moments. What I was really asking, of course, was, are her eyes all right? This kind, warm, and very friendly nurse replied, "We still can't tell, dear. She is very tiny, you know, and we don't want to force them open. In a few days, she'll do it on her own. Just be calm now and enjoy your visit Mommy!" patience was at a premium for me at that time in my life. We had to know, and the seconds and minutes dragged on ever so slowly until finally, on the fourth day, the verdict was announced. Jerry, Nannie, and I held our collective breath as we were led to the incubator, dreading what we were to learn! "They're perfect in every way!" we were told. And our relief knew no limit. Our Nance with the laughing face would skip through life with two of the prettiest blue eyes ever to gaze on God's universe.

PART 7

Memories of an Unusual Play Time Activity!
1958—1963

Chapter 28

"Can't You Hear the Whistle Blowing?"
Lyrics from the Song: "I've Been
Working on the Railroad"
John Denver and Others

Only with the passing of time did we realize that our picture of life in the suburbs was a mirage, and that in reality the greater part of the population of Croton was struggling just as hard as us to keep their heads above water. There was one phase of suburban life that had to be an improvement over city dwelling: despite the weekly editorials, complaints, and petitions, no one could deny that we were a people obsessed by the toot of a distant train whistle. Those who didn't work for the railroad traveled on it. Even villagers who remained at home set their pattern of life in accordance with a horn that blew periodically to signal the three shifts for railroad workers down in the Croton-Harman Train Yard. Even as small toddlers, Linda and Nance would bargain to be allowed some more precious moments of television watching because they would say, "We haven't heard the second horn yet." What they were referring to was the first toot that signaled the start of lunch time for the second shift at the railroad yard. Twenty minutes later it would toot again, indicating the end of the railroaders' break.

For Jerry and me, commuting on the old Central had to be better than straphanging over the shoulder of someone who had just consumed a clove and a half of garlic, and like it or not, we were soon as much slaves to the train's diesel engine as we had been to the IRT subway system.

Who said country folk take life easier than city slickers? They race just as fast to the station, struggle for a parking space, run breathlessly to overtake trains already in motion, swear they'll never do it again, and then repeat the entire process in reverse that evening.

Commuters, we found, were a breed unto their own with habits that no stranger had better try to alter. They rode the same cars, morning and night, sat in the same seats, and adjusted the window shades and footrests in an identical position day after day. And if, by chance, anything caused a deviation from this routine, in their mind they could become justifiably irate.

For instance, if by some twist of fate, the conductors failed to collect tickets before Ossining, the first stop on the A.M. train bound for Grand Central in Manhattan, or by 125th Street on the northbound train back to Croton in the P.M., things went downhill quickly. The copy of the New York Times could not be folded into the starting position, the coffee cup could not be lifted, and what was worse, the poker game could not begin on time. One night we saw a very well-dressed gentleman grab his window seat, open his expensive-looking briefcase and draw out his pillow and a box of Cracker Jacks to fortify himself for the ride home.

"So, this is affluent Westchester," I whispered to Jerry, as we watched the guys in front of us dropping tens and twenties for each hand of poker as though they were confetti in a windstorm. Jerry thought for a minute and whispered, "Yes, but don't let them fool you. Playing as they do day in and day out, the law of average tells us that they're bound to break even over the long haul, so who wins or loses on any given night isn't all that important!"

"Maybe, not," I said, "But you just try coming home some night telling me you just lost thirty dollars, just try it!" Jerry grinned and remarked, "I can see me now begging into a game like that with all of $2.23 in my pocket. Sit back and read your magazine! There are people out there who would think that what you are holding is beyond their means!" I sighed and said, "Good point!" resigned, I opened my copy of Good Housekeeping to finish an article I had been reading the previous night on the ride home.

One morning shortly after we had moved to Croton, we were the subject of conversation among a group of fellow riders just behind us. Now, it had never been our custom to eavesdrop, but when people talk across aisles and over the roar of the train's engine, it is hard not to overhear. "Say, did you see that new ranch on the same street as the Harmon Firehouse?"

Our ears became antennas homing in on the conversation. Goody, goody, someone had noticed our arrival. What would they say next? Be careful what you wish for, my Mother reminded me earlier in life.

"Yeah," said a second man. "I understand that the people who built it are blind."

"Well, that's not surprising," commented another. "After all, they're just like veterans. They get huge pensions from Uncle Sam and oodles of money and perks from those agencies for the blind." Jerry seemed to be trying to swallow his Adam's apple and his otherwise perpetual dark tan was fast becoming bright red like the fire trucks next door to our house. Before he could blow up, I nudged him sharply in the ribs, and whispered, "Let it go. Even if we told them the truth, they probably wouldn't believe it, so just cool it."

"Okay! Okay!" he groaned. "But I hate like hell having these guys think they're picking up the tab for us." Their reaction was typical, and no amount of logic or protest could convince them that we, and thousands like us, weren't milking their tax dollars, taking handouts left and right, and sitting back while they toted that barge and lifted that bale.

Well, let's be fair, we have all seen some blind people with their guide dogs, stationed on a given street corner begging for a few coins, but they are clearly in the minority! As long as Jerry and I commuted together, we had one another, and the sea of faces swimming by each day failed to touch us. So, all work and no play was not in our rule book. Stay tuned and I'll show you what madness draws thousands like us to let our hair hang down!

Chapter 29

What in the World Is Keglomania?

If Mr. Harris or Mr. Gallop wants to take a poll of blind people across the country, finding just the right cross-section might not be too difficult. All they need do is wait until the end of May, and then pinpoint any of a dozen large cities that annually host the American Blind Bowling Association Tournament. In this group of thousands, they would find men and women from all walks of life who have scrimped and saved all year for one glorious long weekend of madness. For blind or partially sighted people to leave the comfortable surroundings of their homes and travel hundreds of miles to a strange city to stay up all night partying and then roll nine games in a row, is certainly a unique form of insanity, called "Keglomania."

If one assumed that we were all a little crazy to go hotfooting all over the country once a year, even stranger was the means of transport we sometimes selected. For instance, one year when funds were particularly low, one lad, who later narrowly escaped a lynching, suggested that we could go from New York City to Cincinnati for less money than by train if we rented a bus to make the thirteen-hour trip. Remember this was back in the 1950s, and airplane travel, where it existed, was quite expensive!

So, we eagerly boarded the bus for this long trip with great expectation of having a blast of a good time, until.... Somewhere along the line a bridge burned down in an electrical storm, and the ensuing detour cost us six additional torturous hours of travel time. To compound our misfortune, the air conditioning broke down, and the windows could not be opened. Nice trip so far, huh! One poor black girl from Long Island filled an entire barf bag in the space of a few short twists executed by that antiquated heap of scrap metal. By the time we reached our destination, she was white and the rest of us were green, pea green from the stench! We hobbled off the bus just four hours before we were due to bowl six games.

That was the year when Jerry let loose with a glass-shattering sneeze, pulled a muscle in his back, and walked hunched over for more than a week before we were to make this epic trip. I'm not sure whether it was the bus ride, the aching muscles, or the scotch he had consumed (for medicinal purposes, of course) but by the time we reached the hotel, he was stony-eyed and oblivious to all around him.

The moment we were ushered into our room, he dove for the bed, muttering something to the effect that he was about to die. In an attempt to ease his pain, I searched for a radio. Music had always seemed to have a calming, sobering influence on him, and perhaps that would help him to get a few hours of sleep.

I finally located a rectangular box just above the headboard with an insert marked "quarters only." How cheap could they get? Paid musical interludes! Well, there was no time to reflect on that now. Sifting through the tangled junk in my purse as Jerry "died" a little more on the bed, I found only one quarter with a wad of gum stuck to one side. Jerry raised his head up ever so slightly to see what was keeping me, and I gently pushed it down just as quickly, telling him that even if I told him, he wouldn't believe me.

Eventually I was able to stick the gummy quarter into the slot, and it was only at that moment that I realized there were no dials for volume or station selection. This was going to be something to behold! I waited, but nothing happened, and I wondered if it had to warm up before we would hear some music that would help Jerry to get a nap. "Oh boy," I said to Jerry, "you are about to feel a lot better soon!" how wrong I was because suddenly the whole bed started vibrating back and forth, up and down and side to side, with a rock and roll beat that would have left even the likes of Chubby Checker panting for breath. With a sudden jerk, Jerry pulled up his knees so that they almost touched his chest and gave an agonized wail as he struggled to throw himself clear of this syncopated torture rack. "What the hell!" he shouted, "turn it off! Pull the plug! Do something!"

Oh my God what can I do to stop this runaway bed! I looked, but there was no plug, only a wire leading to somewhere down behind the gyrating bed. "Can't you read what the label says on that monster?" he pleaded. "I can't! Not unless you can tilt the wall so that it faces the light." In a last gasping effort, Jerry raised himself off the bed, yanked the wire for all it was worth, and as the perpetual motion came to a halt, slumped back completely exhausted, but happy, oh so happy, to be free at last! Free at last! After a few hours, he looked almost like a new man again, if one was not too particular about posture and facial color.

Later he was laughing because he recalled an incident not long ago. "You know, we've got a thing about messing around with these coin devices," he remarked. "Do you remember the last time?" I sure did. It had been a long drag, and I suppose there were times when we both thought that Easter Sunday back in 1954 would never come. You see, on our wedding night we stayed at the Commodore Hotel in New York City, and, characteristically, Jerry's opening thought was for some smooth sexy music to set the mood. This time there was an honest-to-goodness coin-operated radio just above our head. As we both settled back in the luxury of the soft, fluffy pillows, Jerry reached up and inserted a coin. "Well, babe," said he. "We finally made it." He reached down to kiss me and at that precise instant from the speaker above our heads, roared a thunderous, "Hallelujah, Hallelujah." "You'd better believe it!" Jerry shouted. We broke up, quieted down, then fell apart again and the voices rang out, "for onto us, a son is born." "Give us time, fellas, Give us time!" I'm sure that Handel couldn't have written a more appropriate overture for our wedding night.

In any case, after the disastrous trip by bus to Cincinnati, the general consensus was that we would leave the driving to them and go instead by rail or plane. But back to the bowling. You may be wondering at this point just how a blind or visually impaired person actually gets the ball down the alley. If the bowler is right-handed, there was a guide rail supported on both ends with two bowling balls at the base and lined up even with the inner edge of the gutter. This enabled the bowler's left hand to slide along the rail guiding the bowler to the point where the ball should be released. Now, if the bowler is left-handed, there is a rail set up in the same way so that the right hand is guided down toward the foul line, signaling that the ball should be released. This sends the ball traveling down the alley or landing in the gutter just as would happen with a sighted person.

Jerry said, "Do you remember when fat Tony first started bowling in the tournament a few years ago?" laughing, I recalled, "Yeah, he hopped up on the lane, put his left hand on the rail, and prepared to make his way forward. He was so strong that he pulled himself, his ball, and the entire guide rail filled with bowling balls along with him. The shocking thing is that somehow he actually bowled a strike!" "I'm sure that no one could ever repeat such a stunt!" Jerry remarked.

Lighthouse bowling team including Theresa and her husband Jerry

Chapter 30

"Do You Wanna Go Party"
KC & the Sunshine Band

Keglomania extended to other forays outside the alleys. In fact, it might have seemed to a casual observer that bowling was merely an excuse for being where we were. Prizes and trophies were important, but it was the concerted opinion of most of us that the most coveted prize of all was to be found not on the alleys but "in the bed, any bed" or chowing down on local fare. At one tournament in Pittsburgh, a quartet of young men set out late one evening in search of high adventure. Finding their just reward in the persons of four lovely ladies of the street, they decided to share their good fortune with the other men of their league. In hushed tones the four blind pimps went about their business, arranging schedules, and signing up prospective customers. They found that there were a number of lonely hearts frothing at the mouth and ready to put their virility to the test. Did someone say something about the best-laid plans of mice and men? Someone should have, because just before the first touchdown, someone blew the whistle, the game ended abruptly, and it was back to the showers (cold).

The other main attraction to these bowling tournaments was food, food, and more food! Of these excursions into abdominal genocide, none could compare with one held a few years ago. The brochure boasted of an elaborate buffet banquet featuring dishes from around the world. Did I read that correctly, a buffet? Eaters, we are. But, serving ourselves, what a disaster that would be! Unfortunately, someone forgot to tell the host committee this, because large-as-life set before our poor blind eyes was one gigantic buffet setup, complete with hot plates full of meats, casseroles, salads, one of the largest cakes I have ever seen, and it was all topped off by urns of coffee.

Don't worry we were told! There will be loads of volunteers to help you. "This is going to be something to behold," I muttered as I slipped into the chow line next to Jerry. "Want me to fill your plate for you?" I knew that although Jerry could see the table and every last item on it from a distance of twenty feet, once up close and personal, he would be lost. Jerry shook his head and said, "Please, mother, I'd rather do it myself! I'll catch up with you later! I am going to look for Johnny, so you go ahead." "Okay, suit yourself, I'm starved!" I was happy to know that there would be helpers to fill their plates because Johnny's level of vision was similar to Jerry's. Alas, just as a group of us approached the serving tables, smoke came pouring out of the kitchen, and the smiling band of volunteers scattered in all directions.

But did this stop us? No. In fact, I tried to assist a pair of friends whose vision was far less than mine. It was only moments later that all hell broke loose behind us, and it seemed that as usual, my own ever-loving Jerry and Johnny Murken were right in the thick of it. Jerry, who was farsighted and Johnny, who was nearsighted, had started along the serving line, Jerry pulling his tray along the track and stabbing at anything and everything in sight that clung to his fork, and Johnny cautiously reaching only for what came clearly into focus. "I was beginning to think I was losing my marbles," Jerry explained later. "The more I heaped on my plate, the lighter it seemed to get. How was I to know that as fast as I was piling it on, Johnny was dishing it off onto his own plate?" "Sweet Jesus," said Johnny. "By the time those poor kids got back in to help, the table looked like a bomb had hit it. You think we were bad! I saw one guy spear a great big piece of cake on his fork and then drop it into the onion dip."

Chapter 31

Adventure at the Smithsonian

If part of being crazy is to be "touched," this most certainly proved true when the tournament moved to Washington, DC, in 1963. Since Linda had reached the tender age of seven and Nance was almost five, we decided that our nation's capital would be a really great experience for them. After touring all day, we entered the Smithsonian Institute just before closing time. In fact, the lights had already been lowered. We managed to grope our way through the dimly lit passageways, and entered the President and First Lady Exhibit, which featured lifelike statues of our past leaders and their ladies.

Now neither Jerry nor I could see an inch in front of us, but apparently, the girls could, for at each stop, Linda read us the accompanying caption. Nance could be heard hollering, "There is a mistake, a big mistake!" we wandered over to her, and with hands on hips she said indignantly, "This isn't the Adams Family 'cause there is no Pugsley or Wednesday. How could they make this mistake? Mommy, you have to tell them!" everyone around us were laughing because to Nance, the Adams Family meant the TV show that she watched at home religiously. "It's okay, Nance, you will learn more when you get older and you study about our presidents in school." With a sigh, she said, "Why is it that I will only understand stuff when I get older? Why not now?"

We went looking for Linda who had moved further into the exhibit. After passing Mary Lincoln, Martha Washington, and Dolley Madison, Linda suddenly exclaimed from a distant corner, "Hey, dad, now I've really got something for you to feel. It's got no marker under it, but quick come see; it's a statue of an honest to goodness nun!" one moment later as Jerry reached out his hand, there came a voice out of the dark saying, "I'm not a statue, dear. I'm real!" "My God!" Jerry said later, "And to think I almost had my hand up her habit!" "Ah, shucks," commented Mike, a fellow bowler who had tagged along with us. "I'm sure she would have had 'nun' of that!" everyone around us groaned!

When all is said and done, therefore, I suspect that as long as there are bowlers and guiderails and the call of a distant "ten pin," this thing I call "keglomania" will keep us coming back for more. So, shrinks of the world, lay off. We really don't want to be cured!

PART 8

Chapter 32

Come and Join the 4:40 Gang

It was not as though Jerry and I arose one morning, checked our horoscopes for favorable positions with the stars, and decided that this was a propitious moment to go out and make some new, sighted friends. We were reluctant to try too hard to impress or reach out too far in search of love and companionship. Somewhere along the line, people had forewarned us that our plunge into suburbia might be something less than socially exhilarating. Since most strangers were met with a certain amount of suspicion, and when they happened to be two handicapped people, there was no telling what the reaction might be.

Others told us that small towns, looked on newcomers as renegades from an ultraliberal welfare state, bent on upheaving the traditions that they held sacred. We knew, being partially blind, that we could expect to be a source of curiosity, and that other visually impaired people who had made the move before us had found the welcome mat retracted, leaving them in virtual isolation. These ominous forebodings troubled us little, for our world in those early years was already filled to overflowing. Jerry and I were in a chin-deep financial battle for survival, and any spare moments were devoted almost entirely to Linda and Nance, who had already been cheated out of a full-time mother.

When our schedules were changed, and we found ourselves boarding different trains in the P.M., I used the precious fifty minutes for an extra nap or catching up with the latest issue of Family Circle. I rarely spoke to anyone except for a casual "Good Evening," or "Wasn't it a Nice Day?" Jerry who had always been far more outgoing only needed a week before he knew a dozen other men on a first-name basis. To be sure, the morning ride was accomplished in almost complete silence, but before long, the first car of the 4:40 was known up and down the line as the "swingingest" coach on the Hudson Division.

To his surprise, Jerry was surrounded by a bunch of men whose status in life was not much higher than his own. "All these guys," said Jerry at one point, "Johnny, Eddie, Bruce, Billy, they're all scraping just as hard as I am to make a buck. I guess I had them pegged all wrong." Each night a group that originally numbered ten arranged to sit together in the head car of the 4:40. Leaving the dozers and the readers to retreat to another car, they began their nightly hoopla as the sane world was approaching Christmas. There they would sit, offering rousing renditions of the old yuletide favorites until soon, dozens of other guys joined in, eager to be included. In between singing and telling stories, you would hear the tinkle of ice cubes swimming in a splash of scotch and the crackle of chips and nuts being shelled! Then, with the New Year celebration behind them, Jerry suggested that it seemed silly to have to make excuses for having fun, so the festivities became a Friday night ritual.

"We're certainly getting quite a reputation," said Jerry months later. "Would you believe, there are guys quitting work early to get in on the action? There's never enough booze around for anyone to get too smashed, and I tell you, it's a great way to unwind and let your hair down!" the following summer, stacking away the lawn chairs after a particularly enjoyable picnic with some of the 4:40 gang, I turned to Jerry and said, "It's not like they said it would be." "How do ya mean, Babe?" Jerry asked as he sacked the trash. "I mean the friends that we weren't supposed to make. Your train gang were so easy to be with, and it doesn't seem to mean a thing to them that we can't see all that well." Jerry stood up from his garbage detail and remarked, "Maybe that's because we don't make an issue of it! Frankly, the more they forget, the better I like it!"

For my Mother and the girls, the friendship trail was even rosier. I had worried about uprooting Nannie from her lifelong friends back in the Bronx but was soon to find that anyone willing to share helpful hints on the gentle art of "green thumbing" was her immediate ally. Linda and Nance, completely uninhibited, spent the better part of their days roaming from one house to another in the neighborhood, being thoroughly spoiled and overfed as they went. Small wonder that by the time I finally corralled Nance into her high chair there was little room left in her tiny tummy for anything as mundane as meat and potatoes.

Nance had always been a perpetual motion machine, bobbing and weaving as I struggled with my shadowy, off-center perception to land the spoon in her mouth one out of ten shots at best! At one point, presumably incensed at having spinach delivered into her nose and ear, Nance decided to take matters into her own hands, and therefore guided the spoon in the general direction of her mouth.

All the time, there was a quizzical look on her face, and I'm sure she was thinking, what kind of weird mommy have I got anyway?

Linda had always been the one continuously at my heels, whereas Nance used 44 Wayne Street as a stop along the way, where she could receive certain perfunctory services free of charge. And yet, when the time came for entry into Croton Community Nursery School, Linda, the mamma's baby, the thumb-sucker, turned on her heels with not a backward glance, while Nance bawled for three weeks before succumbing to powers greater than herself. I would have guessed their reactions to be completely the reverse, but then, what do mothers know about their own offspring anyway! What was important was that they had made their grand entry into the community of Croton-on-Hudson, and as parents, each night we would await their occasional trips homeward, just to renew old acquaintances.

Chapter 33

"Roar Lions, Roar!"

Another group was soon to enter our lives, although at the onset no one could predict how we would meet and how important they would be to Jerry and I moving forward! It was at a regular Friday night meeting of the Lighthouse Bowling Club. You see, we were in trouble. The Club had contracted to host a national tournament at the Hotel New Yorker, a task that was no small order for a scant group of twenty people. Even today, I can still recall the look on the face of the hotel's convention supervisor when Jerry and I announced that we were there to arrange accommodations for several thousand blind people, their human and dog guides, and guests.

"You say they're coming here for a bowling tournament?" she asked doubtfully. "Yes," I explained. "Bowling is probably the one sport in which blind people can participate without special rules or exceptions." "But how does a person who's blind know where to throw the ball?" she asked looking perplexed. Even after explaining how it was all possible, she was still lost for words, but Jerry and I were determined to make the tournament happen. But here was a reality check. The facts and figures were there on the table. Thousands of dollars would have to be raised and the old raffle book gimmick had worn itself thin. The Committee needed something new and different.

It was at this point, after all else had failed, that my bright-eyed partner, the organizer, came up with one of his brainstorms. "Why don't we run a sort of mini tournament, buy up some trophies, offer them as prizes and pocket the rest? We could enlist the help of a few local organizations and even maybe have a night when a handful of us could compete with some of them!" At first, there was silence, and then suddenly the idea began to take root. Why not? There would be little or no risk involved, and what could the Committee lose. The question was, where?

"How about Croton," said Jerry. The others applauded, he smiled from ear to ear, and I smoldered. "Sweet Jesus," I asked him later when we were alone, "How in the name of God are we going to publicize a tournament when we hardly know a soul in town?" "No problem, Red!" I could kill him. He was always so damned sure of himself. He continued with great enthusiasm. "We can get in touch with the local Lions Club and ask for their help. After all, they are committed to assisting blind people with their sight conservation projects."

"Yes, but we always hated begging! And to ask total strangers," my words faded off. There was nothing I could say that could dissuade him now. "We're not begging, just asking for their cooperation, and anyway, it's not about requesting them to lay out funds or make a donation." I decided to throw in the towel, I had met my match!

So it was that through John Nommik, president of the local chapter of Lions International, Jerry was put in touch with Gordon

Bradfield, who had just organized an all Lions league in Croton. "On first meeting," Jerry told me, "This tall, distinguished looking man in his fifties, an administrator with the New York Central Railroad in the local Harmon Shop, was a unique combination of leader, father, and spark plug for all those who chanced to pass his way." Both of us knew from the very beginning that we had found ourselves a friend, one who had traveled the road of life, and who stood ten feet tall because of it. Not only were the Lions willing to cooperate, they were ecstatic. And when Gordon insisted that instead of a straight exhibition of blind bowling at the end of the week, two teams from his league should roll against two of ours, how could we refuse?

"We'll probably have more volunteers than we'll have room for," he said after lighting his ever-present pipe. And when Jerry mentioned the fact that none of us were championship bowlers, Gordon laughed and said, "Most of the members of the Lions league were just learning to keep the ball out of the gutter. Jerry laughed and continued, "You don't have to worry about us clobbering you; besides, we'll all be using a handicapped system, which puts all of us on an equal playing field!"

During the following week, two members of the Lions Club met Jerry and me at Starlight Lanes, got on the loud speaker to publicize our tourney and raffle, registered those who wished to participate, and remained until midnight tallying up the money we had brought in. To our delight, the notion conceived out of desperation was catching on, and we were, in fact, realizing a nice, healthy profit for our Lighthouse Bowling Club.

When the time came for the Saturday night main event, I'm not sure now who was more scared, them or us. But when one of the Lions, Frank Danna, ditched the ball into the gutter, and Frank Garcia, a local contractor, yelled, "What's the matter? Are you blind or something?" the ice was broken and from there on it was more like a carnival than a serious bowling competition. The near-capacity crowd that had come to witness the fiasco hooted and cheered as one or another of us made or missed a shot. Fortunately for our egos, we all bowled above average. At one point, they threatened to take away the guiderails, so they could catch up. One thing was certain, a group of perfectly sighted people, most of whom had never met a blind person before, were laughing, joking, and forgetting awkward barriers.

"You know, I once met a guy with a cane on 42nd Street," commented Fred Harmon, an executive with Nedick's, a fast food chain back in the day featuring hot dogs and an orange drink that still makes my mouth water with delight. "I offered to help him across the street and by the time we reached the other side, he had sold me three cases of soap and had hit me up for a book of raffle tickets." All of us roared. And Fred continued, "You guys don't waste any time and the worst thing about it was that the soap gave me an awful rash and I had to throw it out!" "Hey, Fred," said Johnny, one of our teammates, "you can assist me anytime. Suckers like you are as scarce as hen's teeth."

Six months later I stood sipping a Tom Collins on the terrace of the splendid Thayer Hotel overlooking West Point, high above the Hudson surrounded by several interlinking mountains. My concentration was focused on trying desperately to appear casual. I just couldn't relax and play it cool as Jerry was obviously doing as he chatted with Gordon Bradfield and Frank (Cheech) Sansavera, so named because there were just too many Franks in the Croton Lions

Club. It wasn't that the women weren't friendly. God knows, they were. I didn't have to search for words with Ag and Patty, Gordon, and Cheech's wives, respectively. The conversation flowed freely.

"What do ya call, I have a recipe for barbecued spare ribs" said Patty, of French Canadian descent. She would sometimes start her sentences with "what do ya call," and I found it really charming. It was Ag who was irate regarding the futility of trying to weed out dandelions or crabgrass, and the proposed shopping center for Croton was a hot topic. They were two fabulous women, down to earth, exhibiting no airs of snobbery and grandeur as I had expected they would. So, why was that lump just sitting there in my chest, defying all rhyme and reason, threatening to explode?

Maybe it was just that everything had happened so quickly, Jerry's induction into the Lions Club three months before, and then, being nominated right off the bat to serve as the club's "Tail Twister," whatever that was. He had been so proud and had told me more than once that if it was the last thing he would do, he would let Gordon, his sponsor, know that this ultimate act of friendship would not be left unrewarded.

I had come to know most of the other women because of our jointly sponsored picnic for the Lions and Lighthouse bowlers, but it was difficult to believe that they were married to bank managers, lawyers, dentists, and contractors. They were so unpretentious, and this reminded me of something I had learned in college. Those who really had the wealth displayed it the least. It was the nouveau riche who were constantly boasting about their forty-foot yachts, what about those three summer homes and their Lincolns! The truly wealthy didn't have anything to prove, so they didn't lower themselves by trying.

My nerves had been too jangled to eat all day at any rate. West Point was to be my own personal "coming out" party, and the specter of what the night might hold for me left me limp. "Have another drink," said Sue Danna, "Frank will get it for us." I was thinking, my God, another Frank to try to sort out from the rest of the pack! "No thanks, Sue, I shouldn't have had that one."

"You must be like me. Two-drink Sue, that's what they call me, but today, I was smart, I had a nice big sandwich before we left." Why didn't I do the same? Well it was too late now. I gave what I was sure was a giddy smile and started to postulate about whether I would be able to stand up without staggering once it came time to move into the dining room.

The last thing I wanted to do was to look over my shoulder at the terrain far below us. High places always made me dizzy, anyway, and now was the time to regain my composure. I sat back, took a couple of deep breaths, which seemed to make a little difference, but I couldn't help theorizing that if I felt this tipsy outside in the cool night air, what was it going to be like inside? I knew my face would turn scarlet red. One drink in a stuffy room was enough to light me up like a million Christmas tree bulbs.

"Time to eat," said Gordon extinguishing his pipe. We were ushered into a gorgeous banquet room, lavishly decorated with potted plants, expensive looking paintings, and a huge chandelier. As we sat there, I couldn't help looking up at it again. It reminded me of the multicolored chandelier they had used in the Phantom of the Opera, a movie that had terrified me as a child. The long spiraling crystals that wove their way up into the main centerpiece seemed to be dancing back and forth, as if to herald our arrival.

"Please rise," said a voice from the center table. Patty had been thoughtful enough to tell me where the flag had been placed, and for a moment I wondered how it was that some people knew how much to do without making a fuss about it. Again, almost hypnotized by its magnificence, I gazed at the chandelier. Why was it that my feet were beginning to feel so wobbly when my entrance into the hall had been so flawless? Was that chandelier really swaying or were my eyes playing tricks on me? Back and forth, back and forth, round and round! Why didn't anyone else notice it?

I swallowed hard and tried to think of the words to the "Pledge of Allegiance." I just wouldn't look up again; that was all. What was this? How could it be possible? A fellow with a clipped mustache at the next table looked just like Adolph Hitler, and the girl next to him looked like a bottle of milk, all dressed in white, from head to toe. They looked so funny, I thought. In fact, the whole thing was a gas, a swinging chandelier that nobody else seemed to notice, a band playing "America the Beautiful," and Adolph Hitler and a milk bottle standing straight at attention.

As we sat down again and some muffled words came from the main table, I sneaked one more glance upward. There they were— not one—not two—but a whole room full of swinging chandeliers, and below them, a pool of swimming, nondescript faces. God, I was drunk and on only two drinks. The next hour passed in total oblivion. I didn't have the faintest idea what had been served or if I had chosen the proper eating utensils for each course, a source of great concern prior to this Dinner. By the time it came to the induction of officers and Jerry solemnly vowed to uphold the motto of the Lions, "to serve," I finally began to come to and to try to consolidate my thoughts. I feverishly wondered what I had said or done during my flight into never-never land.

Only later, while driving home with Gordon and Ag, did I finally have the nerve to ask what had transpired during the main course of the meal. "Nothing," Ag assured me. "You were full of fun and totally relaxed; you were the life of the party!" good grief, I wasn't sure whether I liked that or not, but knowing Ag's sincerity, I hoped that she meant nothing more than that. "I'll tell you one thing," I said finally. "What's that?" Gordon asked. "The next time we have one of these shindigs, I'll know enough to have one drink and eat something beforehand."

Once properly inducted into the Lions Club, Jerry was soon to find out that there was a bit more to his new officership than his pledge as club "Tail Twister" to uphold the general spirit and well-being of its members. As a matter of fact, it soon became abundantly clear that the tail of the Tail Twister himself was the only thing getting twisted! "You know, it's my job," he explained, "To impose fines for infraction of rules, and one of the most important one is that all members are to have their Lions pin on their jackets at each meeting. The first night I faked it, but I wasn't foolin' them for one minute. They knew I couldn't see the damned pins. I was having enough trouble seein' the guys themselves no less. The second night, I decided to let my wits take over where my eyes left off, and so I started feeling their lapels." "Did that work?" I asked. "Yeah, except every time I leaned over to find the darned pin on the guy's jacket lapel, one guy was goosin' me from the rear, and the other one's dickin' me from the front." Jerry continued, —"I've learned to keep my good eye on my beer, too, since at the very first meeting, Frankie and Carl doused it with everything they could lay their hands on, cheese, salt, catsup, hot pepper, the works! They couldn't get over it, when I didn't taste a thing until I hit bottom." Once I stopped laughing, I said, "You don't have to tell me about your cast iron stomach. They sound like quite a bunch!" Laughing Jerry replied, "They are. They're forever razzing me about that cane I'm carrying around. Just trying to get sympathy, that's all. You're not really blind, that's what they tell me!" "I am so happy that you have met a bunch of ball busters who are your equal," I replied.

As a matter of fact, it had been on my insistence that he had started to sport a white cane at all. "One day," I told him, "someone's going to haul off and slug you when you bump into him." "I know. Right now, I'll bet half of them think I'm either perverted or drunk, but I tell you, it gets to be a bit too much when old ladies on crutches start getting up in the train to give me a seat!"

September came and passed and with it, the expansion of the Lions Bowling League. "Hey, why don't you bowl partners with us?" Patty Sansavera said one chilly autumn evening. "Sure," said Cheech. "I'll take good care of you." "I know, pal, just like you did with the beer!" and so, it was that our assimilation into a sighted world was complete. Our weekends from then on would be crammed full of as much social gratification as we chose to take on. More than this, a group of beautiful people had entered our lives and before a year would pass, we would know through them, how the true meaning of Lionism would reach out to touch us all.

Theresa's husband Jerry was a life-long member of the Croton Lions Club, and is pictured here receiving the Lion of the Year Award. He was president of this Club three times over the course of his membership.

PART 9

One Moment in Time Changed My Life Forever!
Christmas 1963—Spring 1964

Chapter 34

It Was Just a Silly Ray of Sunshine!

How often we look back and wish, if only we had a second opportunity to change that one moment in time, but the truth of the matter is that we would probably make the same mistakes. It is only in the sober light of retrospect that we come to realize how a single instant has altered the course of our life. Even now, I am unable to arrange that instant in its exact place in time. All I know is that it was the spring of 1964 and fast approaching the day when Linda would receive her First Holy Communion.

"Mrs. Clean, you're up to it again!" Nannie looked down at me on my hands and knees applying a fresh coat of wax to the children's bedroom floor. Continuing, she said, "The way you're tearin' around, you'd think that the Pope himself was comin' next Sunday!" I looked up and smiled but I hadn't really heard. I had always been a compulsive person; in childhood, it had been food. As a young adult, studying; just then, it was the need to keep busy.

Blot it all out, don't look back and dwell on the past, I told myself, think only of the future. But would the months ahead be any different from the six that had just passed? There seemed little hope. The Christmas holidays in 1963 had marked the darkest moments of my life up until that point. Nannie was in the hospital following a massive heart attack. While back at home, Jerry was in one bed with Walking Pneumonia and the two girls in another with Chickenpox.

Jerry had lost his job, or to be more accurate, had voluntarily transferred from one New York State Commission for the Blind, sponsored vending stand to another, in the hope of effecting an increase in his salary. Although the prospect at first seemed bright, Jerry, like thousands of other blind men throughout the country, soon found himself caught in the battle between man and machine. All around him coin-operated vending machines were slowly sapping money out of the blind operators' tills and into a federal pension fund, from which he could claim only a small part. Stands were being relocated, pushed off to the side out of the main stream of traffic, and all that any of them could do was to move on in search of something better. For months before Christmas, all that Jerry could salvage each week was a scant fifty dollars take-home pay, and as the weeks passed, we fell deeper into debt.

We owed everyone; the druggist, the butcher, and most of all, the doctors. Over the past few years, Linda had needed four additional operations to help save her one good eye. Nannie had been in and out of the hospital with various ailments before this last heart attack. Finally, I had added insult to injury when I had decided that the pain from Glaucoma in my bad eye had become unbearable, and I had gone and had it removed.

Would you believe this? At this point I had asked the doctor if we could pay him back in monthly installments? He had replied,

"You should have been prepared for such emergencies; go out and borrow it!" Can you imagine, how cold hearted! Did he forget that he took the Hippocratic Oath? Each morning I dreaded opening the mail, for there seemed no way in sight that any of the bills could be paid.

Chapter 35

Is There Really a Santa Claus?

On that Christmas Eve, however, I was stunned to note that our balance owed to the local drug store had been whittled from hundreds down to nothing. When I checked further, I learned that it had been paid in full by some "friends." I knew it had to be the Lions! The tears flowed freely down my cheeks in shame that it had all come down to this. Later in the afternoon, Ag Bradfield arrived with the makings of a complete Christmas dinner, right down to a homemade apple pie. "None of my bunch likes turkey anyway," she said cheerfully. "I got this bird for nothing as a Christmas gift from my employer Reader's Digest, and it seemed a shame to let it go to waste!" I grinned, hugged her and prayed for my friends! God had been good to me and my family; I was not alone!

"Are Daddy and Nannie going to die?" Linda asked, as I tucked her into bed that night. "Of course, not," I replied. "Christmas is a time of joy when we think of birth not death." "Besides," added Nance with great enthusiasm, "Santa Claus is coming tonight, isn't he, Mommy? Santa wouldn't let anything happen, would he?" Linda sneered, buried her head in her pillow and said nothing.

The next morning, when the girls awoke, there were no presents under the tree. "Didn't Santa come?" Nance asked with tears in her eyes threatening to spill out over her sweet little cheeks. Yawning and wrapping my arms around her, I replied, "He sure did, but instead of leaving the presents under the tree, he left you hints and clues and jingles so that you could have fun finding them!" for the next hour and a half, amidst shrieks of joy with discovery, I silently congratulated myself for having contrived this delaying tactic that succeeded in disguising what would have seemed all too meager if placed under the tree.

With the ushering in of the New Year 1964, our luck seemed to take a remarkable turn for the better. In utter defiance of all predictions, Nannie had survived. "Ah, sure," I might have to go a little slower for a while," she said after several months had passed. "But I'm not about to lie down and die!" by the time the snow had melted, and her beds of mountain pink were starting to bloom, she was back out there, digging and hoeing and raking, living life in the way she knew best.

"It's the only sensible thing for us to do," Jerry had said as we approached the entrance to Westchester County Savings and Loan in April of that year. "We're borrowed out, and we stand a good chance of losing everything unless we can get an extension on our mortgage. This way we can consolidate our debts and hang on until something comes through for us. Both of us are alone, honey! There's no one around who can help us now, with Pop close to death and your Sister and Dan with five children to support. It's the only way out!" I didn't dare give vent to my innermost feelings, which I was sure he shared. Eight years of scrimping and budgeting down the drain, and now we'd have to start all over again.

My thoughts returned back to the present. The wax had dried on the bedroom floor, and now it was time to really make it shine! My mind was made up and as I untangled the buffer cord and glided the machine over the freshly polished floor, I revisited the plans I had mapped out so carefully over the past few weeks. The children were getting older now. Linda was going to receive her First Holy Communion this upcoming weekend, and next fall Nance would be going to school all day for the first time. It was about time I got myself out there and found a job, where or how I wasn't sure, but I did have a skill, typing, and was sure I had not forgotten how to prepare various kinds of documents and letters. I would have to wait until after the summer, but the idea of going back to work was really beginning to appeal to me since I knew only too well that there was no immediate hope of transfer on the horizon for Jerry.

Why was it that today of all days I couldn't keep my mind on what I was doing? Thinking too far into the future, that's what Nannie would say. Ever since childhood, there had never been se-crets between us. I had run to her with all the little hurts, real and fancied. She had always come up with the appropriate treatment, whether in the form of a cooling lotion or a moment of reassurance. This time was different. Confiding in my mother now was out of the question. She must never know how close we were to the brink of financial disaster.

During a brief respite, my gaze was drawn toward the window, where a gallery of pink and white ballerinas were being tossed to and fro in the breeze against a background of blue Dacron, and then as the wind subsided, one pirouette and their dance was ended. I paused and waited, half expecting them to join together in a final curtsy.

The humming of the buffer as I flipped the switch brought me back to the task at hand, and as I glanced down at the floor there appeared to be something white, perhaps a cloth I had dropped directly in the path of the spinning brushes. If it got caught in the brushes, what a mess I would have to clean up! Quickly, I reached down to pick it up and in that split second, the millionth of a speck in time, it was over and there could be no turning back!

Chapter 36

As the Curtain Falls!

"On This Day, O Beautiful Mother! On this day, we give thee our love." I hadn't heard this hymn since childhood and as the double row of boys and girls proceeded down the aisle of Holy Name of Mary Church, I choked back the tears that were threatening to tumble down my cheeks for all to see. What of it, even if they did? Everyone in this congregation had to feel the same way I did. The sweet young voices, chanting out the carefully rehearsed responses to the prayers, the hush as they were solemnly assured that they were now indeed children of God, then finally the procession, with clasped hands and bowed heads pressed forward in single file they returned to their seats. It was all too much to bear!

Jerry lifted Nance up to a better vantage point. "Daddy, when Linda eats the host, can I have a Life Saver?" like her older Sister, Nance had reverently passed up breakfast, saying that if Linda was going to fast, she would too! Now, as I followed her glance and pointed my finger toward the front of the church, I became aware of a certain fuzziness in my visual field. It was probably just my long-standing difficulty, acclimating my eyes to sudden darkness, I thought, but still, it had never seemed quite that bad.

Later, as I squinted through the camera view finder, something was wrong with what I saw or failed to see. I had always been the one to take most of the pictures up until now as Jerry's vision was not suited to the task. "Let Bob Friend take the picture for you." Jerry suggested, thinking to himself, this is odd! He continued, "Bob is a pro, and we don't want to let this shot get away from us." Although I had no way of predicting it then, that one snapshot taken by Jerry's fellow Lion and buddy would come to have a very special meaning in a way none of us could have foreseen on that lovely day in May.

The day after Linda's First Holy Communion, I was standing in what we loosely referred to as the outfield, but which in reality was a vacant lot adjacent to our home. I was out there for the purpose of playing center and nothing could have pleased me more. No visit from Dan and Helen whose brood now numbered five, could be complete without a knock'em sock'em kickball game, and as far as I was concerned, despite the grunts and yelps and mighty attacks on the ball, it rarely came out my way and when it did, there was usually ample time to catch sight of it.

Now it was the second inning, and Danny hit a high soft drive straight out in my direction. I moved toward it, camped under it, and heard it drop ten feet away. My Godson was understandably gleeful, but my teammates wasted no time in letting me know that I was no Joe DiMaggio. I shrugged my shoulders helplessly, and then moments later Helen lobbed the ball to me. Again, I spotted the ball and lost it. "I guess this just isn't my day," I said and promptly forgot the entire incident.

A week later, I was browsing through the Sears catalog in search of summer clothes for the girls, and spotted a white dress with red polka dots and a bright red sash. Even though they were not twins, I just loved to have them dressed alike in the same color, especially red, the one color that for me (a redhead) was out of the question. When I looked for the catalog number to order those dresses, suddenly the letters before me became fuzzy and indistinct, and the lines began swimming back and forth, even to the point of converging at times. My glasses would just have to be changed; that was all. It had been too long since the last checkup. Then I began to have trouble recognizing faces, even those that were familiar to me. This problem was not my glasses, since I never wore them for anything but reading. What in the name of God was happening to me?

Finally, one day when I was bringing laundry into the girls' room, I found myself silently swearing under my breath. Nannie was at it again, switching off the lights all over the house to save electricity. "Why couldn't she leave them alone?" I groaned. Reaching out my elbow to flip the switch, I found that it was already on. How could that be? Could all three bulbs have burned out simultaneously? I automatically looked up in the direction of the ceiling fixture and to my horror, I saw that all the bulbs were shining bright as the day they were first installed.

In total disbelief, I tossed the pile of clothes on the vanity, not caring about the few that toppled onto the floor. I stared straight ahead. The pair of twin beds with their pink and white bedspreads, the set of gleaming white French Provincial Furniture that stood at right angles to one another, the desk, the lamp in the corner between the two, the clock, even the flock of stuffed animals and the international dolls; they were all there. Nothing changed. They were all still clear as a bell. Slowly, ever so slowly, I raised my head toward the ceiling, praying that what had happened a moment earlier had just been a bad dream or one that at least had a logical explanation. But it was not until my head rested on my shoulder blades that I was able to bring the light once again into focus. All that lay above dead center was lost in a pool of yellow and brown fuzz.

I darted out the door and ran in the direction of the dining room window, relieved at the thought that Nannie and the girls were out of the house. The sky would be there, bright blue in the noonday sun to reassure me, just as always! I closed my eyes for a second and brushed away any excess moisture from my face. This time I had to be sure that there was nothing obstructing my vision. When I finally opened my eyes and stared outward and upward, the top of my world was a ball of crimson, and all the blinking and squinting in the world could not change that fact. My God in heaven, what was happening to me? Mine was a static eye condition that had little hope of getting better, but almost no chance of worsening. This was what every eye doctor had told me since I had been a child visiting the Columbia Presbyterian Eye Institute Clinic. That was it. I would go see the head retina specialist down at Columbia. He had my records, and he surely would be able to clear this thing up. It had to be an infection or a cold or something, and there was no sense worrying Mom and Jerry about it.

During the following week, Jerry will be in Washington pressing for legislation that would benefit the blind; so, I announced to Nannie that I was taking the girls for a train ride. I'm not sure to this day what possessed me to take them along, unless it was the growing fear of traveling alone. To my chagrin, when we arrived at the clinic, I found that my eye doctor was on vacation in Europe. Cynically, I thought that some of Jerry's hard-earned money had helped to send him there. I agreed to see the specialist who was taking his place, reassuring myself that he, too, would be in possession of all that was pertinent for making a final diagnosis.

After a thorough examination, he announced, "Mrs. Marafito, there is no change in your vision whatsoever according to your chart." "That can't be," I protested. "What about the reddish-brown spots swimming around in the top of my eye?" "There's simply nothing there, dear, but you must remember it's very difficult to do a thorough workup on you since your pupil is so tiny."

Dejected and confused, I walked out of the office with Linda and Nance at my side, but when we emerged into the glare of the afternoon sun, my heart dropped to my toes. The drops that he had used during my examination had so distorted my vision that all I could see ahead was a dirty screen of white. Oh, God, how was I going to make it home with two little girls depending on me for protection? There was no way I could share my panic with them or even begin to explain what had happened. They should be leaning on me, not I on them, for direction out of this jungle of steel and cement. One step at a time that was the only way to deal with this thing, and my most immediate concern was a six-lane thoroughfare that had to be traversed. I would worry about the subway and the rest of the trip home later, but I knew I would have to find some way to get the girls to help me without letting them know they were.

"Let's play a game." I said. "It's going to be called", I paused a minute searching for some spark of inspiration, "It's going to be called: 'who can see it first!'" "How does it work, Mommy?" Linda asked. "Well, it's easy. We're going to see who can tell first when the light turns green, and then, we're going to find out who's going to be the first to spot a car coming around that corner over there." "I see it! I see the green light! I win, I win!" Nance said, jumping up and down. I knew she hadn't since the cars were still whizzing by. "She's cheating, as usual," said Linda. "How can she see it if it isn't even yellow, yet?" thata girl, Linda, I thought, remembering how cautious she had always been about tearing through traffic. We'll make it. We've got to make it. God wouldn't let anything happen to us, not this way!

Oh God, thank you, I thought as we crossed the boulevard without an incident and finally made our way down the stairs into the subway. By this time, I had no qualms about asking Linda to read the sign on the train or on each platform. At this point, both girls had become accustomed to doing the seeing for me when first we entered out of sunlight into darkness. We continued with the little game I had started, each time Nance being outflanked by Linda in her haste, until at one point, Nance reached up and whispered, "I'll bet I see something she can't see." "Really? What's that?" "It's not a thing, it's a who" she said stretching her finger out in the direction of someone who was obviously seated further down in the car. "It's not polite to point, Nance," I said clasping her little hand in mine. Both of them giggled until in desperation I turned their attention elsewhere. A few moments later, after the source of their amusement moved on, Linda turned to me and said, "Mommy you've got to do something about that kid. You know who she was pointing at?" "No, who?" "A rabbi with a skull cap sitting there reading his Bible or whatever he reads!"

That night, after Jerry had gone over all the details of his trip to Washington, including the fact that the Senate was going to be far too involved with welfare legislation and foreign affairs to care about a bill that affected only a small segment of the population, we decided to turn in early as both of us were exhausted.

Gloomily, I lay there wondering how and when I was going to tell him. I know he would be devastated with the horrible news that I just had to find a way to tell him! What would he say? Was this too much for our marriage to withstand? He had to know now, that is for sure. There was no way to beat this thing without his help. Try though I would, the torment of the day's ordeal seemed to boil within me and before I knew it, I was sobbing in his arms. I poured out the whole story from beginning to end including my confusion in having been told that there was absolutely nothing wrong with my eye.

Jerry pounded his fist into the pillow. "Screw the doctors of this world who won't give us credit for knowing what our own eyes can see. Don't worry, Red. We'll get you to another doctor; we'll see ten doctors if that's what it's going to take to get some answers. We're not going to get burned again, I can promise you that!" but with each successive examination, the responses became so bewildering. Here is what we were told: The first specialist stated, "It could be an infection." Then there was one doctor who said, "My God, I've never seen anything like that in my life!" another doc nearly got a taste of Jerry's size 8 EEE planted where the sun don't shine when the idiot proclaimed, "You never had much vision there to begin with, did you?" and there was the so called expert who stated with authority, "You could have a Detached Retina." On and on it went, each ending with the same question. "Did you have a blow to your eye in recent months?" my answer was always, "Of course, not. Surely, I'd know if I had!"

Finally, we settled on one doctor in Ossining, a nearby town, who seemed willing to attempt to cover all bases at one time. He started to explain but seemed rather unsettled, "The problem is that we cannot be sure what is happening to you until certain tests are performed." "This means hospitalization, doesn't it?" "Yes, Mrs. Marafito, but until we can get a bed, and that may not be for a week or so, you'll be started on massive doses of cortisone. If it is merely an infection, drugs alone should do the trick." The days seemed to drag on forever. Each morning as the girls skipped out the door, running as they always did for the school bus, I longed to hold them back, squeeze them and tell them Mommy might get the call to go to the hospital today! If so, how long would it be before I would hold them in my arms again? Instead, I laughed and sent them off. But those two cherubic faces seemed so dim and distorted, and no matter how I tried to squint, it was just no use. With tears in my eyes, I thought, how could I remember them and cherish them when distance would separate us? Suddenly I recalled the snapshots taken by Bob Friend on the day of Linda's First Communion. Eagerly I ran to the television set where special family photos were displayed, snatched them up, and held them close. They would always be there whenever I wanted a reminder of a very special picture no one could erase from my memory.

Nannie took the news like the real trooper she had always been in my childhood when one crisis after another set in. At a time when others would normally go to pieces, she was at her best, drawing strength from that veritable pioneer spirit that had always sustained her, that and her devotion to St. Jude who could be called on to fix whatever was wrong and all would be right!

Weeks later found me sitting in a wheelchair in front of a set of heavily paneled oak doors while within a group of some of the finest surgeons in the country were pondering my fate. I had undergone just about every type of eye examination known to mankind including an Electroretinogram that was unable to get a really deep look into my eye. The bottom line was that they could not be sure what exactly was the cause of my deteriorating vision, not without doing an exploratory operation. Feeling that I had no other recourse, I sighed and said, "Well, then, let's do it and get it over with!" and so, I had been delivered back to my room while the formalities were attended to in distant corners of the hospital, lining up an operating room, an anesthetist, photocopying my Blue Cross card, and getting that all-important signature that stated for all to see that I had been in complete agreement. What other choice had I?

The flickering sound of the defective fluorescent light just outside my room alerted me to the fact that I was about to be transferred from my stretcher and onto a bed just across from the window that looked out on the rooftops of New York City melting under the heat of a late afternoon sun. I felt safe and secure. All apparently had gone well, and there had only been a few minor complications, a little excess bleeding but nothing of any great import.

My thoughts drifted back to the actual operation. I had been awake during the entire procedure, which is normal for eye operations and I never knew precisely why this is so. Laying there on the operating table, I had listened to Dr. Taylor and to his two assistants piping out orders for clamps, probes, and tweezers. I had heard them send out a hurried call for some tiny instruments to be brought in from the baby lab for use in especially vulnerable areas in my eye and had felt the cool damp cloth applied to my forehead as beads of perspiration flowed freely down into my ears. At one point, possibly due to the mild anesthesia I had been given to relax me, I had found myself wondering what would happen if I had to sneeze with three sets of hands gingerly working on a two-inch area. Not only that, what if I had to tinkle? It was all over now, and the worst had not happened. My relief at having it all behind me was profound. Much to my consternation, the next two days did not bring any further enlightenment as to my condition since something seemed to be covering my entire eye.

"We'll have to wait a little longer and give the eye a chance to heal before removing the bandages. We know that you are justifiably nervous and anxious," said one of the doctors making their morning rounds. "But in the meantime, we insist on strict bedrest for you, no moving around here!" I promised to obey orders while deep down was the gnawing, unmistakable realization that with the passing of each day, the light I could see under the bandages had taken on a bewildering bizarre shape, neither round or oval, not elongated nor pinpointed, and I silently vowed that another night would not pass before I would peel the bandages off and in the privacy of my room make my own diagnosis. I had to know. The long weeks of sleepless nights with drugs administered intravenously around the clock had converted me into a quivering hyperactive junkie, and double doses of sleeping pills had failed to calm my nerves.

I waited patiently for that time when all the nurses would be scurrying round, handing out pills and juice. The light overhead was on since one of the nurses had commented on the fact that it was too dark, and the switch had been flipped on. Slowly and painstakingly I eased the wide tape that held the bandage in place. It wasn't difficult since the heat of the evening had left large drops of moisture in and around my eye. In those days, only fans cooled each room, no air conditioning! What I saw as I stared ahead left me numb and motionless. I moved my head toward the white-clad bed of my roommate. There was absolutely nothing that I could discern clearly. My eye was a sea of crimson, full of red, squirming, shapeless inhabitants, and all the blinking in the world could not erase them from view. I had seen enough. Quickly I replaced the bandage and sank back onto my pillow shivering with fear and dread. I never cared about being alone, but now the loneliness threatened to completely overwhelm me. I thought of ringing for the nurse as I was sure I was going to be violently ill, but my arms seemed immobilized. I had never been one to make unnecessary work for the nursing staff, but this time I didn't care. If it was to happen, I would just let it out and let them take care of it.

Why hadn't the docs told me? How could I tell Jerry, Helen, Nannie, and most of all, my two little babies? My thoughts were suddenly interrupted by the steady humming of some sort of machine being pushed into our room.

"I know this is one hell of a time to polish the floor," said a heavy voice, "But we've got a bunch of VIPs coming through tomorrow, and orders are orders. Hope you ladies don't mind. I'll be out of here in short order." I settled back almost grateful for the temporary distraction, and as the buffer wheels spun and the motorized whirring moved back and forth across the floor, I suddenly burst into hysterical sobbing laughter. "What's wrong," cried Mrs. Michael, from the other bed. "Do you want me to call the nurse? Are you in pain?" still laughing and crying at the same time, I replied, "Yes, I guess there is something wrong with this whiz-kid brain of mine if I could have forgotten something that happened only a few months ago, and when they asked me about a blow to the eye, I told them, can you believe it, I told them no!" my howling grew even louder and with more depth, and my neighbor and the maintenance man must have thought that I had lost my mind or was having a seizure or something.

By this time, I was upright in my bed, mindless of pain or the pulling of stitches; the walls seemed to cave in around me, pressing down on me, and making each breath a desperate gasp for survival. Between fits of hysteria, I continued, "And you want to hear the funniest part of it all? It was all for nothing! Do you hear me? Nothing! When I was buffing the girls' room, I reached down for the cloth on the floor in the path of the buffer and there wasn't a damned thing there, just a white beam reflecting on the shiny polish. I reached out to catch a silly ray of sunshine and all I caught was a tank full of bloody fish to haunt me for the rest of my life."

It was true. That fateful morning in April I had caught the handle of the upright buffer square in the center of my eye when I reached down. I hadn't even paused to take an aspirin. I have no recollection of what happened then. I suppose I was forcefully knocked out.

The next morning at the hospital was as much a blur as the hours that had passed between dusk and dawn. Several doctors came into my room and stood talking in subdued tones. Suddenly aroused, I felt compelled to ask the one question that had been eating away at my insides since first having peered out through the grotesque ocean of red. "What happened to me?" I asked. "We're not sure, perhaps some superficial hemorrhaging," one of them replied, still engrossed in charts and orders for future medication. "Is it going to clear up?" I asked afraid of the answer. "That's up to someone far wiser than all of us," said one of them finally. "What the hell kind of an answer is that," I screamed, but by this time they had moved on to Mrs. Michael's bed and were absorbed in a discussion of an upcoming fishing trip.

I listened incredulously, for my life and my whole existence was hanging in the balance while they talked of bluefish and imported reels and lines. I wanted to scream, "If you've got to talk about fishing, go do it somewhere else. Don't you care that my whole world is shattering into pieces? Get out! Get out!" Instead I buried my head in my pillow and wept. My poor sweet Jerry! What had I done to him? I need not have worried because years of hardship and illness in our family had hardened the core in him, and he stood as ever the steady rock I could lean on.

"It's going to be all right, baby! You'll see. We've made it together this far, and if anything, we're all the stronger for it." As his large tanned hand clenched mine tightly, the two of us sat there in silence, no words were necessary. There was now a very special bond between us that no kind of adversity could destroy. Jerry continued with conviction, "Day by day. That's how we're going to tackle this! We can't lose! You'll see!"

The next day Dr. Taylor was in bright and early. "Where have you been for the past day or so?" I asked with great impatience. Looking at my chart he replied, "I was called out of town on an emergency. Why, didn't they take good care of you?" "I guess so," I replied unconvincingly, "But they certainly don't hand out much information, and I've been wasting away here wondering what this blob of red is that I'm seeing!" "I'm sorry, Terry. I really am. I wanted to explain things thoroughly to you two days ago, and then I got called away, and I suppose my team thought that there was nothing that couldn't wait until I returned." As we proceeded down the hall to the examination room, I wanted to make it very clear about my feeling that even residents should be aware that a patient's mental attitude is as important as, or more vital perhaps, to their overall recovery than the battery of pills or shots they could prescribe, but I decided to drop the matter. Certainly, this doctor, who was full of warmth and compassion, could not be held responsible for the thoughtless actions of others.

Then suddenly I remembered the blow I had given my eye back in the spring and concluded with the rather sullen remark, "I suppose if I hadn't been so stupid and overlooked this before, no operation would have been necessary! How could I not remember that blow to my eye?" "Not true," said Dr. Taylor, feeling very sure of what he was saying to this very scared and courageous woman. "This would have been all the more reason to go in and establish for sure whether there had been any degree of retinal damage. Fortunately, there wasn't." "I don't know whether I am sad or glad about that," I said in a shaky voice. "So, what's with all that red stuff?" "When you gave that eye a jab, you started some retinal bleeding. The reason your vision was blurred on top was because you probably struck your eye on the bottom. As you know images and even bruises are delivered upside down to the screen at the back of your eye. Then when we went in to operate, there was some more minor hemorrhaging of the blood vessels around the back of the cornea."

Impatiently I asked, "What does all this mean in terms of my future?" Dr. Taylor sighed and reluctantly replied, "It means that the bleeding has left some scar tissue. Unfortunately, to date, we have not found a way of dissolving scar tissue; so for all practical purposes, you can expect it to be like this for months."

Two weeks before I would have considered such a forecast as bordering on the lopsided end of absurdity, but now in comparison to what might have been, my relief knew no bounds. "I can wait this thing out for as long as it will take," I said. "Just knowing that tomorrow the sky will be bluer than today, that's enough. Do you know what I mean?"

"I sure do," he said soothingly. "Now stay with us here for another week or two so that we can keep watch on any changes happening around that cornea of yours."

The two weeks turned out to be three, but the time passed quickly with Jerry, Helen, friends from our old bowling league and from Croton popping in and out. Helen brought me a huge get-well card drawn and colored in by two of her children, Eileen and Eamon, and I had one of the nurses paste it up on the wall. "Someday," I told Helen, "I'll see that card. Just you wait!" each morning, long before daylight, a priest would arrive asking whether I wished to receive communion. For the first week, I simply shook my head and turned him and God away. I was angry, bitter, and disappointed, and through the long sleepless hours of the night I would lie there pleading with Him for the answer to the inevitable question. Why me? Dear Lord, why me? Why had God forsaken me? How was I supposed to live the rest of my life?

Just when Jerry needed me most to pitch in and help financially, when my children needed me most for all the things Mommies were supposed to do. They would need me to be class mother, participate in PTA events, whipping up dozens of cupcakes for cake sales, taking them on shopping trips, I had become half a person and life would never be the same again!

At one point when Mrs. Michael and I were talking about our adjustment to our present circumstances, a nurse nudged me and said, "Well now, you're not so bad off. Think of Helen Keller!" I bit down on my tongue hard and simply nodded a weak acknowledgement, while deep down, I thought that if one more person mentioned Helen Keller to me in my lifetime, I would scream. Certainly, this woman had risen above tremendous obstacles and was leading an active, productive life, but to compare her to me was ludicrous. She wasn't married as far as I knew, and didn't have to cook, clean house, rake leaves, or read bedtime stories to her children. Her own daily routine was not intertwined with that of anyone else. There were no little faces looking up at her for guidance or direction. Helen was her own person, and a fine one she was, but being compared to her now only added to my own misery.

In the end, I could look closer to home to find a more suitable analogy. My childhood friend Josephine had two children, and despite being totally blind, was leading a normal life, with of course, some adjustments being made. Then there was Anna Amendola and Fran Allen, each with visual impairment, who also were coping with day-to-day life very well indeed.

Linda makes her First Holy Communion and she celebrates this Special Day with her younger Sister Nance. This photo would become very important to Theresa in about six months later.

Since Theresa was a redhead, she felt that wearing the color red was not an option for her. Here's the photo of Linda and Nance in white dresses with red Polka dots and bright-red sashes. You might be wondering why her girls are wearing the same dress. There're not twins! Theresa just decided that while they were young she will dress them alike.

Chapter 37

A Brief Seating on the Pity Pot!

If fame and fortune are said to be akin to one another, then my guess is that the two have a sister named "Lady Luck." In the year 1964, and the two that followed, Jerry and I were convinced that at the poker table called life, we were playing against a loaded deck. Our debts before my accident and at the time of our mortgage extension agreement seemed like a pittance in comparison to those we had amassed by the summer of 1966. Jerry had been shifted from job to job left and right down in the city. As the bills mounted up and one disappointment led to another, and another, he came home to a wife, who for months must have seemed like a stranger in the house!

On the outside, I was the same as ever, laughing, gay, almost spastic with energy. Yet he knew, as surely as any man could know, he understood the upsetting moments when I would gaze at my children through half an eye. This was when I would send them off, lest they see for an instant the tears of hurt and despair bottled up inside me.

Even as the months passed, and as the sea of red began to dissipate, contrary to all predictions I knew, deep down that I would have to walk forward through life dizzy from distortion, blind to color and certain that never, never again would the sky above be blue for me!

"Use your fingers. Learn to feel with your hands for the time being," was the advice given by Jerry. "I can't! I never learned how! I don't want to be blind!" I said trembling with anger. Why had God forsaken me? Jerry continued, "You can still be independent! You can learn to use a cane just as you advised me to do!" with tears of rage I countered, "And have everyone looking at me and feeling sorry? never!" By this time, I was boiling over with tears pouring down my face, and I continued with my misgivings. "Besides, how are you supposed to use a cane when you live in a small town where lots of streets and sidewalks are not paved as yet?" Jerry reached out and held me in his arms, desperately trying to find a way to make things better. With a sigh, he continued, "Then get a dog!"

At the moment, I wasn't sure that I really wanted to use the word hate, but I said, "I hate dogs and so do you!" Jerry said, "How about this make a list of the things you can do and work on them one by one! Remember how you did it before and figure out how you will be able to accomplish the task the way you are now!" blowing my nose, I sighed and said, "That'll be the shortest list on record!" "That's a lot of crap, and you know it. You have too much inside bubbling over to just sit back and give up! Besides Nannie and the girls won't let you."

As time went on, I knew he was right, and it became harder and harder to indulge in self-pity in the shadow of one who loved and believed so deeply in me. My children, too, from the very moment

I returned home from New York Hospital, seemed hell bent on denying the inevitable, and in so doing, making of me the "seeingist" visually impaired mother in the whole wide world. "Take us shopping," they would plead. Linda added, "Just like we used to do, only this time, we'll pull the carriage, and you'll hang on." What they left unsaid was, then no one will know, and I could never argue with that. Once Nance remarked, "Today a lady told me that we had no luck. Is that true?" "Not for one minute, Nance. We have a lot of luck 'cause we've all got each other, and don't you forget it for one minute!" with a big sigh, I concluded, if my family could do it, so could I, but it was going to mean having to start all over again, teaching the kids to throw clothes into the hamper when they were dirty rather than waiting for me to do it, putting things in my hand, rather than simply pointing or telling me, "over there!" I wondered if they could ever be made to understand. Only with the passing of time did I come to know how baseless my worries had been.

Linda and Nance are shown holding their fluffy bunny rabbits

Here's the photo of Linda and Nance in their Girl Scout uniforms.

PART 10

Two Weeks Spent at a Special Summer Camp
Summer 1964

Chapter 38

"Summertime, and the Livin' is Easy"
Ella Fitzgerald

Summer is many things to many people, but for us, especially during our lean years after first moving to Croton, and for hundreds of other blind and visually handicapped people living in the greater New York metropolitan area, there would have been no summer at all were it not for the generosity of the Visions Organization funding Vacation Camp for the Blind, known as VCB, located in scenic Spring Valley, New York. Some of us were more fortunate than others, for we did not have to flee from the drudgery of a tiny sweltering apartment in rundown city neighborhoods. My family already lived in the suburbs where water and clean air were supposed to abound. Why, then, were we drawn to a camp where our individuality would have to be, in part, sacrificed in the name of order and expediency?

We were fortunate to have many of the same formal trappings at this camp right in our own back yard, swings, a sliding pond, and an eighteen-foot above-ground pool. My family knew the taste of a barbecued steak smothered in peppers and onions and the serenity of rocking away the steaming twilight hours on our front porch in the company of friends and relatives. What then, was the special attraction that propelled us into a flurry of frenzied preparation and anticipation weeks before we were scheduled to leave for camp?

As our taxi driver Joe Rose made his way across the Tappan Zee Bridge, we knew that in twenty minutes we would pass through the camp gate and finally arrive at the lodge known as Hofheimer. I have often pondered the magnetic pull this camp held for many of us, and I think this fascination can be summed up in one word, "people!" This was an opportunity to come together with those we had known off and on since childhood; these were people with whom we could simply relax. The fact that we had so many sighted friends back in Croton added to our enjoyment of camp life, rather than detracting from it. My family could find pleasure in the vast array of campers and know that, unlike so many others, we had several couples back home that Jerry and I could spend quality time with either sharing dinner together or just simply relaxing on our patio with a cool drink. These people were fast becoming lifelong friends who gave of themselves freely for the good of us all.

One common denominator was our inability to afford the sort of vacation fellow Crotonites considered part of their summer routine. Where else could a family of four find a resort with every recreational facility imaginable, a cabin with a private front porch, and a team of well-trained counselors to supervise the children, morning, noon, and night; all this for a voluntary donation, not in excess of twenty-five dollars? Now if some campers were unable to pay, no one was the wiser for it. They were entitled to every privilege extended to the rest of us. It was not until Nance was five and Linda eight that we first heard of Vacation Camp for the Blind, with its swimming pool, lake, arts and crafts, gym, and literally miles of guiderail-lined paths connecting every part of the camp. Of course, we were amazed with the family unit complete with kitchen, laundry, separate cabins, and a fully equipped playground featuring a life-sized dollhouse that provided the setting for the dozen or so families enrolled for each two-week period during any given summer. I had just come home from New York Hospital and, despite the fact that I was severely depressed and for all practical purposes, almost totally blind, Jerry and I still decided that it would not be fair to cheat the kids out of what could be a really unique experience for them.

The very select group of young people chosen to work at Vacation Camp were drawn from all walks of life, college campuses, the Peace Corps, and private industry. They had to be pretty damned special to put up with us, especially our little clan as we were fun-loving instigators and would give some of the counselors quite a headache all in fun. Keep reading, you will see what I mean.

The great majority of these young volunteers, I'm sure, had never come across a blind person in their entire life. I suppose, before the opening of camp, they were put through a mild sort of indoctrination or orientation program. The counselors had to be taught to direct a camper by means of words rather than pointing a finger. It was essential they had to learn not to fall apart at the seams if a blind person tripped over a chair or walked into a wall. The most difficult challenge for them was understanding how to give help without dishing out too much or too little.

I suppose the acid test came when the first of many carloads of campers started arriving from local communities and were joined by a couple of buses from New York City as well. The various vehicles drove up to the gate to unload what was undeniably a diverse group of human beings. They would meet the young children of blind couples, usually well dressed and far cleaner than those they had seen in their city communities. The parents of those boys and girls, whose annual income ranged anywhere from three thousand to ten thousand a year were as excited as the kids to get settled in their cabins. The next group eagerly awaiting their turn to get off the bus were a bunch of young visually impaired singles, some very mobile and self-sufficient, and others having multiple handicaps. Finally, the counselors would come upon a large group of older blind individuals, most of whom were living in either homes for the aged or surviving on welfare. Whether or not the group of counselors were able to take it all in one gulp, was, of course, up to the individual. Most of them would tell us later that once past the first hurdle, very little adjustment was necessary.

The first afternoon in camp was like old-home week for us, since it brought together all our blind and visually impaired bowling cohorts from way back, among them George, with a water pistol the size of a sawed-off shotgun. And there was Chuck with a new supply of raunchy jokes, and Anna and Armando, who had sprouted two children. Anthony was just a tot, and Dominica was about a year younger than Nance. Jerry had known a very handsome young man named Eddie Allen from the Institute for the Blind, where they both went to school. His wife Fran became my best friend, and our close relationship would endure and flourish through the decades to come. Eddie had been an orphan, and we would watch this warm generous man raise two children of his own, Robert and Richard, two boys as different as apples and oranges. Also, Jerry and Eddie knew another woman from the Institute who owned a home in Mount Kisco, New York. Anne and her husband Lou and young son Randy attended camp with us and shared many holidays together in the coming years. No one could forget her and two other women who treated us to some of the best yodeling that could rival any heard in the mountains of Switzerland.

I need not have worried about the youngest member of our family adjusting to camp life, for every time I managed to catch up with her, she, Dominica, and Linda were up to their eyeballs in mud, sand, and would you believe, sugar? Don't ask where they got the many packs of granules! After expressing my thoughts to those who had gathered around us, Fran reasoned, "They must have taken them off the dining room tables." "Do you suppose we are raising future criminals?" Anna asked as the rest of the group of people hanging around the pool joined in laughing. "You can't have fun without getting dirty!" Nance said, as I tried to extract some pebbles from her ear.

I had never been a person who was particularly comfortable with other people's small children. Somehow, they always started bawling their heads off, no matter how I coo-chee-cooed them. Anthony was definitely the exception. Every time I picked him up, he snuggled deep in my arms, jabbered away, and seemed perfectly content to put up with my shortcomings.

You see, Anthony's family had the cabin next to ours, so it was natural that we were in and out of each other's quarters constantly. One morning I heard Anna, who had never been known for being particularly soft spoken, was fussing around in her cabin and obviously in great distress. I made my way along the path, and even through the closed door, I could hear her screaming, "Anthony, where's your shoe?" he was only a tot. Did she think that all of a sudden he would start talking? "Holy cats, Anna. That mouth of yours would wake the dead. What's wrong?" "Here," she said, handing over Anthony to me. "Hold him while I get the broom, before

I really blow my cool! Every time I go to get him ready, I can't find one shoe!" "How's my little boy," I asked kissing his pudgy cheeks. "Your mommy's flipping her top in there, isn't she?" this time, however, I was surprised to find that instead of snuggling up to me as was his custom, Anthony was pulling away and was apparently pointing to something. "Gaba goo! Gaba goo!" He said, as though he was intending to relay some sort of message to me. "Next time," said Anna sounding even more frustrated if that was possible! "No there's not going to be a next time. When I put him down tonight, I'm going to tie his shoes to the bed post. That's what I'll do!" with the passing of each moment, Anna's rage swelled, and the net result of all her sweeping was a very neat cabin with not even a trace of anything resembling a shoe to be found in it.

"Gaba goo, gaba goo" howled baby Anthony getting very agitated! "Anna, before you burst a blood vessel, I think he's trying to point to where it is, and since I can't see, you'd better take a look!" "Okay, okay but first, I am going to check the bathroom. I don't think he knows where it is any more than I do!" at that point, Anthony wanted to be put down. He let out an exasperated grunt and the next thing I felt was a sharp rap on the head. I reached up automatically to find what it was that could have landed on me quite that hard, and sure enough, down it came again, only this time, its shape was unmistakable. "Ata boy," I said to Anthony as I gave him a big hug and patted the place on my head where he clobbered me. Laughing and clapping his hands, he said again, "Gaba goo, gaba goo!" "Hey, Anna! I hate to tell you, but I've found the shoe. This poor kid has been waving and puffing like a steam engine, and we were both too dumb to pay any attention!" Anna picked up her squealing Anthony and said, "My smart little squiggles!"

Chapter 39

Let the Fun Begin!

Every once in a while, we would come upon a counselor who considered her stay at camp to be a penitential pilgrimage, wherein she alone could atone for the sins, injustices, and ignorance of mankind. This young lady was the type who would preach to anyone who would listen how awful she felt when she met a blind man who wandered around for two hours after breakfast in search of his cabin, or how she could have cried when that young fellow over there had asked another guy to dance, thinking that he was a she. Now, we all thought that this sort of thing was uproariously funny and certainly not deserving of any great degree of pity, but our friend would plunge into another of her sermons on the need for love and understanding. As I promised you earlier, my Jerry and another conspirator decided that enough was enough! Here's what happened next!

Harry Dando, a young man with a cherubic face, remarked, "I'll bet there isn't anything she wouldn't do for any of us. I'll bet she'd even teach us how to row a boat, if I asked her!" "Row a boat," we roared. "Why you're one of the best crewman in the whole camp!" "I know that and you know that, but she doesn't. I wonder how long it will take before she catches on. Probably just a few minutes, if I give her a good dose of my charm!" "What's the point?" we asked. "The point is to get her mad, so she'll forget about being so damned sad. As far as she's concerned, we're the dumbest, most pathetic aggregation of misfits ever created by the left hand of God and someone's got to call her bluff."

Several days passed and Harry's impending venture was almost forgotten in the interim, although I must admit that some of us did hang around the dock a bit more than usual. Finally, one afternoon, he announced that he had had quite a productive morning at the lake. "Good God! You did it!" we said, knowing what he was referring to. "I said I would, didn't I?" he then went on to relate in fine detail the account of his supposed virgin voyage and his single-handed crusade to convert one very gullible young lady.

"Well, you see, it all started out like this. I went down to the boat dock when I knew she would be on duty. She spotted me and asked if I wanted to take out a boat. I hesitated a bit and mumbled something about not knowing how to row. She was right there, Johnny on the spot, ready to give her all to teach me. I agreed cautiously, telling her that it was very sweet of her to offer." "She went on to say, 'Oh sure thing. You know I'd do anything to help you out. I think it's just marvelous that you're brave enough to want to try.'" The bunch of us sat transfixed to our lounge chairs around the pool, wondering what would come next. "So, I asked her if she would help me into the boat since I was afraid of falling! 'Sure, I will,' she said with great enthusiasm. And then she continued, 'Now just step over the side of the boat!' then I asked her, 'Could you help me to put my foot over the side?'" "Oh, this is getting good!" Jerry said laughing and nearly spilling his beer.

Harry continued, "Well, she not only lifted up one foot at a time, she even held my shoulders while I tried to find the seat behind me. It wasn't hard to miss but I still managed it, almost chopping a piece out of my ass in the attempt. She apologized profusely, telling me the next time I would do much better. 'Now,' she said, 'Lift the oar straight up and back until it's behind you in line with the boat.' At this point I held the oars sky high and almost broke her chin with the hand grip. I said I was sorry and I really was." "After catching her breath, she said, 'No, that is not how to do it! Just ease the oars back gently. Here, I'll hold your hands to guide you.'"

"Oh, that's so nice," I said, "...and with that leaned forward and plunged the oars down so hard that it sent a waterfall streaming down over both of us. I was sure she would begin to get the message that no guy, blind or not, could be all that stupid, but I was wrong. 'Gently,' she urged. So I slowly raised my arms high enough to pull both oars out of their locks. When the first fell overboard, there was no reaction at all, just a deep sigh, but when the second landed in the drink, I was sure the game was over, and that she would let me have it with both barrels." "Did she finally see that you were giving her the business?" Eddie asked as he sipped his favorite drink, a Bloody Mary. "No, there was a long moment of silence, during which she leaned over and retrieved the oars and then the two of us just sat there. I fumbled around and managed to reseat them in their locks again and I started to row just as awkwardly as before, only this time, I managed to scoop up a lot of seaweed on the oars."

The crowd thickened around the pool as he continued this saga! "Finally, I said to her, 'Could you please clean my oars off?'" "You didn't," we said in unison. "I did and what was more, she took care of the problem, only this time without a solitary word to let me know what she was thinking. We ran through that gig a few more times, and she was very soaked with all the splashing and bending to clean off my oars. I was beginning to run out of ideas and feeling a little guilty, too, when suddenly she put her hand on mine, stopped me dead and asked, 'In all sincerity, have you been putting me on?' I just couldn't take it anymore. In a minute, the two of us were laughing so hard that we nearly fell out of the boat for real." "What did she say?" we asked. "Was she mad?"

"Nah, she took it like a real sport, and what was more, I think she got the message 'cause when we came back to the dock, and I asked her which way was out, she turned on her heels and said, 'Find it yourself, sailor!'"

"Hey, Jerry now it's your turn to tell them what happened when we agreed to take out a couple of elderly Jewish ladies for a boat ride!" "What did you do Jerry?" I asked, not sure if I wanted to know. "Harry and I were rowing our boats with our passengers seemingly having a good time, when all of a sudden Harry started an oar war with me!"

"What did you do to those sweet women?" I asked after sipping on my frozen Tom Collins. "Well, both boats were rocking quite a bit when the battle grew fierce and my lady, cried out, 'Take me back to the b-i-t-c-h, take me back to the b-i-t-c-h!' Remember, they were Jewish ladies, and the more we ignored them, they continued, 'mein God, I'm gonna drown!' I replied, 'That isn't possible. The lake is not that deep,' and I took my oar and showed our ladies that when I was standing it up straight, half of the oar was out of the water."

Jerry stopped for a moment because he was laughing so hard, and once he caught his breath, continued, "They just kept howling and what they said in Yiddish, didn't sound very good at all!" "Serves you right for scaring the bejesus out of them!" I said half laughing and crying!

The baseball diamond served a multitude of purposes. At night, it was turned into a gridiron. By day it was used for track and field, baseball, and a game known as "barn ball". "Come on, Red," said another camper, Tony. "You'll get a real bang out of this game. It's like nothing you've ever played before." He continued, "The object of the game is for the team on the field to get the ball past the row of opponents lined up against the barn wall. The rules are that the ball has to be hit with a bat, a fist, or a foot on at least one bounce after hitting the ground so as to alert the opposite team as to its location."

"Why not," I said to Tony. "It looks harmless enough. After all, that's only a great big old yard ball you're using." The cry of "play ball" brought a sharp line drive in the direction of our left rear guard. With the poise of a Brooks Robinson, Jimmy Corrigan, who had extraordinarily good vision, lunged for the ball and batted it away into foul territory. "You're out," we screamed. "Well, now, this is pretty easy," I said. "This might be fun after a…" I never got to finish my sentence because I heard "Bam," as the next shot came screaming past my ear on its way to the wall. "Hey," called Jerry from the other end. "Why didn't you stop that, Red?" "You're a riot, Jer," I said. "I mean a real riot," checking the side of my head to see if it was still intact.

The next few minutes could have only been likened to a boxing match with me at the receiving end of the TKO. The first shot hit me in the cheek, the second, in the bread basket, and the third, "menza goshe." No translation necessary. As I hobbled off the field, unashamedly clutching at my playpen with one hand and at my raspberried cheek with the other, I could hear Jerry giving Ralph, the last man who had batted, a good-natured belt, saying, "What the hell are you trying to do? Ruin my sex life for the rest of the vacation?" Then, catching up with me, he said, "Sweetheart, are you alright?" "A lot you care," I muttered slumping to the ground under the cool maple tree. "A lot you care!"

At night, there was always something on the fire to appeal to groups of all ages. While the kids slept under the watchful eye of the team of staff members, there was bingo in the dining room for the older set, trips to the local gin mill in town for some of the more parched members of our lot, theatre trips to Tappan Playhouse, social dancing, or for those so inclined the ageless joy of girl watching. Yes, there were many who could see quite enough for that, and what they couldn't see could be supplemented by a three-dimensional cinema-scope imagination.

At times, they were even able to put odds on which of the fairer sex was getting zonked down by the lake or in the dollhouse up in the family unit. There was even a thought, for a while, among the married couples of putting a lock and key on the latter and charging rent by the hour, but that was voted down as being anti-heterosexual and downright un-American. Sometimes our choice of recreation was far less pretentious. If there was a counselor around with a tandem bike, this always made a hit since many of us had never known what it was like to fly past buildings and trees, our hair getting mussed in the cool air and our feet pedaling like crazy.

As with all our trips to various bowling tournaments, the card sharks were ever present. Any casual observer tuning in for the first time on one particular Italian game known as "Briscola" might have thought he had stumbled upon a bunch of sex maniacs or a gang of hoods for Murder Inc. This game was played with two sets of partners, and although Cheech back in Croton assured me that sighted people spoke not a word from one deal to the next, this sort of silence in Spring Valley would have ended in a stalemate. After all, how was a blind person supposed to see his partner wink or touch his nose, when calling for a trump? No, our way was much better and certainly more fascinating for any eavesdropper.

"Have you got anything for me?" Anna asked. "I sure do, baby. I've got a great big load I got to get rid of!" Jerry said half laughing. "Can you cover me if I lay down my loads?" Eddie asked. "Sure, I can, unless he's got a bullet to kill it!" answered Fran.

Eventually when one of the fellows quit and took off for greener pastures, I was able to join in for the first time, playing the game with Tony Parise as my partner. There was, I was told, one very strict rule, that no conversation whatsoever should transpire during the first hand. Each player was on his own. It didn't take me long to get the hang of the game, and so, one evening Tony and I were playing against Jerry and Frank Castrigno, one of the sweetest, quietest guys in camp. This was to be the tie-breaking rubber game to decide the championship, and the cards were slowly dealt out. The first three of us laid out our cards. There were thirty points on the table. Unable to contain his emotions, Frank jumped up, pounded the table, and screamed, "Jerry, kill it!" Tony immediately called "default," and in an instant the game was ours all in spite of the fact that Jerry had the ace of trumps in his hand ready to play all along. From that day on, Frank never lost the nickname we all pinned on him that fateful evening, killer Frank, and I guess we'll never let him live it down.

The last day when we drove past Director Minkoff's cabin on the way to the main gate, I wondered whether we would ever be back again. We would miss the warm and wonderful people who worked there, the campfire, the swimming meets, the hayrides, and even the receding lake, filled with seaweed. Summer would never be quite the same again, and all I could do was shrug my shoulders when Nance asked what we would do next year.

Theresa and Jerry are enjoying camp with their long-time friends, Fran and Eddie

PART 11

Stand by Your Man!
It Happened in the Spring of 1966

Chapter 40

Eureka! We Finally Have Our Own Business! Hurrah! Hurrah!

Real luck of any type that comes in green with pictures of presidents was soon to arrive on our doorstep, and I must admit that when "The Lady" finally smiled down on us, we just happened to be in the right place at the right time. You see, it started with Gordon Bradfield rushing up the walk. Now, this was quite unlike Gordon, for he was not one to move quickly; rather, he was easy going, warm, and compassionate, but never effervescent.

"Jerry, I think I may have something that is just up your alley," said Gordon, as animated as he could be. Having finished watering the lawn, Jerry put down the hose and asked, "What's that? A cut-rate room in the poorhouse?" "No, a newsstand three blocks from home!" "You mean down in Harmon Station? Are you kidding, Gordon? The unions have those stands tied up as tight as a crab's ass!" Jerry was so hopeful, and now to hear where this stand was located, really bursted his balloon of enthusiasm! Lighting his pipe, Gordon continued, "Well, now not so fast. What would you say if I told you the railroad is looking to get the unions out and give some of these stands over to private operators? This one has gone way downhill since the end of the Second World War and will take quite a lot of time and patience to restore it. Folks around here have sort of given up on expecting any kind of steady service."

Jerry pounded his fist against the supporting pole on the porch, and declared, "Goddamn it, just a few blocks away, right under my nose? Where do I go? Who do I see? I'll get down on my knees and beg if I have to!" for the first time in his life, Jerry got a "yes," with no strings attached! No complications! And no commitments he could not keep!

"The railroad is just interested in the restoration of service," said Mat Collins, Director of Real Estate. "Just supply those people with their daily newspapers. How you do it is your business, but get them off my back!"

"Rich!" Jerry screamed as he whirled me around. "We're going to be rich! No more counselors breathing down my back, telling me what to order. No one saying we can't help it if there aren't enough jobs to go around! Nothing. All we do is plunk our rent down the first of each month, and it's ours! Can you believe it? All ours!"

He was right and wrong. True, there would be no interference from the railroad, but we were soon to learn that one doesn't just say send us a thousand newspapers, and we'll pay you later. There were deposits that had to be made to signify one's good faith, all expected in advance and in the shape of endorsed pieces of paper with "Pay to the Order of" printed smack dab in the middle. Here again luck was on our side. There was Tony at D&H News, Mrs. Feldman of Feldman News, and George Neustadt from Adam Winter Tobacco and Candy Distributor who seemed willing just this once to allow our ship of hope to set sail.

At first sight, the object of our dream, the tiny ten-by-six concession stand, could only have been described as very sad, and on second look, downright pathetic. So, we just stopped looking at the mess and started to cart away any junk, mended broken display windows, and installed new lighting fixtures. The men of the Lions Club came to our aid, refinishing wood and scrubbing until finally it almost looked habitable. The bets were made, the chips were placed on the board, the die was cast, and we were as committed as two chickens without a pot could be. The previous Friday we had tapped the last remaining source of liquid assets available to us, when Mr. Giglio, our man from Metropolitan Life Insurance Company, produced a check for $300 to cover the purchase of our initial stock. "You know, you're playing with fire," he warned. "Borrowing against your life insurance policy is never a wise decision!" "I know, Gig," said Jerry. "But when you come right down to it, this is my life rolled up right here in this contract and if it doesn't work, I'm as good as dead anyway!"

The Sunday before our grand opening, we could just as well have stayed up all night playing knock rummy for all the sleep we got. There was no use kidding ourselves, we knew that there was more at stake than just a cozy home in the suburbs, the warmth of a fireplace, and a cupboard full of food. There was the pride and dignity of a man who had seen everything he touched crumble beneath his feet. There was a woman who had to stand by helplessly and watch, and there were children who still believed in Santa, the enchanted fairy, and the pot at the end of the rainbow!

"It's no use," I said finally. "If we can't sleep, let's talk." "I could think of something else we could do besides that," leered Jerry, but I just groaned. Giving in, Jerry continued, "Okay, let's discuss about what?"

"Well, try this for openers. You're only going to be at the station until seven o'clock because you still have to work a few more months down in the city. Now, has it ever occurred to you that I know nothing about making change? I've never worked behind a counter in my life and don't know one cigarette from another. I know my own brand, Newport, but after that…" Before I could finish my sentence, he was ready with a reply. "Ah, come on, Red, you know you can handle it. The first day I was hired down in the city, I was thrown in cold and believe me, when you know that you're in there on your own, to sink, swim, or muddle through, you give it all you have." "I suppose so. It wouldn't bother me half as much if I had the kind of vision I used to have, but you know how it is lately. One day I see everything within range of a few feet. The next it's like looking through a bowl of milk. It's hard to believe that I can see even that much after the accident that I had two years ago." Jerry yawned and said, "Then you're going to have to find a system that works for both situations."

Next morning, as I made my way down the station hallway that led into the waiting room, I suddenly realized that staying home playing Mama for so many years, I have forgotten what this place looked like during the hours between six and eight in the morning. Outside in the traffic circle, there was the inevitable maneuvering for parking spots, the slamming of doors, screeching brakes when one guy cut in front of another, and the incessant honking of horns while one chick or another leaned over to give her bedfellow a lingering peck for the road. The life of a commuter is orchestrated by a time clock, a train schedule, and a newspaper; it would be our job to see at least one portion of the morning routine run smoothly every day without a hitch.

"Come on in, Red," said Jerry as I approached the door to the stand. "The water's fine. Now remember when they call for cigarettes, just turn around, stick your hand out toward the rack, and they'll tell you whether to go right or left." "I could think of a few other places they might tell me to go, that's for sure!" I replied half laughing. The next half hour can only be likened in retrospect to a collage of deep voices echoing in the distance, colors, lights, coins swimming before me, and what seemed like a million hands, reaching, grabbing, waving, and shaking! In the middle of this cacophony was my own voice speaking to the customers, but for the life of me, even today, I can't recollect what my response was to their requests.

Taking a deep breath, I said, "I'll never make it," after the first wave of people had passed through. "Sure, you will," said a voice from in front of the counter. It was Gordon. I should have known he would be there. What I did not realize until much later was that we had a silent partner. "Let her know what you've got," I heard him whisper to one man. "Tell her it's a ten-dollar bill and put it in her hand." What he was doing was circumventing a suggestion we had received from some of Jerry's friends in the city to put up a sign to the effect that visually handicapped people operated this stand. We both discussed the idea and were sure there was some other way of handling this issue. It was only natural to expect some pretty strange reactions. After all, it is not every day that one comes across a lady news dealer who can see a customer's hand, yet needs to be told the denomination of the bill the person is holding! And yet, there was no reaction except for a few who thought if they shouted out their order I would be able to see them better. I realize now that if I had had six heads and fangs no one would have noticed.

To move the line through faster, we experimented providing a large money dish on the counter where customers could deposit their coins and bills and make their own change. To handle each purchase individually would be an enormous waste of time, and commuters are always dashing through with seconds to spare to run down the stairs and dive into their train. This was an honor system they had never seen, but in time, the process really caught on. Both of us had to trust that people would not cheat us making their own change. If a customer needed cigarettes or something else on display behind the counter, I would take care of that type of transaction. Amid the chaos, it was also my job to empty the dish, wrap the coins, and prepare packs of 50 singles to be deposited in the bank later in the day. Here again, the ticket agent, Betty, took our remittance to the bank for us, saving us a cab fare.

It's hard to imagine how we could have gotten our little business into high gear without help, and it seemed no matter where we turned, there was always an outstretched hand to help. Even though the station was only three long blocks away from home, there were no sidewalks for Jerry to follow in the early morning. Before he could even ask (and I'm not sure he would have), if it wasn't Vince Polcini, one of our local police officers, Victor Sperano, who made a habit of getting up with the chickens, or Frank (Cheech) Sansavera offering him a ride to or from work.

When Jerry was finally able to devote all of his energy to a full-time operation in Croton, it was Eddie Powell, one of his old 4:40 sidekicks who took over while the rest of us went to church on Sunday. And help was to come in the form of kid hours put in by our young girls and their friends. Linda, who had always been tall for her age, was initiated into the program at the tender age of ten, and before a month had passed was firing off suggested improvements with the zeal of a veteran efficiency expert. Guess this was her training wheels for becoming an accountant, moving forward.

"You don't have enough of the good magazines, like McCall's and Good Housekeeping. We're always running out of them too soon," Linda was quick to point out. She continued, "You get a lot of kids coming through on weekends, and they want magazines about Barnabas and The Monkeys, not to mention the comics." Placing my hand under my chin, I thought about what she was suggesting. "Let's see, Barnabas, I know. He is the spooky vampire from the Dark Shadows daily soap whose picture adorns your bedroom wall, isn't that right? But The Monkeys, what were they?" putting her hands on her hips, Linda sighed and replied, "They're not a 'what,' Mother. They are a 'who.' Kids think that they are a real cool rock group, and they like to read about them." Linda's message was well received. To sell magazines and have several hundred titles in stock, it was necessary to know your clientele and gauge the orders accordingly. Sort out the sleepers and double up on the ringers, this was the name of the game if we were to realize any profit at all from the sale of magazines.

As time went on and Nance's nose peeked just over the counter, her older sister condescended to train her personally. The first issue was to get her a high stool so that she could reach over the counter to collect the money and put candy and mags into paper bags for the customers. The first day Nance worked, she wore down a path between the stand and the ticket office, replenishing coins for the cash drawer. Linda finally assessed the problem and got things straightened out in short order. "What was going on?" we asked. "Was she giving out the wrong change?" Linda laughed, caught her breath, and went on to say, "No. She was just giving out the wrong kind of change!" "What do you mean, Linda? This should be interesting!" Jerry said, not sure what she was going to say next. "When a man bought a roll of Life Savers for a dime, she gave him back three dimes, eight nickels and twenty pennies, that's all!" we all had a good laugh about little blue eyes!

Although Nance had charmed her way through life and especially school, we had a terrible time getting her to say "thank you" to each customer vocally, in anything more than a whisper. No amount of prodding and coaching seemed to help. "Don't worry about her," said a woman customer. "I came in here to buy a candy bar and before she got through with me, I was dishing out money for a toy and three magazines."

We were soon to realize that we were missing a load of customers who were parking in the lower lot and were walking up the overpass steps to reach the platform. Jerry bought a large cart where he could pile tons of newspapers and some other sundry items and proceeded to use the baggage elevator to bring the whole lot down to the train platform. To reach the other end, this meant he had to wheel the monster in and out of the crowds packed on the platform.

"You should have seen it!" he announced the third morning. "There I was with the sun in my eyes and scared as hell I'd pitch one of those commuters down onto the tracks, you know how they like to hang on the edge of the platform. Well, anyhow, I got halfway there, and I decided enough was enough. So, I yelled, 'Hey, blind man coming through!' and boy did they scatter!" many of those watching Jerry must have admired his guts, for soon all sorts of helping hands were offered. One pair belonged to Tommy Travis, a baggage man with the New York Central. "I'll be a son of a gun!" he announced one cold snowy morning. "Here I thought I'd give Jerry a hand, figuring he would have a tough time seeing, and no sooner do I take over than I send the whole damned thing down on its side, papers and all!" "You're a good guy, Tommy" said Jerry slapping him on the back. "You were only trying to help." He countered, "Yeah, but by now you know where every bump and nick on that platform is, and it's only a stubborn old fool like me who'd think that he could do it better!"

They grew to be great friends, these two, and if it wasn't Tommy climbing all over Jerry, then it was Walter Rupert, Tommy's partner. From all outward appearances, Walter looked as if he should have been a priest or an insurance salesman. He had a baby-faced innocence that fooled even us for quite a while, but directly below that veneer of respectability beat the heart of an imp. Jerry had long hours in the afternoon to work out various improvements that he thought might increase efficiency or at least provide more working area. At one point, he cut out, sanded, and varnished a gorgeous cigarettes rack that brought sighs of admiration from everyone, that is, everyone except Walter. "What do you think, Walt?" Jerry asked, knowing what was coming. "It's crooked," was the reply from Walter, smiling from ear to ear. "Your ass is crooked!" Jerry whipped back.

Soon after, Jerry installed a large wooden rack above the cigar counter to hold small periodicals such as the Reader's Digest, Pageant, and Coronet, but this time I felt Walter's comment was justified. "It's too low," he said. "Okay," said Jerry. "Tomorrow, I'll bring some tools down and raise it a little."

In the meantime, however, everyone who approached that portion of the stand was cautioned to watch the low-hanging obstruction. Finally, just as I was about to go off duty, a tall, thin man, well over six feet approached the center counter and asked if we sold cigars. "Yes, sir, quite a variety," I said pointing to the display. "But watch your head on that rack."

"Oh, sure, no problem!" he ducked his head under, meditated for a few moments and then cried out, "Oh, you have Coronas!" and with that, jolted back suddenly, and there was a sickening crash as flesh meshed with the wood. "Oh God, did you get hurt?" I asked rushing toward him, but by this time, he had staggered past Walter, his hand still pressed against the swelling on his noggin, and had dropped the cigars limply to the floor. "There's one thing you've got to say about your husband, Red," said Walter, after helping the man to his car. "He really knocks them dead, doesn't he?" later, when Jerry was told of the incident, his only remark was, "Well, I always wanted to make a good impression on people!"

At this point we didn't sell coffee, so each morning, there was a hassle as to which one of the workers in the station was going to spring for the coffee. A fellow Lion had built a very fine coffee shop directly across from the station. One morning, when the whole Northeast was digging its way out of a fierce snowstorm; plows could be heard outside, banking and piling the snow into drifts; and there was a half foot of slush under our feet inside the station. As usual, the haggling went on as to who would be the one to spring for the coffee and donuts. "Forget it, you guys," said Jerry. "Today, I'm buying." Nobody objected. He donned his hat and coat and set out on his way, returning twenty minutes later covered with snow, his face beet red, and droplets of water running down from his glasses. The coffee, nevertheless, was safe and sound. Shortly after, when Jerry had gone to the bathroom, one of the sanitation men wandered by the stand obviously very bewildered. "Did a guy just come in here with a batch of coffee containers?" he asked. And Walter replied in the affirmative. "Well, that's the darndest thing I've ever seen. There we were piling the snow up against the fence, just finished making a wide, straight path from the coffee shop clear through to the station entrance, and what do you think happened? This guy comes out of nowhere and instead of following the path, the damned fool is trying to climb up over the mountain. For every two steps forward he took, he slid back four and I'm saying to myself, 'what gives with that nut?'" "It's a long story," Walter commented. "And you'd never believe it anyway."

Jerry and Theresa start their business together, at the Croton Harmon train station, in the spring of 1966, and would work together hand in hand for decades to come.

Chapter 41

People Say and Do the Darndest Things!

Since Croton-Harmon Station is the transfer point for all trains bound due west and north, we see a good number of visitors from other countries. I've managed to get some pretty startled looks from some when they hear this chick with the map of Ireland plastered all over her freckled face spinning out salutations in Spanish, French, and Italian. What they don't know is that even though I can recite "Le Petit Renard" in French and "Si Mi Chiamano Mimì," in Italian, I'll be damned if I know how to say take the staircase on your right and go to the middle platform. The ultimate insult was, of course, when I charged a man fifty cents for a cigar that should have cost fifteen simply because I got the two numbers confused in Spanish. He was on his way, scratching his head in disbelief, long before I could recover enough to refund the difference.

No one can deny that we are all victims of habit. Commuters walk in the same door every morning, buy the same items, and sit in the same seat. So, too, they always avoid selecting the top newspaper on the pile as if it were contaminated with some rare disease. Once our buddy Eddie Powell placed a five-dollar bill inside the front page of the Daily News, the first one on the stack of hundreds. There it sat for one hour, untouched by human hands. In the meantime, over one hundred papers were extracted from beneath that first poisoned paper. At one point when Jerry fell ill with the flu, Linda and I mistakenly placed a stack of New York Times to the left of the Wall Street Journal where the New York Daily News should be. Dozens of men raced, by snatched up the paper, and then returned screaming, "Who put the Times where the News should be?" we have always contended that we could set out a pile of blanks, and no one would know the difference until the train had reached Tarrytown.

Speaking of newspapers, we thought that we should mount the peaks of Sinai and add an eleventh commandment: thou shall not be deprived of thy paper! No greater infamy can we commit as concessionaires than to stand there, blank-faced and impotent, while those before us froth at the mouth. Their wives can leave them, their dogs can bite them, they can be on the verge of bankruptcy, and they will not care. But tell them we have just sold the last copy of the New York Times, and they become screaming maniacs. "Red, you're not going to tell me you don't even have a torn copy?" piped a very troubled commuter moments before shedding tears, and soon a bunch of fellows chimed in. "The Sports page? The Crossword Puzzle? Nothing? Tell us it isn't so, baby! Tell us it isn't so!" how can we expect them to understand that we have no control over the reading habits of a thousand or so people? How can we make them understand that commuters buy more papers on Monday and fewer on Friday? The answer is that we cannot. When the home team has a good day and Reggie slams a four bagger, or if the Stock Market takes a leap, we sell more papers and the best that we and Feldman

News can do is try and guesstimate and hope that over the long haul our predictions will prove valid.

People, I've learned, believe anything they see in print or on television, especially when the something they hear concerns blindness. One day for instance, I was holding a pack of cigarettes close to the corner of my eye, by now I could see clearly enough to read through only one small tiny area. "Pardon me, Miss," said a man. "I bet I know what you're doing!" "Oh, what is that sir?" I was sure that what he was gonna tell me would be ridiculous! "You are able to feel the letters and symbols on the pack, isn't that right? Or is it that you are getting mental vibrations through your hand that tell you which cigarette you are holding?" all I could do at that point was shrug my shoulders.

Listen to this, one day shortly after we opened for business, one commuter asked, "Can you feel Lincoln's beard on my five-dollar bill?" there was simply no answer that I could come up with that would make any sense, so I just replied, "Aha! You guessed right!"

We had our share of drunks and hoboes passing through, too, but my feeling here was that as long as there was a counter between us, they could do me no harm. The week between Christmas and New Year's Eve seemed to be open season for all of them, and there were times when they really put on quite a show. One evening in the height of the holiday traffic, two well-dressed men who were obviously pretty well crocked, started waving at the loud speaker behind the clock on the wall, telling the voice that they would come in and fix him good if he didn't tell them what track their train was leaving on. Finally, as the two of them staggered merrily down the stairs, I expected to hear a loud thud, and when there was nothing, I reminded myself of the old adage that God takes care of idiots, children, and drunkards and naught can do them harm. They were not the only ones to tip the glass a bit too far, for many a Christmas party had laid a man low, well before his arrival back in Croton. "Honey, got something for my breath, so the little woman won't suspect?" they would ask. As I offered them one thing or another, I knew full well that nothing sort of a gallon of Listerine could hide that smell. But these same men would appear again the next morning, refreshed and safe as another day began, and both Jerry and I would pretend that there had never been a night before. You might say that whatever happens at the stand stays at the stand! Okay, I can hear you groaning!

Chapter 42

The Dark Side of Humanity

Even in those first few months, it could hardly be said that life was all lollipops and roses, for we were to learn, the hard way, that there were still creatures on this earth who lived only for the sheer enjoyment of bringing destruction to it. About one in the morning, two or three days before Christmas, the phone in the dining room rang. I was the first to stumble out of bed to answer it, still half dazed. It was the railroad police, informing us that a gang of kids had broken into our stand. Ten minutes later, we were able to see firsthand what a few minutes of malicious vandalism could do to an otherwise peaceful country station. The three display windows in front of our stand had been smashed to pieces, broken by a few of the metal weights Jerry kept outside to anchor his papers in the morning. Candy bars were ripped open, cigarettes stamped on, the money drawer torn from its hinges, magazines crushed and laden with mud from boots, and even the tiny little Christmas pins, the bells, the holly wreaths, and the mistletoe, all pulled loose from their cases. There were cartons of cigarettes strewn all over the station, down the staircases, and even out on the rain-soaked platform, apparently dropped in the course of the ensuing chase.

Jerry and I were sick, but not because of the few dollars they had stolen or even the merchandise they had ruined. Why? We wanted to know. If they were poor or hungry, why didn't they just take what they wanted and go. Why did they have to destroy? The thing that also hurt was that they ripped the dollar bill we had tacked up on our shelf, the first buck we had earned on the opening day of our business!

In the aftermath, even though all fourteen kids were caught, we were soon to find out that law and justice did not apply equally to the innocent and the guilty. They were all under the age of sixteen and, therefore, only to be treated as youthful offenders. Each one could claim that it was the other who had planned and perpetrated the crime, and there was no way of proving beyond a shadow of a doubt which among them was the leader. Lay low, we were told, for these were the years of racial unrest after the death of Martin Luther King Jr. "It's the principle of the thing," said Jerry disgustedly. "Just because they're a minority, they think they can grab up everything and that we owe it to them to sit back and try to understand why. It's not fair!" Jerry's anger was reaching the boiling point as he continued, "Just because I can't see well, I never expected the world to make it up to me, and yet, these little snots can get away scot-free. Next time, by God, if there's a next time, I'll bash their heads together and ask questions later!" there was a next time and yet another, although not with the same group involved. As we went through the process of installing bolts and chains and locks, it was almost like closing Fort Knox every night, so numerous were the keys on our ring. The world was slowly changing but not in a good way.

PART 12

Hurrah for Us, My Jerry Had the Midas Touch!
The Golden Years Began in 1967

Chapter 43

Perk, Baby, Perk!

For some, the road to becoming rich is paved with a killing on the Stock Market, an unexpected inheritance, or a thousand-to-one hit on the numbers. For us there were no Dow Jones dabblings! No plump old aunts ready to kick the bucket leaving their all to us! And no numbers except those on our Braille playing cards!

"Don't give up, yet," said Jerry one morning, a year after our grand opening. "There's still a 'pot' out there at the end of the rainbow waiting for us!" "Yes!" I replied smiling from ear to ear. "But who would have thought it would be full of coffee and that the gold would turn into beans?" patting one of the party perks, Jerry continued, "You just give it a while, Baby, and you'll see! If we put both coffee pots right up front where it's easy to access, they'll go for it, and then we'll see what color of gold is in that pot! My bet is that it'll be brown!"

The notion was simple. The coffee shop across the plaza was gone; the territory was wide open, and the cup was empty. Jerry was very enthused about trying new ways to serve our customers, and in turn, they would help us pay the mortgage! He seemed to have the Midas touch! "Let them serve themselves," said Jerry totally animated now. "Pull, push, slurp, they are on their way, and all we must do is keep the pots clean and use good quality beans!"

"I bet," said one commuter, "if that guy could figure out a way to empty the toilet bowls and bag it, he could even peddle shit if he put his mind to it!" "Go ahead and laugh," said Jerry. "Columbus discovered America, and I figured out how to convert coffee beans into gold!" laughing and smiling from one ear to the other, he continued, "so, drink, I need the money!" Gradually, ever so gradually, Jerry's "folly" caught on, and although the two 100-cup party perks never led us totally down that elusive road to fame and fortune they at least started us on our way!

When Christmas rolled around, something new was added to the coffee for one wonderful staggering day. The magic ingredients were scotch and anisette. Our Coffee Royale and all that went with it, donuts, rolls and bagels, were on the house, our own small way of thanking the hundreds of people whose patronage had made us believe, at long last, the real makers of miracles were right down here on earth all the time. We found that each year that commuters were deliberately missing their normal morning train to stay a few more minutes to celebrate with us! This would be a tradition that would continue every Christmas for the next five decades to come.

Chapter 44

Oh Goodness! Trouble in Santa's Workshop!

That year, as in the past, ever gluttonous for punishment, we had our bout with assembling the children's toys for Christmas. Thanks to our loyal customers, we were finally able to buy some more expensive gifts for the girls. Mindful of Jerry's past encounter with the fire truck and the wayward Wise Men, we decided that it might be expedient to purchase toys that required little more than the installation of a battery. Also, we had to make use of our precious leisure time, as it took many man hours to keep our business going with our rapidly growing customer base.

"It's just perfect," I said to Jerry one afternoon. "Linda's got her heart set on a Chatty Cathy doll and Nance is gaga about this goofy little dog that's supposed to move along spirited solely by the sound of a human voice. What could be simpler? No forty-page manuals, no screws or bolts, nothing. All I have to do is slip this little disc into the side of the doll, and old Chatty will do her thing!"

"Yeah, this is going to be a breeze," said Jerry as he made his way downstairs to test the pooch. As he faded from sight, I proceeded gleefully to pull the cord at Chatty's side, fully expecting her to whisper, "Mommy, I need to tinkle" or "can't we go out to play" what about "hey, big Mama! Where's the grub?" Instead there was nothing! I gave the cord another yank, this time with a little more force. Just silence! My frustration was beginning to reach new heights! "Damnation!" I muttered. "How could I have goofed now?" I raged at the thought of having been sold a talking doll that wouldn't even mumble! Angrily I pulled open the tiny pamphlet that had accompanied her in order to discern a model number.

At this point Nannie asked, "What are you getting so excited about my dear?" with a huff and a puff, I said, "I need the model and serial numbers for this dumb doll!" she was able to find what I needed, and knowing my luck, the store would probably want my blood as well! It seemed lately that no amount of information had been quite enough when demanding a refund. If I had the sales slip, they would demand the checkout stub. If I had both, they would insist on seeing the warranty card, which more often than not had been long since tossed away or misplaced. I know those of you who are reading this story are probably nodding your heads in agreement. Well, this time I had everything, and no sales lady was going to give me the business. I'd show them a thing or two, I would!

I was about to put my plan into action when Nannie tapped me on the shoulder and said, "There is a line headed by a word CAUTION in big black letters." Beyond frustrated now, I yawned and asked, "Nannie what does it say?" continuing, she said, "It says, there is no need to insert a disc at the start, since this doll comes with one installed at the factory." Laughing I declared, "guess some surgery is in order; perhaps we'll take out her appendix while we're at it! Remember what a great dentist I was when I was young!" twenty minutes later, with the help of a bobby pin, a knitting needle, and a pipe cleaner, the abdominal surgery was complete. Only then did my thoughts turn to Jerry, who, by now, should have had that pup tearing across the basement floor. It couldn't have taken him all that time just to insert a couple of batteries!

As I descended the stairs, I could hear him barking out orders. That was it, my overgrown boy had simply gotten engrossed with that pup! There on the floor was the reincarnation of Sargent Preston screaming, "Go, you damned mutt! Move your ass!" spotting me and feeling just a bit ridiculous, he shouted, "I've begged! I've yelled! I've pushed! I've sworn, and that dumb dog just sits there!" In the end, after rechecking the instructions, we learned that the batteries had been the wrong size. "Doggonit," said Jerry now totally exasperated, "I couldn't have been that dumb, but I could have sworn the man said C batteries and not D!" I'll tell you what, with our track record around the holidays, maybe next year we'd better just give the toys to the kids and let them take it from there." "Amen to that!" I said after hoisting myself off the cold basement floor.

Chapter 45

"You Want to Buy What, Sir?"

"Let's finish the basement," Jerry said without any prior warning, as we were closing up the stand one evening and ready to ride home with Rudy Vander Heide, a railroad cop. "Finish it? Finish it?" I repeated. "We never started it!" I checked the candy rack, as was my custom before cashing out for the night. Let's see, three Milk Duds and three Hershey's would have to be filled in. When I returned in a minute, to restock the missing bars, four more were gone. Now how could that be? I hadn't sold a thing. It was only then that I thought of looking up. Sure thing, there stood Rudy with a sheepish grin on his face. Half laughing, Rudy asked, "Having trouble?" hands on hips, I replied, "I should have known you would be up to your old tricks!"

Rudy was one of the very rare human beings I had met who seemed to know exactly how much I could see at any given moment, and this sort of talent certainly did not come easy, since my vision varied greatly from day to day. He knew, for instance, that I could not read the labels on the packs of cigars, and when I had trouble in identifying two that were of the same size and height, he had shown me a foolproof system. Rudy explained, "Look, one pack has one long black line and the other has two." It was simple enough, but I was amazed at the insight that caused him not to question why I could see two thin lines and not bold black letters that were four times as large.

Because he was built like a Sherman tank, Jerry had always called him Chubs or Chubby, but there had been occasions when he had been known to substitute other epithets. One evening Jerry had been checking through the novel rack and was attempting to arrange a trilogy by the same author in appropriate rows. Knowing Rudy was just behind him and without stopping to glance backward, he said, "Hey, Big Dummy what number is this?" Rudy stepped back just far enough for a huge black man to come between them. "Let's see now, man. That's number two." Jerry turned on his heels, his mouth open half a foot and found himself staring straight into the belt buckle of a veritable giant. "Oh, excuse me," said Jerry recovering just a bit. "Sorry, my buddy standing next to you is always playing tricks on me!" "That's okay, man! At least you didn't call me big black dummy!" there was no sense trying to explain, and Jerry decided it was better to quit while he was ahead.

Getting into Rudy's station wagon, Jerry commented, "You know, someday, Fuzz, you're going to get me flattened!" that was the way he was, and as long as Jerry kept on bouncing back, the more Rudy was more than willing to dish it out in triplicate!

Now, the next evening at the stand, when the subject of our finished basement had arisen again, Rudy jumped in feet first, while I stood there wondering which of the two was the greater thorn in my side. I had stopped to fill in some cigarettes on the rack when

Jerry made his proclamation. "We'll put up nice oak paneling," said Jerry becoming more enthused by the minute. "And oh, yes, we've got to have a bar!" "Shh, Jerry," I said shaking my head. "Everyone's going to think we're millionaires!" "Right," continued Rudy, pretending to ignore my comment. "You'll have a great big bar, 'b-a-r', and a hundred bottles of liquor!" I shook my fist at Rudy, but it was no use. "Let's get out of here." I said, "It's quitting time, anyway." "Okay, Terry, I'll wait for both of you out in my car, and then we can all go home and talk about your bar, that's 'b-a-r'!" out in the circle, we jumped into Rudy's car. "I'm sorry sir," said Rudy in an effeminate voice. "You're in the wrong car." Laughing, Jerry replied, "Don't kid yourself, Rudy! Once we really did pull that stunt off. Remember, Red?"

One of Jerry's old buddies from the old 4:40 gang, had given us a ride into Peekskill and when there had been no parking spots, he had suggested driving around the block until both of us were finished with our shopping. As luck would have it, that day we purchased several huge boxes that we barely managed to drag out to the curb. A car looking just like Bruce's station wagon drew up, tooted its horn, and without further ado, we opened the back door and shoved ourselves and the bundles in. "What the hell are you doing?" said the voice from the front seat. "Do you think this is a goddamned taxi?"

Meanwhile back at the ranch, Rudy, Jerry, and I went down to the basement and proceeded to lay out plans for the massive finishing job. The main part of the cellar was twenty-by-thirty feet wide and there were four other rooms. With a sigh, I said, "It's going to cost a fortune." The master organizer, replied, "Nah, we'll do it a little at a time. Cheech is going to be home for a while, and he's promised to give me a hand. We'll buy materials as we go along, and we won't tackle one room until we finish the other." So, phase one was put into operation, and we dove full speed ahead with a project that never would have been possible were it not for those two coffee pots perking away down at the station.

The next order of business was to buy a saw, but this was not just any saw. It was to be a ten-speed radial arm saw that could have ripped off a man's arm with one rotation. "It's still safer than using a handsaw," said Jerry with confidence. Not stopping to even take a breath, he consulted the Sears catalog and continued, "This big one has a lock and a guide and a million safety devices, and besides, it's the only way I'll get a really straight cut!"

As it happened, there was a sale on the saw that he wanted, and I don't think that the salesman or I will ever forget our encounter. Finding the model that he wanted, he asked, "Would you please show me how to operate it?" As the man explained the procedure to be followed, Jerry extended his hand in order to size up the equipment first hand. "Now this is the motor," he continued. "Where?" Jerry asked, stretching his hand out in the direction of that part. "Right, here, sir," said the man pointing to the motor. "And here is the blade." Again, the same routine, Jerry inquired "Where is it?" I could see the poor salesman starting to back off. "Sir, pardon me for saying so, but if you don't see very well, maybe you should be thinking about buying a simpler machine. Now I have another one over here." "No sweat, man," said Jerry urging him back in the direction of the monster. "I worked with one like this in school. I just need a refresher course, that's all!"

By the time the order had been signed, sealed, and delivered to the loading platform, the poor sales man was slightly the worse for wear. As we made our way down the escalator and out the front door, I said, "That poor guy. You know he's not going to sleep tonight thinking about you slicing off part of your hand!" Jerry replied with great confidence, "No problem, Red. I've got it down pat, now!"

The children were warned that the shop was one room that was strictly off limits for them. This machine was no toy, and when Daddy was working, they were to stay clear out of sight. The last thing he wanted was for one of them to come up behind his back and startle him while the button was on. In fact, he had no cause for worry, since they were scared silly of it as were Nannie and Jerry's Mother, who was now living with us for part of the year.

The next phase of our Grand Design was for all, except Jerry, the most enjoyable since it involved the actual selection of materials to be used. In this, Jerry felt thwarted and put upon by those around him who dared to suggest shopping around for a better price. "That's fantastic. This will really look good," he would say, after a salesman had brought out the first of hundreds of panel samples for us to choose from. "That's beautiful, look at the way it shines. We'll take it!" Jerry concluded. He didn't even know the price. This was a minor detail as far as he was concerned, one which could be settled later.

"Isn't there some way we can leave that guy home?" Cheech finally asked after one of these performances. He continued, "If we don't stop him now, you're liable to wind up with sterling silver door knobs and imported Italian marble on your floors. There are so many variations that would do just as nicely, but with Jerry around, determined to blow his bankroll on everything he sees, you'd be back in the poor house, for sure!" finally, Diamond Jim relented and left the pickin' and choosin' to Patty, Cheech, and me, but I should have known in advance what he would be like once money started burning a hole in his pocket.

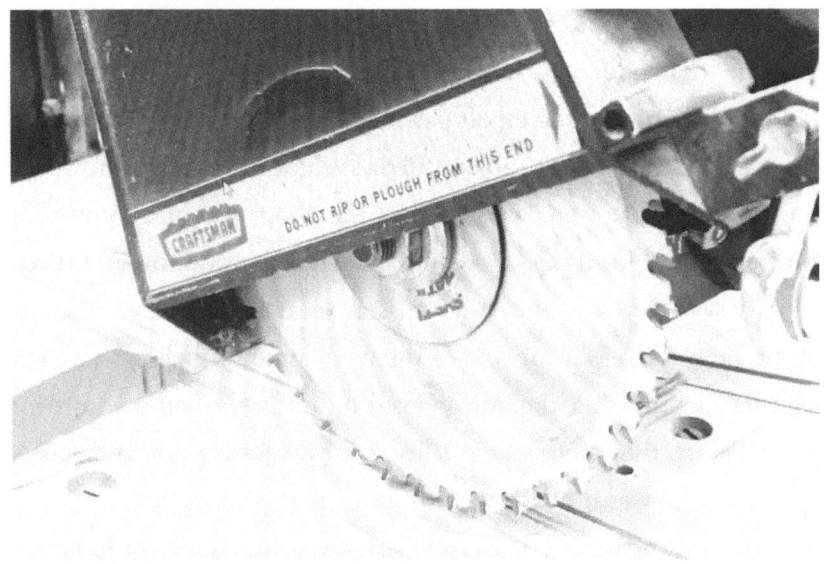

Theresa was worried about her husband Jerry who was partially sighted working with, of all things, a "Radial Arm Saw!"

Linda is sitting at Jerry's much talked about "b-a-r"

Chapter 46

"Hey, Cash Register Lady!"

For the first time in many years, I too was able to luxuriate in the joy of drifting through stores and being able to buy as well as look. Now living in a suburb where public transportation was at a minimum, this caused us to depend on some of our closest friends, but implicit in our friendship was the understanding that they had the right to say, "no, not today, or I'm busy!" never depend on relatives, we had been told by one blind person after another. If they do something for you, you'll hear about it, and they'll let you know you're imposing. The trouble with relatives is that they either ignore you or smother you to death and pretend you can't do anything for yourself. We had heeded the warning, although, again, I suppose that our situation was the exception rather than the norm. No couple could have asked for finer relatives than ours, ready to act on our bidding. Jerry's Nieces and Nephews along with my Sister Helen and her Husband Dan could have so easily felt imposed on, but the will to do whatever we needed was always there.

There were isolated instances when we dared to venture out on our own, just to prove that we could still do it. No one needed to remind us that the soft life we had been leading had spoiled us, perhaps beyond repair. All this riding around in cars and being constantly accompanied by the girls had taken the edge off what had once been a very keen sense of awareness of how best to use whatever vision we had. It was easy to get out of practice. For the most part, the both of us did very well despite the fact that it was Jerry now who was doing most of the seeing, not I. What vision I had left was hardly useful for unfamiliar surroundings, and I had never been one to use anything other than physical appearances, which helped me to locate my point of destination.

Jerry had always been aware of minute details. For instance, in Peekskill, that an Army & Navy Store was three establishments in from Jones. There was a crosswalk at Division and Bank Street, and so on. I had picked them out in the past by simply looking at merchandise in the windows, reading signs, etc. In short, I had depended completely on what I could see, since there had been no reason for me to do otherwise. Now the tables were turned, and I wished that I could remember the way Jerry did, and I hated thinking that; for me, there would never be a day when life would again be so casual. I would have to listen harder, react faster, and change my whole lifestyle. I wasn't sure that I wouldn't strike out without ever having the bat leave my shoulder.

None of our escapades were very spectacular, and only a few were what one might call eventful. Everything was A-O-K unless, as once happened, the proprietor decided to remodel his store without consulting us first, and in so doing stuck a plate glass window where a door had originally been located. The both of us were able to do some shopping for our basement venture on our own as long as the packages were manageable for us when traveling by bus.

There were times when I swore I would never again go shopping alone with Jerry. It was just too embarrassing. He was so completely uninhibited. I can recall being in the basement of a small department store, and after making our selection, Jerry asking a passerby, "Where do we pay?" "At the checkout counter," was the reply of a harried shopper who only stopped for a nanosecond to answer. Now, checkout counters usually have registers or adding machines, both of which make some noise, thus aiding our kind of folk to find them. This time, there was dead silence. Finally, after walking up one aisle and down another, Jerry shouted, "Hey, cash register lady, make some noise so we can find you!" I was about to disown him completely for making a spectacle of himself, when suddenly from a far corner of the floor came a "ding-a-ling, ding-a-ling, I'm over here!" "You are too much," I said, "just too much!" "Maybe so, but it beats standing around twiddling our thumbs."

Chapter 47

What a Three Ring Circus!

"Grandma," I said a week later. "You're going to have a ball cooking up a storm while I'm at work each day." She could understand more English than she could speak. Grandma just nodded, and the little gold rings that she wore in her ears danced with delight! If this were anyone else, asking her to take charge of the kitchen would have been an imposition, but I knew in advance that this was the one place where she felt truly at home. Grandma loved to eat and was delighted to see others "mangia." Many was the time I had seen her spend hours in the kitchen, fussing around, and even rewashing pots and pans that had already been scoured.

Nannie took care of the housekeeping details, including washing clothes and stringing them out on a line that Jerry had put up in the backyard earlier that year. Of course, since it went over the pool, she would often have to fish out a shirt or other garment that the wind had blown into the drink.

Now in any home, I don't care how special it is, it is not very easy for three generations of people to live together. To make it work, there must be compromise and reciprocity on the part of each member of the clan. I had always cherished my role as chief cook and bottle washer, but now that I was going to be working twelve to fourteen hours a day, while Jerry and Cheech worked in the basement, there was nothing left but to relinquish my title. It must have been very confusing for the girls, who now had four adults handing down orders to them, but they took it in stride, and although there were occasional flare-ups, as long as Linda and Nance catered to each Grandmother's whims, they were able to maintain a reasonably steady balance. Individual idiosyncrasies and petty annoyances, if permitted to be blown out of proportion, could, we knew, break down the smoothest-running family wheel. Grandma, for instance, had a habit of coughing up what sounded like part of her intestinal track into a wad of tissue at least once every ten minutes while the rest of us choked back the impulse to heave. Nannie ran around the house turning off light switches and drying out old paper towels and garbage bags, so they could be used again. She remembered the Great Depression and knew it was her duty to save money when it was possible. Nance left peach pits wrapped in Kleenex, shoes and slippers all over the house. Linda left the bathroom mat in a state of total saturation and half cups full of hair in the drain every time she took a shower. Jerry had a way of walking into the living room and starting a conversation right in the middle of a hair-raising thriller on television, and I never walked out of the kitchen without leaving at least four or five cabinet doors open.

More than once, with any group so diversified in age and temperament, there was bound to be dissention within the ranks. Nance would tearfully holler, "Mommy, Nannie said I can't go out to drum majorette practice tonight!" Nannie would put her hands on her hips and cry, "Nobody wants you when you're old!" Grandma would put in her own two cents saying, "Tesa, you have to do something with those kidsa!" Jerry would go out to Lions Club meetings every other Thursday. After one of these events when arriving back home, he didn't turn on the lights in the living room, and all I heard was a crash and then him hollering, "Son of a bitch, Terry, what did you do!" Jerry limped into the bedroom, nursing the lump that was slowly blooming on his leg. Yawning, I said, "Well, what I did was to rearrange some furniture in the living room."

I became the mediator who had to soothe ruffled feelings, shove the girls into another room, or tell Jerry to go smoke a cigar. So, all was quiet on the western front for now! There were many occasions when I was sure I was going through change of life, even though I was only in my thirties, for each of these minor skirmishes left me hot and cold all at once.

When the initial purchases of equipment and material had been made for our basement-finishing project, Jerry charged through the cellar casting aside heaps of junk that had been piling up over the years. "Why do we need three toasters and four broken clocks?" he asked. "Because Nannie thinks we'll be able to use them some day," I replied. Thus, the junk we hauled out to the sidewalk for the weekly pickup would have put a twinkle in the eye of any flea setting up a market.

With the antiques disposed of, the two Grandmothers turned their attention to a friendly, but spirited, competition to see which one of them could spoil the rest of us the most. They hung up the girls' clothing, made their beds for them because they hated to wake them up early enough for them to do for themselves before running out to school. Jerry's glass beer mug was placed in the freezer each night, so that the poor, dear boy could enjoy his brew with chips of ice tingling through his gullet. Also, I was not permitted to lift a dish from the table. Finally, at dinner one night, I tapped my fork against my glass and proclaimed, "This has got to stop," I announced.

"This is all very sweet now, but think of what it's going to be like around here when Nannie, you spend time down in Queens with Helen and the kids! What about you, Grandma, when you travel down to North Carolina to visit with Kay (Jerry's youngest Sister), what will we do? From this moment on, the honeymoon is over, and it's everyone for himself. Do you dig, ladies?" "We get it," said Nannie, "but I've said all along that Grandma was the one who was going to spoil those kids." I shook my head and expected that Nannie would want to have the last word on the subject! So, before a new battle took hold, I got up from the table and cleared the dishes with Linda's help.

Chapter 48

Jerry Went Up the Hill to Fetch a Pail of Water

My expanded working horizon brought me in contact with many strange and wonderful people. A self-service coffee pot with multiple spigots on the end seems a simple enough operation in itself. Yet, I often had to race over to point out as gently as possible that the safest way to obtain a cup of coffee is to actually hold the cup under the spigot. Although many have tried, we have not figured out a way to deliver the brew into the cup of an outstretched hand by means of magnetic attraction or metallic osmosis. We've also not discovered to date how best to keep customers from scalding their hands as they search in vain for a slot in the side of the pot where they may deposit coins as payment for their brew. Or watch as in frustration they give up completely, lift the lid, and dump them into the grounds.

There are those among us who cannot begin their day without coffee, but then, too, there are many who insist on tea, hot chocolate, or yes, even soup. Things got interesting, because we had to have some pots of hot water for cleaning up. We did not have access to a sink nearby; the only one, in the station maintenance closet, poured out a pint every five minutes. Now Jerry could juggle all these pots of coffee and water if we had ample electrical outlets, but that was not the case! We only had access to two. As usual Jerry had a very good system to make all this possible, however, there were occasions when we were bound to run out, and invariably, this moment would coincide with the arrival of Alex or Joan from the taxi stand eager for their cup of Jo! "What the hell are you doing with all the water?" Alex would scream. "How could anyone use all that? What are you doing back there, Jerry, delivering babies on the side? Now, make up your mind, it's either midwifing or coffee making. What's it gonna be?" "you know, I just don't know how you do it all," remarked Joan and she continued, "Jerry, you wind your way in and out of here every morning with steaming vats of water, and you'd think people would know, by now, to get out of your way!" "Nah, Joany, I'm wearing glasses, don't forget. As far as they're concerned, there's no problem, and I can't kill them for what they don't know; even when they wait just long enough for you to reach the door and then slam it right in your face." Jerry was on a roll and continued, "Yeah, even then, I've learned to count to ten when one of them comes up and asks me for change of a quarter, seeing I've got both arms full, and when I tell them 'get it at the newsstand,' they say, 'what newsstand'?"

There was one man, recently arrived in our midst, who looked on our infant coffee concession with even more endearment than us. Emil Laemmle was the night baggage man. "Do you see what you just did?" Emil asked one evening. Jerry was gathering the leftover newspapers to be thrown away and stopped to inquire, "Did what?" "The cloth you put on top of the pot to dry, well, I hate to break it to you, but the lid was off." "Oh, my God, what do we do now? I sure can't go over there and fish it out in front of customers!" laughing, Emil continued, "You might not have to bother. A lady just poured herself a cup, and now she's just standing there trying to figure out how a coffee pot could have a green tail hanging out of its spigot!"

Our friend Emil, was shy, especially with women, but once I was able to find the key that could turn him on, he was reading jokes and cartoons out of Playboy along with other mags to keep me informed with the latest goings on!

Every going concern is bound to run into snags along the way but in the winter of 1969 when the entire plumbing system in the station gave up and quit, we were sure that our embryo coffee business had roasted its last bean. It wasn't that we hadn't enough water around. Lord knows, we did. It was just that we had it in the wrong place! It came pouring through the broken panes of glass during every rainstorm and down through the cracks and holes in the roof. A trip to the ladies' room was like a voyage into the undersea world of Jacques Cousteau.

Now, you can't brew coffee without water, and it was only after the well had run dry that we first came to truly comprehend how often in one day we hit that faucet. "I'll get water if I have to pipe it in straight from the Croton Reservoir," Jerry proclaimed. When an oasis in the desert was finally found, it lacked the availability of unemployed camels. The only resource open to Jerry was to become a suburban Jack on the Hill, complete with pail. Up and down he would go on the elevator hour after hour and before long, the muscle in his arm was matched only by the four-letter words he had added to his private collection.

Chapter 49

"I'm Sittin' on Top of the World!"
Al Jolson

Meanwhile, while we were having all sorts of water fun down at the station, our gorgeous basement was nearing completion, including the pièce de résistance, our bar, 'b-a-r.' I had prevailed on Cheech and Jerry to reconsider the size of the bar, feeling deep down, that one which measured twenty by twenty, was just a bit too ridiculous.

Now, as the last of the tiles were being set in place, I offered to scrub the floor as my final token of gratitude. "Tell you what, Jerry, I'll do the washing and you can do the polishing." Remembering my accident with the buffer several years earlier, he replied, "No sweat Red!" two hours later, I was on my hands and knees scrubbing the floor behind the bar, while Jerry was upstairs apparently having started his shower. As I gazed down at my reflection, suddenly and without warning came a deluge of water from above. It seemed to be coming out of everywhere, the pipes, the ceiling, and the walls. "Turn the water off," I screamed, "turn it off!" but by now, my voice was being drowned out by the noise of the shower and Jerry, a.k.a. Jolson, from on high singing, "I'm sittin' on top of the world, just rolling along, just rolling along." What was I going to do? The turn-off valve, I knew, was hidden behind a fortress of 2x4's and unused wood paneling. Yet, if I waited to go upstairs, the world my dearly beloved was sitting on top of might as well be floating right out from under him.

I jumped to my feet, slashed my head open against the bottom rim of the metal pail that had been sitting on the counter, knocked over the can of polish, and slid and slurped across the floor to terra firma. Three hours later, water finally turned off, the plumbing reha-bilitated and the floor dried and rewaxed, all I could say, throbbing head in hand, was "There's got to be an easier way. There's just got to be!"

PART 13

Would My Faith in God See Me Through, Yet Again?
The Year of Our Lord, 1970

Chapter 50

The Culprit Was a Cigarette!

The year 1969 had been very tiring for me as I was working a forty-hour week with Jerry going home after the rush hour to work with Cheech on the basement. So it was that we were looking for a part-time employee to help us out. In the early part of 1970, Mannie Morales came onboard. He was all we could have hoped for in an employee, honest, conscientious, hardworking, and genuine. This man wore many faces. With little old ladies, he was the proverbial knight in shining armor ready to render assistance. With those who tried to put something over on him, he was hard-nosed and uncompromising. In our book, he was the means by which through added time off we could finally keep our eyes open long enough to appreciate the new life we were building for ourselves and the girls. He was a Godsend for several months moving forward, and now you will read why.

The summer of 1970 had finally arrived, and the girls were happy to be out of school. Linda had graduated from Pierre Van Cortlandt Middle School, and Nance would start there in the fall.

Grandma was faithfully watching the Late Night Show with the host whom she called, "Johnny Cashew!" to this day, I have no idea what she got out of that program as his wit was very quick, and she only could understand some English. But there she would sit with a glass of ice and, would you believe? A bag of crushed red pepper, which she chomped on just the way you would eat peanuts! Grandma still had every tooth in her mouth, and to my recollection, never needed to see a dentist as long as I had known her.

Nannie and Grandma would sit in the afternoon together watching the soaps, especially Days of Our Lives. However, if you asked them what was going on, their answer would be very different! One day, I saw Nannie watching with rosary beads in hand, and she was praying for Addie, a character who was supposed to be dying of cancer. I asked her, "Who are you praying for?" reverently she replied with a tear in her eye, "Ah, my God! That poor woman is dying, and she looks terrible!" I remarked, "Nannie that lady is just a person playing a role on the show!"

Before I could finish speaking, she continued, "Oh no, don't you see her?" I tried again, "Nannie, remember the bug spray commercial that you like?" she nodded and said, "Ah, yes, but so what?" feeling even more exasperated I sighed and continued, "This woman here is the same actress in both the insect spray commercial and this soap!" feeling even more sorrowful, she finally said, "Ah, no, look, she is dying!"

I gave up and turned my attention to Grandma, and the next scene that day had to do with Julie who had slept with every male on the show. Grandma said, "Julie, she is a pregga!" "Wasn't she pregnant last year?" Grandma replied, "Julie, she is a niza girl, she was kissie, kissie thata other man and then bumba, bumba, bumba she iza pregga." Nodding, she said defiantly, "Julie isa a niza girl!"

Giving up, I went out to the kitchen to start preparing dinner. Later, Linda broached the subject of putting a phone under our awning-covered patio in the backyard. "I don't want to miss calls from my friends when I'm swimming in the pool." Nance, the so- cialite of the neighborhood chimed in, "Suppose one of my friends wants to meet by the wall across from Carvel, and I don't know about it!" grinning, I said, "Heaven forbid!" remember that in those days, there were no cordless phones, to say anything of an answer- ing machine or a local paid service that would record any messages we received. It was Jerry's turn, "Well ladies, I have the situation under control! I spoke to the part-time summer ticket agent and he agreed to come over tomorrow and install a jack for us out there." "Fantastic, I said. "Do we have an extra phone to use?" "Yup the one now sitting on the bar downstairs." Nance scowled, "Yuk, that ugly thing? What if my friends see me talking on that hunk of junk?" Jerry replied very sternly, "For now, it will have to do!" the sub- ject was settled, and we all dug into our macaroni and meatballs, a Tuesday night favorite.

Before the girls got up from the table, I asked them, "Isn't this the night when you change your monthly sleeping arrangement?" "Oh, yeah," said the girls in unison, and off they went to gather their things. Nance would share her room with Grandma since there was two twin beds in that room. Linda would bunk with Nannie on her double bed and so it went that every month the girls would change places.

About a week later, someone came up to the counter at the stand, and I have no recollection of whom he was, because I was in shock! "Manny is on his way here to take over for you!" "Huh? He's not due to work for at least a couple of hours!" this same voice continued, "There's an emergency at your home!" "What kind of emergency? Does Jerry know about it?" I asked frantically! "He asked me to tell you that he got a ride home, and the baggage man would bring up the cart soon from the platform!" Half in shock I managed to reply, "Thank you very much!" for the next several minutes, while I was waiting for Manny to get there, I had no idea what I said to any of my customers; I was on autopilot! Did something happen to one of the girls, Grandma, or Nannie? I couldn't imagine what else it could be! Soon Manny arrived. I blew by him and ran out of the station and jumped into the first cab I could find, and luckily, it was Alex.

"Do you know what happened at the house?" I asked him totally out of breath. "All I know is that there might have been a small fire in the kitchen!" I was shocked and dumbfounded, I felt that our domain had been violated. We worked so hard to build our beautiful house.

The tears started to fall, and I'm not sure that I ever paid Alex for the ride!

Linda met me as I got out of the cab, and all I smelled was smoke. Somehow, I managed to ask her, "Is everybody okay?" "Yes, let me tell you what happened." Linda took a deep breath and continued, "I awoke because I heard a noise and couldn't figure out what it was, and so I looked out the window and didn't see anything unusual in the backyard. I then heard what sounded like someone uncorking a bottle of champagne." Still out of breath, she continued, "I knew it had to be something, so I got up out of bed to investigate, opened the door, and was met with thick smoke from the ceiling down to my belly, and it took several seconds for me to realize that the house was on fire. I didn't see the flames. All of a sudden, my instincts kicked in, and I yelled to Nance to get Grandma out of bed. Nannie had joined me by now and was frantic. She wanted to go out toward the kitchen, but I wouldn't let her and instead ushered all of us out the door leading to the front lawn. Now, I remembered that the phone had been installed in the backyard and led all of us back there and called the police. It was a chilly morning, and we all were cold because there was no time to change." There was an awful lot to process especially in my state of numbness.

By now we were in the backyard, and Nance ran up to me. We hugged, and she said, "Some nice ladies in the neighborhood brought us some coats to put on!" after checking that Grandma and Nannie were alright, I turned to Jerry, who was speechless and asked, "How did you find out about the fire?" he started to speak slowly as if he was in a trance, "I was on the platform with the cart, selling the papers and coffee, and suddenly I saw a plume of smoke up the hill and wondered what was on fire. The next thing I knew, Vinny rushed over to me and told me that he got a call on his police radio to go to the house. Once he saw what had happened and realized that everyone was okay, he came down to the station and found me to tell me what was going on. One of the baggage men, honestly I was so shocked I don't remember which guy, told me to leave and he would take the empty cart back upstairs for me. Vinny then drove me back here!"

Feeling totally overwhelmed, I asked, "Do they have any idea what caused this fire?" soon a fireman came over to speak to us and said, "It appears that the fire had started in the garbage pail under the sink in the kitchen. What your daughter heard was the faucet popping due to the pressure buildup under the sink." He continued, "Thank God she heard that, or this fire could have been far worse. The entire kitchen will have to be replaced, and of course, there is severe water damage to the rugs in the living room and dining room. They'll have to be thrown out. You will not be able to live in the house for at least a month." Finally, he said, "I am giving you a sheet of instructions that will explain what property needs to be disposed of and which articles should be washed in a machine off the premises." "Thank you for all you have done!" Jerry said still in shock and waiting patiently to go inside the house to assess the damage for himself.

Next, I went over to see how Nannie and Grandma were doing, and Grandma was nowhere in sight. "Where is Grandma?" I asked Nannie. Shaking her head, she replied, "That damned fool woman went into the house, said she had to wash her clothes."

"Oh, good God!" I said running around to the front of the house to go inside and get her.

Later Jerry and I figured out what had happened. Nannie must have finished her breakfast after smoking her cigarette. She must not have completely put it out, but had thrown the contents of the ash tray in the garbage and gone back to bed. Jerry declared to all of us later on, "If anyone smokes in the house, water must be splashed into the ash tray before tossing the butts into the garbage pail!" he continued, "Mom, I talked to my Nieces, and they will come to pick you up later in the day. You can't sleep here for a month!" next, I said, "Nannie, I spoke to Helen, and Dan will be up later to pick you up also." "Where will you and the girls sleep?" she asked. "Oh, great accommodations, the motel at the Montrose exit is where we will stay!" Nannie shook her head and continued,

"I've seen a piece in the newspaper about that place and from what I saw, you shouldn't take off your socks and, well, it is nothing more than a flop house. They should call that place the 'No Tell Motel.'" Feeling disgusted, I remarked, "Oh wonderful, this will be a great education for the girls! But we had no choice in the matter because Mrs. Feldman agreed to have the newspaper truck stop at the motel and pick up Jerry to take him to the station in the early morning!"

Linda was scanning the list the fireman gave us, and she was shocked! She nudged me and said, "It says that all canned food, everything in the refrigerator, freezer, and boxed food has to be dumped out as well!" "Canned food?" I said, not totally understanding. "What else does it say, Lin?" I asked, not sure whether I wanted to hear more. "All linens, towels, and clothes have to be washed in a machine outside of the house and not returned to the closet and drawers until a month has passed." "Good grief," I said, "it's a good thing that we hired Manny because there will be plenty for me to do here at the house. What a Godsend he will be for us!"

As if all this wasn't enough, what I found out the next day from the insurance adjuster just put the icing on the cake. It seems that we can't just buy some burgers and steaks to grill outdoors, no. We have to go and eat at an actual restaurant or diner. After fierce negotiation, they agreed to let us buy breakfast and lunch from the local deli or pizza joint.

By the end of the summer, Grandma and Nannie were back with us, and if any of the family even dared to ask whether we could go out that night to eat, they would risk being strangled! Linda hollered, "If I see one more salad, or hamburger and French fries, I will barf." Nance added, "I used to like macaroni and cheese, but I'll never eat it again, never!" as the fall was just around the corner, there was more drama to come for my family!

Chapter 51

"And the Eyes of the Blind
Shall Be Opened"
Isaiah 35:5

Although we have all come to reject the classic whitewash and demand a greater degree of realism in literature, it is innately apparent to us that where suffering has been endured, we cannot write our own final chapter. People have been conditioned to expect that for every ailment there is a cure, and we need only thumb through the pages of the greatest book of all time to find a precedent: "And the crooked shall be made straight, the lepers shall be cleansed, the deaf shall hear and the eyes of the blind shall be opened!" I would certainly like to say that one day there came unto me a miracle and that after a short surgical procedure, I was once again able to bear witness to the beauty of God's universe. Unfortunately, quite the opposite was true. There was an operation, a Corneal Transplant, a last-ditch attempt to relieve the agonizing pain resulting from a blister-ridden degenerative cornea. What no one, least of all the specialists in the field, could predict was that the first incision would bring forth a deluge of blood and from it cause a permanent scar on the retina. How does the old saying go? The operation was a success, but the patient died? Not quite, in my case: the transplant was a success, but the patient will still be totally blind for the rest of her days.

From the first awful moment when I opened my eyes to impenetrable blackness, death would have seemed almost a blessed thing. "It'll come back, Mommy," I heard Linda and Nance say. "It'll be like before you'll see." But even then, my girls and my poor Jerry knew as I did that it wouldn't. Nance threw herself across the bed and I could feel her hot tears of disappointment pour down on my pillow that was already drenched with my own tears. "It's just not fair, Mommy! Why couldn't it have been me instead of you?"

Trying hard to reply to her with confidence, I croaked out, "It's going to be all right, Nan. You'll see." "Mommy's right," said Linda, pulling her sister back into her arms. "We Capricorns don't give up easily." Her voice was shaky but resolute. "We'll work it out together, but first, Mommy, come home so we can all be together!"

Then, after Jerry ushered the girls out of the room, we were alone, just the two of us. "It's all my fault," said Jerry! "I was the one who kept pressing you to go through all this!" taking his warm hand in mine, the man who was my rock, my fortress, and my soulmate for life, I replied, "That's ridiculous, and you know it. It would have only been a matter of years, maybe months, before I would have lost it all anyway, and I went into this thing with my eyes wide open." Half laughing and shedding tears, Jerry managed to say, "That's the lousiest pun I've ever heard, Red, but the girls are right. Please hurry home, 'cause God, how we need you!"

I settled back on my pillow after my beloved family had gone and laughed aloud. "Need me, did they? For what? What could I do for them that they couldn't do better and faster for themselves?" soon after, I must have slipped into a moment or two of fitful delirium. Lucifer was the judge with gavel in hand and was about to deliver my sentence with my two girls ready to hear. "Wish that you were dead? Cry on if you will! And then you'll lose your precious girls, too!" with one sweep of his arm, gavel in hand, the two of them were gone. "Come back! Come back!" I screamed. "It's a deal. I'll never cry again." Though consciously aware, in the aftermath, that it had been a horrid nightmare. The impact of what real misery would be like left a lasting impression on me, enough to make sure that there would be few tears shed thereafter.

The day I returned home was the best and worst in my life, for there was love, but no light, laughter, but no color, companionship, but emptiness. Why had I taken it all so much for granted, that God-given gift of sight? Could I really remember enough to last me a lifetime, or would there be times when I would miss the beauty of a snowflake dancing outside my window or a spark glowing in the fireplace? At night, I would dream of silver planes soaring through the night; Times Square at dusk with lights shimmering in the twilight; and red, orange, and green beach balls rolling along the sand of pure white under a sky of silken azure. I'd remember! I would! I wouldn't let myself forget!

There were times when my preoccupation with color would spill over into my day-to-day existence when I least expected. A week or so after my return home, I found myself seated at our dining room table with my Nephew Eamon and my Niece Eileen. They were engrossed in a set of coloring books that I had Jerry bring home from the stand along with a giant box of crayons. "What color should I make the sky?" Eamon asked his younger Sister, as though her opinion really counted for something. Eileen thought a minute and said, "Well, silly. That's easy. Look outside. What do you see?"

Eamon replied right away, "I don't know, clouds, rain, and all that kind of junk." "So, you have your answer," said Eileen impatiently. "Okay, then, color it gray!" she said finally. Suddenly I lunged in the direction of where the crayon would be. "No, Eamon, not gray. Always color the sky blue!" I'm sure I startled him as I could sense his eyes fixed on me. Eamon asked feeling slightly confused, "What difference does it make, Auntie?" "All the difference in the world, Eamon. Gray is dark and ugly. Color the sky blue, the way it is when it's beautiful, and then you'll always have that to remember when it's not!"

Chapter 52

"Now nothing's impossible, I've found
for when my chin is on the ground,
I pick myself up, dust myself off,
and start all over again!"
Frank Sinatra

In the months that followed this last and final disastrous operation, when my own sanity and well-being was hanging very much in the balance, it became a toss-up whether the gun, the bottle of pills, or some more socially acceptable outlet might help me rid myself and my family of this cross that I had to bear. The love of my family helped me somehow to cross this line, not to say I enjoyed it, but I accepted it. I assured myself that I would give my all to live through the rest of my life navigating these uncharted waters.

In the weeks that followed, I found that the name of the game was "Concentration." All the old involuntary reflexes were now, by necessity, deliberate and measured. No longer could I walk across a room without forcing myself to remember that to my left was a chair; to my right, a sofa; in front of it, a coffee table: and that dead ahead were probably two pairs of feet belonging to my two carpet-bound TV watchers. Since they were both now in their early teens, I supposed I would have to wait until they hit menopause before I could expect to find them sitting on anything as conventional as a couch. But in the meantime, it's just like playing jump the brook: there was no water to leap over, only two pairs of feet and hands!

"Hey!" Linda said finally, laughing. She continued, "It's getting downright dangerous living around here!" "If not dangerous, it was at least bewildering; the trouble is that no one around here understands me," I said pettishly one day. Continuing, I asked, "Don't I have the right to whine once in a while?" "Sure thing," Linda said with conviction. "Okay it's our turn," said Nance, getting into the conversation. She put her hands on her hips and declared, "Yeah, well, you've got to admit that it's just a little weird coming home with one of our friends and seeing you sprawled out on the bed sound asleep with all the lights on. They ask, 'Boy, how does she do that?' and we would say, 'skip it, you wouldn't believe us if we told you!'" "Yes," I admitted, "That must seem quite weird."

As I look back on those first few years after this last and final operation that would leave me totally without any sight for the rest of my life, I knew that all the functions that I was able to accomplish before as a partially sighted woman and mother would have to be altered to fit my new world moving forward in the dark. I thought about the futility of my work as a trained teacher of visually impaired children years ago, having encountered fierce criticism for my forward thinking. Was it so bad wanting my students to explore the world around them, pushing the envelope to experience everything that they could with their visual handicap? What if I had the chance to make a difference for blind children and adults now, so many years later?

My opportunity came in 1975 when I was asked to mentor a group of college students seeking degrees to teach blind and visually impaired children and adults. So, to help you, my readers of this memoir, to understand the very difficult adjustment that I had to make in every channel of my life in 1970, would be to share some of the information I would teach those young eager students moving forward.

"Okay, students, here is some of the stupid things that I did shortly after becoming blind." Taking a sip of water, I continued, "it isn't as though I haven't given my family just cause to wonder about my sanity, and it isn't every day that one finds a Mama like me who brushes her teeth with preparation H." "Yuk!" my eager students howled in unison. Laughing, I went on to give another example. "What about opening the scoop on the side of a box, and then pouring Cream of Wheat into the dishwasher. Talk about baked-on stuff! What about this one: I have also measured out detergent carefully and then proceeded to dump it into the washing machine with the lid still down! What a mess I had to clean up!" laughing a little, I continued, "I graduated Magna Cum Laude supposedly making me more intelligent than the rest of the pack. Well, before I smartened up and started using primitive labels in Braille and stacking cans according to content, it was a real adventure into the unknown, shaking them up and down, jiggling cans left and right, trying to guess. Is this tomatoes or fruit cocktail? There is nothing quite like having one's Husband saunter into the kitchen drawn by the scent of pineapples and cherries simmering in onion and garlic. Try that with your spaghetti! I told Jerry, and I could sense that he was shaking his head and smiling at his crazy wife!"

One of my students said, "Ding, ding!" just like the sound the popular Jeopardy program uses. "Yes," I said. "Can you tell us how you fry stuff in a frying pan? How would you know where the food is?" "Great question," I said. "The trick is to use a large pan and only fry one food item at a time so that it is easier to turn it over and it won't land on another cutlet or egg. Another thing, when possible, use a fork instead of a spatula to manage this. Here's an exception to my rule. When working with fish, place a finger near the top of the fish that needs to be turned, slide the spatula under the fish, and slowly turn it over. Yes, it does take practice, and so what if some of it breaks apart!"

Now getting animated, another asked, "How can you tell what color clothes you are wearing?" I answered, "That is difficult, if I don't have Nannie or the girls to ask. I try to place like-colored shirts, pants, and skirts together in the closet, and the same with the rest of my stuff in the drawers." Laughing, I said, "I never ask Jerry because he is Color Blind and can't see the difference between black and blue or between red and green!" it would be several decades later when Braille labels could be fastened to clothing. In more recent times, a lot of us use a voice-activated color identifier to help us become more independent.

I went on to explain to my charges that "Hearing has become so important to me, although contrary to universal belief, it does not get better once the lights go out. I just depend on it more. Too much noise, like nonstop rock and roll is as bad as too little, like an acquaintance at a crowded cocktail party who won't grunt or yawn or belch during pauses to let me know they are still sitting there!" my students were taking all of this in as they frantically scribbled tons of notes while giggling about the stories I was telling them.

A student with a great announcer's voice, named Jack, asked, "Were you able to go back to work at the stand? How could you possibly know what customers had in their hands? Weren't you afraid?" "Here's what happened when I went back to work at the stand not long after my operation in the fall 1970. 'You'll fool 'em all,' Jerry had said just before my return to work. He continued, 'Just like always, they will never know for sure what you can or can't see.'" Taking another sip of water, I continued, "you see, students, to my surprise, they didn't. It wasn't hard to pull it off, for I was, after all, in familiar territory, but still I would have bet my whole jar of jellybeans that they were just being kind."

"Here is something important to remember when teaching visually impaired or blind children and adults." Down went their heads, preparing to catch every word I was about to put forth. "It is essential to level with people when it becomes necessary. I would say, 'I'm sorry, Madame, I can't see!' and the irate customer replied, 'Well, if you didn't want to help me out with the price on this magazine, you could have just said so. You didn't have to make up a cock and bull story like that. You should be ashamed of yourself, making light of something as tragic as that!'" when I had barely finished telling about this encounter, my students all howled with laughter. I continued when the giggles subsided, "You win a few and you lose a few! Maybe there's another way. So here is what I tried next with another customer. 'What do you have, sir?' I asked smiling. 'A quarter!' he replied instantly. 'I know that, but what did you want to buy?' he was getting agitated and replied, 'This!'" again, my students laughed, and I am sure they were wondering about their teacher. I never said that I was "normal."

One very quiet student, I think that her name was Cindy, asked, "Did the customers ask about your operation?" framing my answer, I said, "First I need to tell you how I felt initially and the wonderful encouragement I received from Jerry. He told me that 'it is really going to be okay.' After my first hour back on the job, I became more confident that I was going to be able to hack it!" with a tear in my eye, I continued, blushing a little, "Jerry said, 'Of course, you are, Toots.' Jerry went on to say something like, that he never had the slightest doubt, and, he gave me a hug."

One of my students seemed to be smiling and said, "What a wonderful Husband you have!" I nodded, smiling from ear to ear and continued, "Yes, he is really special, and he is my everything!"

"Now, back to your question! The commuters were still just the same, rushing, pointing at stuff and, oh they were as nice to me as before. I can't tell you how wonderful it was to be back working with Jerry! Invariably, several of them asked, 'How'd it all turn out, Red?' and I didn't have the heart to tell them anything other than what they wanted to hear. So, my answer was, 'I'm feeling fine and glad to be back.'"

"Here is another issue that is important to talk about" I said to my eager students. "The customer's voices were still the same and oh, how I tried to measure my gaze so that it would fall somewhere in the vicinity of the person's face. I was sick of seeing blind people in movies with their heads tilted toward the sky as though the rest of the people on the planet were hanging from the rooftops!" John, one of my students piped up, "Yeah, I have seen blind people always looking up in the air!" I went on with my story, "Before my complete loss of vision, I often thought to myself, how even a blind person could be that dumb? Now I knew for sure that the greatest concentration in the world is required to keep one's gaze focused on a person in the absence of any visual stimuli. The inclination is so much there, to relax and permit my eyes to close, and then I remember and pinch myself back into reality." "Finally, students, some concluding thoughts on this subject. So often I have found that blind people tend to forget that although their world is dark, others around them can see. If I was going to have to paddle my boat in a sighted world, I must look the part of a sighted woman! You see, the only other alternative was to let myself go completely, and in so doing, make it impossible for anyone normal to relax within ten feet of me."

After treating my students to pizza and soda, they were eager to hear more and so, I would continue telling them about something that really bugged me. "Someday, I would love to catch up with a guy who invented the boob tube. He certainly couldn't have had my kind of people in mind. It seems that they do it every time. There would be a thriller on the screen, bringing us to the tense moment of climax, and suddenly everyone stops talking. We hear the grotesque sound of someone grunting, an agonized scream, and five minutes of motorcycle roar, fadeout, a commercial, and the end! Once, so incensed was I at being left back at the gate that I raced into the girl's room, flipped on the light switch, ran across the room, almost killing myself on the throw rug, pushing the "on" button on the TV, and shaking Nance out of her sleep. 'What's happening on the screen?' I pleaded. 'Nothing,' Nance said yawning, 'just a guy hanging in the ice house! Good night, Mommy!' feeling enraged, I said to her, 'What the hell do you mean, good night? What else do you see?' all I got was a kick in the thigh and an exasperated groan. She said, 'Go 'way, Ma. Go watch Boston Pops or Sesame Street. Ya can't lose with either of them!' But still, I remain a glutton for punishment. I will not give up my all-time favorites, the fuzz shows. New or old, such as the Rookies or Dragnet, I am drawn like a magnet to them and yet week after week, as sure as there is a bullet in Sergeant Friday's gun, there will inevitably come an interlude when one car is chasing another up and down the freeway, or one lone bandit is scaling a cliff and a cop is shown leading a fearless lawman across the rooftops of the city. All of this is done to the pound of a drum, the ominous blast of a trumpet, or the shake of a single castanet."

Taking a breath, I continued, "Sound, music, and action we can really appreciate, but someone needs to be talking or the whole scene is useless to us! I slam the on/off button and swear I'll never watch this stuff again! For similar reasons, the old picture show, just isn't what it used to be for me, either." Almost in unison, my students declared, "We never thought about this; guess we took for granted how much would be lost to a blind person." It would be a few decades later before there would be narrated TV shows and movies that would open a new door to a world blind people never experienced.

Another student, whose name I think was Tom, asked, "Did you have to learn Braille when you were a kid even though you didn't need it because you could read?" "Yes, when I was in the Sight Conservation class, they made me try to learn Braille, and when I first used it in a normal class setting, I gave it up quickly because it was impossible to keep up with the lessons being taught. Also, I missed thumbing through magazines and cookbooks. I find it genuinely amusing that in rehabilitation programs so much ado is placed on the necessity for bringing Braille into the life of one who has been recently blinded. Certainly, for a child or even a young adult, it is essential, as it is one of their chief means of communication, but for a person past the age of forty, it is a joke. It takes years of practice before this system can be mastered and one can read with any degree of speed or accuracy.

I came into the world of midnight madness with a working knowledge of this crazy system of dots acquired in childhood, and my fingers are, I suppose, as agile as the run-of-the-mill sighted person. Yet, with the exception of short articles and an occasional recipe, I can say without any equivocation that old Louis didn't do me any favor when he invented the stylus and six-point cell. And, so many folks getting on in years find themselves with numb fingers from the pain of arthritis. For them, too, Braille is a farce." Thinking a minute, I declared, "Far better are thousands of records and cassettes provided by the American Foundation for the Blind and the other agencies assisting visually impaired or totally blind like me with an anxious ear to listen."

There are few dollars that are spent more wisely than those that go into providing the wherewithal by which we are kept in touch with a seeing, reading public, and there are no reading volunteers more greatly appreciated." It would again, be a few decades before this reading material would be available digitally and could be consumed on a handheld device with a mini-card that could hold dozens of magazines and novels. Also, it would be several years before there would be a home computer with a state- of- the-art piece of software known as "Jaws" that would open up the information highway for visually impaired and blind users. Every key pressed on the keyboard would be verbally repeated back to that person. Long and short articles could be written, the Internet could be surfed, and social media would be opened for visually impaired people.

Returning to the present, you would think that by now my students would be exhausted from their notetaking and rapt attention to all that I could explain to them, but they begged for just one more helpful guideline that I could share with them. "If the ears have learned to listen and the hands have learned to feel, the mouth has done little in the way of learning how to eat like a civilized human inhabitant of Mother Earth. I don't know why it is, but the knife has become my number one enemy. How often, for instance, have I found myself at a formal dinner methodically hacking away at a large slab of cow only to find that the piece deposited in my mouth is nothing more than a gristly chunk of fat? It then becomes a toss-up as to whether I should attempt to swallow it anyway, thereby increasing the chances of my upchucking a layer of, as-yet undigested shrimp and noodles, or better yet, spit it straight across the table, square into the eye of one who is probably sitting there thinking, 'Christ, it must be hell to be blind.'"

As I walked my students out to their cars, I said to them, "I sincerely hope that you can make a great difference to those children and adults that you will be tasked to teach and mentor!" they were very appreciative of the stories and lessons that I tried to share with them. Even though it wasn't cool to hug adults, each of them in turn gave me a big bear hug that made me feel warm all over.

PART 14

The Four Day Squeeze! Spring—Summer 1971

Chapter 53

"New York State of Mind"
Billy Joel

The year 1971 brought with it the news that the railroad was about to relocate the station building to one that would be ground level with accessibility to the lower parking lot, which was the biggest parking facility at our train station. This new venture would involve a huge expenditure of money, and even though our infant concern had set us on our feet, it could hardly be said that we were rolling in dough, remember all of the loans. "Where are we going to get the money?" I asked Jerry, the optimist. "Well, you're not going to believe this, but I actually think there's an agency in New York State that can help us." He replied. Flabbergasted, I declared, "Agency?" I boomed. "You are getting senile! Since when did any agency help any of us without taking over both our private and public lives?" with a sigh, Jerry continued, "Of course, you are right, but there might be one that I just came across that could be different." I was skeptical but continued to listen to his explanation. "It is the Small Business Administration, and it's connected with the Division for the Visually Handicapped in Albany. It's a brand-new agency that helps out people who are already in business or who have one lined up but need financing for equipment or fixtures."

Reluctantly, for there was no other choice, we contacted Mr. Lloyd Wellman and Mr. Dave Dobson in Albany and put our cards on the table. At our first meeting Jerry explained, "We know there's going to be red tape, submission of financial statements, and medicals," said Jerry. "But we've got to know ahead of time whether we have a chance." With a deep sigh, he continued with conviction saying, "Otherwise, we'll just have to get funding somewhere else. Where, I haven't got a clue."

Did we hear correctly, are our ears deceiving us? Mr. Weldman excitedly said, "Yes, yes, there is a chance." We had all we could do to keep listening, and I pinched myself to make sure that this wasn't a dream. "The philosophy," as Mr. Wellman explained about this brand new group, "is that in helping to finance a blind person in business, the state will eventually reap the greatest harvest in the form of taxes to be derived from the increased income forthcoming from such investment."

Only with the passing of time did we come to know how really innovative and revolutionary this agency could be. Throughout all the months of negotiating, no one up in Albany told us what stock and supplies to order or let us show them where fixtures like a super modern coffee urn would be placed. We would finally have a sink with running water that could be piped automatically into the center well of the coffee urn. What a blessing, I thought. There was no one looking over our shoulders reading our inventory reports or analyzing bank deposits, and both of us were assured that once the case was closed, it would stay that way with no further big wigs poking their heads into our business. As Dave Dobson put it,

"After all you've been in business already for a handful of years, and you've been successful. Therefore, we must assume that you know what works best for you, and it would be ludicrous for us to try and dictate otherwise."

Jerry's enthusiasm with our new venture was contagious and went on to say, "There is no doubt about it. This new stand of ours, in gleaming white and black Formica is a beauty, functional down to the last detail, easy to clean, and as spacious as we had ever dreamed possible for so small an enclosure! It is amazing how you can take fifteen feet of space and with some ingenuity from people in the know, can create a working capacity of over forty!" now, this next statement is one that I will always remember, "We found ourselves a second home," Jerry remarked triumphantly, "and here we'll stay until we're both old and gray!" we had no way of knowing then, that this prediction would never come to pass!

Getting into the spirit of our new project, I said to Jerry, "The railroad workers have been asking for some food for the afternoon hours, and with the space we now have, we can try selling hot dogs with all the toppings!" "Good idea," said Jerry, "An all-American favorite!"

Chapter 54

Now, What Do They Say About, "The Best-Laid Plans of Mice and Men...?"

For the first five years after taking on the concession at Croton-Harmon Station, we learned firsthand that getting involved in a business that serves the public on a daily basis meant relinquishing the right to take a vacation as a family. Therefore, whatever summer fun we had was of necessity squeezed into occasional long weekend trips.

In winter 1971, it happened that Anna, Armando, Dominica, and Anthony were visiting us in Croton, and by chance the TV was showing a scenic tour of Disney World filmed at the grand opening not long ago. Suddenly, Nance jumped up and declared, "Why don't we go to Florida?" this triggered a chain reaction that rocked the living room. After simmering down a bit, the adult faction reminded the younger set that it would probably take a king's fortune to finance such a venture. "Sensational!" Linda said. "We could go down there for a week or even ten days!"

"Week or ten days!" Jerry roared. "Would you believe three or four? Armando and I both have businesses to run during the week, and if we can manage to sneak away on say, this fourth of July weekend, that'll be as much as we can take without having a couple of thousand commuters on our backs." Armando and Anna agreed. "If we went at all, it would have to be a hit-and-run deal."

"They have all sorts of packages," Anna said. "I've heard they give you the whole works all for one price, excluding food, and if we all leave our stomachs home, we've got it made!" this time, however, Armando announced solemnly, "We'd better leave the arrangements to a travel bureau or agent or something. We don't want a repeat performance of the Washington, D.C. fiasco!" "Amen to that," said Jerry.

Here's what happened on our trip to the nation's capital, and to say that it was a fiasco is an understatement for sure. There was no doubt from beginning to end, that short-lived trip had been a disaster from the get-go. I had dialed the free exchange 800 number, thinking this was the fastest, cheapest way to make hotel reservations, and when the price quoted was $23 per room, we had immediately settled for three rooms to accommodate eight of us. Several weeks later, a hotel confirmation came in the mail but none of us could really make much sense out of the maze of punched out numbers on the cards. It looked as if everything was in order, and with this matter settled, we set ourselves to the task of mapping out a tentative budget, including in it the cost of food, recreation, tours, and a few souvenirs.

I recalled that Armando said, "I'm taking fifty dollars extra, just in case!" and then Jerry remarked, "We will, too, but I'm sure we'll never need it!" he continued, "With all this planning and budgeting, how could we go wrong?" we could! We did! And what's more, we hadn't been in Washington ten minutes before we knew it!

After receiving a soaking at the hands of a pair of unscrupulous cabbies, we arrived at the hotel, with spirits high, and slightly aggravated by the experience. All of us made our way past the deserted rows of cushioned sectionals to the desk marked "Reservations only." "Yes, is there something I can do for you folks?" asked a big bass voice from behind the counter. Jerry produced the cards we had received in the mail several weeks before. The man disappeared into a small antechamber and after a wait of about ten minutes, returned, asking with puzzlement in his voice, "Which three of you will be staying with us this weekend?" "Which three?" Armando echoed. "Why all of us, of course!" the representative cleared his throat and continued, "All of you? I'm sorry, gentlemen, these cards hold reservations only for three single rooms for $23 per night." "Singles!" we all gasped in unison! The desk attendant continued, "Now, we do have three rooms available for doubles and they just happen to be all situated together!" "Okay, no problem," Jerry said with a sigh of relief. "Splendid," said the man. "We'll have you checked in in a matter of minutes. Now just fill out these three cards, and we'll have you on your way in no time at all!"

"Wait a minute," said Armando hesitantly, "How much will it be for each of these three rooms?"

"Well, we should be charging more for each of the three bedrooms, but since we were in part responsible for the mix-up, we'll stretch our policy and only charge you $47"

"$47 for all three?" little Anthony asked. Laughing the man continued, "No, sonny, $47 each."

The kids let out an acappella scream that soared up and down the scale just once while the rest of us froze, like deaf mutes lost in a traffic jam. Simultaneously, we all moved back from the desk as a private conference was definitely in order. There was just no way that Jerry or Armando could afford that sort of money for a three-night stay. There were only two options, therefore, within our reach. Either we would stay one day less in town, or we would have to settle for two rooms instead of three. The kids balked at the idea of cutting short our vacation. It would already be hard enough for us to see everything in the time allotted.

"Okay, it's settled," I said slightly dejected. "We'll take one room and your family can take the other." Then Nance put her hands on her hips and asked, "Say, why can't we take one room, and you old folks take the other? The three of us girls can sleep in one bed and give the other one to Anthony. We can work out some kind of arrangement." "Terrific," yipped Anthony. "Can we, Dad?" Sighing, Armando said, "I suppose so. It'll be sort of like a commune for us old folks, but if they don't mind, I don't!"

Talk about togetherness. This was ridiculous as we were soon to learn once ushered into the room we were to share. It looked as though it had originally been a single but had been converted into a double without taking into consideration whether two people, much less four, could live in a space appropriated for one. In order for one of us, for instance to pass through on the way to the bathroom, everyone else in the room had to perch on the beds. The three hangers that hung in the closet were typical of most hotel rooms, so we squeezed all that we could into the two dresser drawers that, again, could only be opened if everyone played freeze.

All the kids thought the whole fiasco was a gas and were sprawled out on the beds, clothes cluttered around them and draped on chairs, already tuned in to the local TV station. "Look at that!" Anna said disgustedly as she came back through the door connecting the two rooms. "They come all the way to Washington, D.C. and the first thing they think of is that stupid box!"

"Hey, Mom, when are we going to eat?" Linda asked from the opposite end of the room. "God, I thought we just finished feeding you kids an hour or so ago!" I said. Linda continued, "Yeah, Mom, but that was then and this is now. I'm not starved, but I could sure go for a hamburger or something!"

It had been pouring since we had arrived in Washington, so we ventured down into the lobby in search of a coffee shop, still dressed in the attire we had sported on our trip to the Capitol. A friendly bellhop informed us that there were not one, but three, places we could choose from right there in the hotel. He ended his explanation with a "but!" We didn't stick around to hear about the "but."

Great, our luck seemed to be changing. The sign, however, over the entrance to the coffee shop read, "Open 8 am to 8 pm." The kids said that it was now 9:13 pm by the clock on the wall. Strike one! The drugstore where we ordinarily could have gotten a sandwich was open, but its lunch counter was closed. Strike two! This left us no resource but to follow the arrow through two heavy oak doors and into a restaurant that was completely deserted. Strike three! Oh, no, not quite, for just as all of us were about to turn on our heels and leave, a waiter, decked out in formal dining garb, rushed up to us and asked us, "Do you have a reservation?" "Doesn't look like we'll need one, does it?" Jerry remarked, glancing around at the empty tables, but old Poker Face in the white jacket just bowed low and with one sweep of his hand, bade us in the direction of a long, narrow table bedecked with a very fancy white tablecloth that had already been set for eight. Anna started to hum nervously as the waiter escorted each of us personally to be seated, saying, "Your place, Madame," or "The head of the table for you, Sir."

Once settled, Poker Face snapped his fingers, and voilà! Four other waiters made their grand entrance, bowing and solemn faced as their noble leader had been throughout. "Would you care for a cocktail first?" one of them inquired. "Now, that sounds like a good idea," Jerry replied, before I could whisper in his ear that it might be a better idea to get a glimpse of the menu first. Once drinks were ordered we would be stuck, and there would be no way that we could just casually slip out and say that we had suddenly remembered a previous engagement elsewhere, anywhere, Hong Kong, Outer Mongolia, anywhere except here!

Now that option had gone by the boards, and as Jerry pointed out, "We might as well stay and make the best of it." When the menus were passed out, and we told the garçon that we would only need four, he gave us a rather whimsical look, but seemed to know to which four of us they were to be passed. Ordinarily given this situation, any one of the girls or even Anthony would have proceeded to read the menus from the appetizers right down to the desserts in a voice just loud enough so as not to be too conspicuous but clear enough to be heard by all. Such was not the case this time. They all sat there, apparently unable to believe the numbers popping before their eyes.

Finally, Anthony couldn't contain himself any longer. In a rather loud voice he asked, "Mom, do you know what they want for chopped steak? Do you know what they want? This is unbelievable!" "Shhh!" we all said. Anna asked, "How much?" Anthony replied, "$9.50 that's how much!" "Yes," added Nance, "and that's a la carte. All the other things are extra." "Madonna mia," said Anna, wiping her brow. "I don't want to even hear what they want for steak." "Now, listen, we've come here to have fun," said Armando, "so we might as well sit back and enjoy ourselves and order a regular dinner. Besides, how's it going to look, sitting here up to our elbows in fancy china and silverware, ordering eight burgers? You people just have no class!"

Within minutes, eight gigantic red goblets of water were placed on the table and in the center, a tray of round, thin wafers for nibbling. Several times during the next half hour there were uneasy pauses in the conversation because it seemed that everywhere we looked, there was a smiling waiter ready to do handsprings to satisfy our slightest needs. The fact that each would be expecting a handsome tip, did little to improve our mood.

Then from the other end of the table, the three girls started giggling in what I thought was too audible a fashion. "What's so funny?" I asked. "Well," said Nance, "Dominica and I were just thinking that this table with all the goblets and everything, looks just like the Last Supper!" Impulsively she took the goblet in her hand, raised it high in the air and said, "Take this and drink, for this is my blood." With equal reverence, the remainder of the three co-celebrants broke off pieces of wafers, chanting "Take this and eat, for this is my body." As they finished their ceremony, poker face who had been standing at Linda's elbow, retreated covering his face with a linen napkin that had been folded neatly over his arm.

"Don't be sacrilegious," I said, hoping to sound like the chastising parent. "I don't know about it being sacrilegious", commented Anna, "but before we get out of here, we might well be leaving both body and blood at the cash register!"

So that was the highlights of an otherwise crazy vacation to our nation's Capitol. Was it any wonder then that, during spring 1971, we should be a bit skeptical when laying out the plans for our trip to Disney World? Even though we were told by Rita at the Croton Travel Agency that everything was under control? There was so much that could go wrong. We were to get our 'Fun-in-the-Sun' booklets not ahead of time in Croton, but at the Orlando Airport when the plane landed. Jerry and I just knew that there would have to be a mix-up there, or if not, then with the limousine that was supposed to pick us up and deliver us to the motel. Then, the Ramada Inns, who had ever heard of them? They were probably some fly-by-night flea-joints that were offering reduced rates to out-of-towners.

I had been told by some people back in Croton that at the entrance to Disney World's Magic Kingdom, long lines should be expected. Not only that, upon entry through the gate, all of the worthwhile attractions were bound to be extra, they always were. On the other hand, Jerry remained unshaken by all of this negative stuff we had learned from others who were supposed to be in the know! "I've got faith in Rita, and if she tells us everything is set, that's good enough for me!"

For once in his life, the cock-eyed optimist was right. The plane took off and landed on time, to the chagrin of the kids, who had hoped to be hijacked to Cuba as so many had in those days. On arrival in Orlando, a representative from National Airlines met us, handed out our booklets, and within minutes, all of us were whisked away in a swank air-conditioned mini-bus to the Ramada Inn, which was far more luxurious than any of us had dreamed possible. We all had rooms looking out on the pool, and regardless of how late we got back from the Magic Kingdom, a starlight dip was a must before bedding down for the night.

Contrary to all we had been told, the trip was speedy and smooth running in every respect. From the moment we passed through the gate and onto the trams that were to take us to the "Castle," the children as well as the adults became helplessly immersed in a world of color, movement, and fantasy, which could have been a million miles from home or right at our doorstep for all the adults knew. All sense of time, distance, and space had been left behind at the last turn of the road.

Ordinarily, touring a place as spectacular and as diverse as Disney World would hold no special kicks for four people with impaired vision, since so much of its appeal was bound to be visual. As far as we were concerned, we were there for the sake of our children, and none of us adults expected to derive any more than the single enjoyment of being there with them to share their special experience.

Even though each of them tried to recount what they had seen through the portholes in the underwater sub, or on the scenic ride high atop "Tomorrow Land," and although most of the intricate detail of what passed in front of us was lost, still for once in our lives, we could not have expected more from our kids. They were too dazzled, too awed by it all, and to have demanded any more of them would have been cruel. Still, in our own way, we were part of it, much more so than we had expected. It just didn't matter whether we knew which country was being represented by the dolls that passed us by on our way through the "It's a Small World, After All" attraction. There was music and laughter and animation, and it was easy to imagine the rest.

I knew, too, for instance, in the "Hall of Presidents," that there were life-sized replicas of our leaders, shaking their heads in disapproval, rising to take issue with one another, or sitting at stiff attention. Although we could never fully comprehend the magic that moved them or caused them to wink or frown, still we appreciated hearing their voices. We were as much a captive audience as those around us. As adults, we could relate to the content perhaps even better than our kids. It was all about the nostalgia of the moment. It would have been nice for just those few days to have viewed the world of make-believe as others did.

There was something about the people who worked there, too, for rather than being cold and superficial, they seemed as if they had a personal interest in making thousands of tourists comfortable and welcome. We were thanked for waiting. We were thanked for staying. We were thanked for buying, and we were thanked for enjoying. Crowds were moved in and out in an orderly fashion, and not once during our entire stay were any of us pushed or shoved. There was just no need for it, and for a bunch of brain-washed straphangers from New York, this was, indeed, a new experience! "How could one trip be so right and another be so wrong?" I asked as we sat in Howard Johnson's treating ourselves to bowls of ice cream.

Now, let me tell you what happened that evening, back at the hotel. Being thoroughly exhausted, all of us were stretched out on the huge bed reliving some of the brighter moments in our day's itinerary, when suddenly a thought occurred to me... "Say, now that I come to think of it. How come, Linda, you kids were getting so shook up when we decided to go on that canoe ride, what was it, Davie Crockett's water tour, or something?" "Oh, Mom, it was nothing. It was just that we could see ahead how they were loading the people on the boat, and it just looked like the kind of scene you all were bound to blow!" seemingly confused, I asked her, "In what way?" with a sigh, Linda continued, "Well, you remember, we had to walk on a small narrow gangplank, then up and over the side of the boat. The more we looked at the terrain, the realization hit me that I could picture all of you sprawled out on your faces and hands after missing one of the bumps. It was just too much! Too much!" Dominica, Anthony, and Nance seemed to have the same reaction. I could almost visually see them nodding in unison. "Now, I don't understand that," commented Anna impatiently. I perked up adding, "Now if traveling alone, we would have simply walked up to the guy, told him about our visual difficulties and asked if he would help us to navigate the entrance to the boat!"

At this point, Anna declared "I'm not ashamed to let them know I'm blind, but you kids get all uptight if you think anyone's going to find out!" without planning it, Anna had launched us into a discussion, the likes of which we had never heard before. Perhaps it had been the heat of the day, our fatigue, or simply the mood of the moment, but for the first time in our lives we were about to see our own kids let their hair down and be totally honest with us.

Dominica stated, "For you to admit that you're blind when alone is one thing, but when kids like us are with you, the whole world doesn't have to know!" Dominica, who was normally much quieter than the other three, was on her feet looking very much as though she might start running if the tide started to flow against her. "Sit down, Dominica," said Armando, the shrink at the moment. "Let's talk about it." Dominica put her hands on her hips and stated, "You're supposed to have a couch for me to lie on when you say that kind of thing, Dad!" "Oh, I'm the sit-on-the-bed kind of shrink;

the other kind is outdated!" replied Armando. Taking a deep breath, Dominica continued, "Okay, doctor, this is it. I certainly don't go around boasting that I have a Father who can't read the newspaper and a Mother who reads with her fingers!" With steam building up in her, Anna asked, "Why not?"

Dominica replied, now getting even more agitated, "Because they would think that my parents are freaks!" "I know what she means," added Nance. "It's not that we never want people to know. Once they come home with us and see that you don't have four heads with horns sticking out of them, I don't care if they know then."

Now it was Linda's turn to get into the discussion, "You know, Mom, when the two of us go walking arm in arm down the street, we get some pretty weird glances. I'll bet they think we're queer." With this last comment, we all roared! Although this was a tough discussion, it was necessary for the kids to really tell it like it is. After all they had grown up quicker than their peers, and of course, we were thankful for all the help that they gave us on a daily basis.

Chapter 55

The Adventure of the Banana without "Appeal!"

Our family and the Amendola clan also planned one-day trips to Palisades Amusement Park, an earlier version of Great Adventure Parks. The easiest way that we found to get there was to take the train down to Grand Central, followed by a subway, and as I write this, I don't remember which one it was, but it led to a pier on the west side of Manhattan. Then there was a short ride on a boat across the Hudson River, and finally we entered the park in Bergen County, New Jersey.

Most of the time we sat on a bench while the kids ran off with some of our loot to get on countless rides. My biggest joy had been the French fries served in a cone, juicy ears of corn, and, of course, homemade lemonade with big slices of lemon plopped in the drink. One day, I decided that we would get adventurous and convinced Jerry and the Amendolas to go on the ride, "Wendy's Teacups." From my point nearby, it sounded like a simple ride, and I figured that it would be good for us because it didn't flip you upside down, so how awful could it be? Jerry and I got on one teacup and

Armando and Anna mounted another. The ride started innocently enough, twisting our teacup around left to right and back. Just as I was thinking that this wasn't so bad, I swear to this day that the guy operating our teacups decided to show us old farts what it is really like taking this unpredictable ride. One minute we were spinning to the left at Mach speed, and then all of a sudden, the cup turned the opposite way, and as we felt the whiplash, all of us were not yelling and screaming, but groaning was all we could muster. As we got off the ride, dizzy from our adventure, the kids saw us and really gave us the business!

Nance looked like she had ants in her pants and said, "Daddy, Daddy, look what I won!" screamed Nance with great enthusiasm. "Here it is; just hold out your arms," and I could hear Jerry groan as Nance deposited her winning into his arms. "What the hell!" "What the hell!" Jerry cried. Nance said, "It's a large banana with a black top hat and black facial features, isn't it neat?" "Let me see it," I said. As the words barely left my mouth a huge stuffed banana was dropped into my arms, I swear it was six feet long and quite an armful. "How will we get it back home Nance?" I asked laughing. "Daddy and Linda could carry it." Replied Nance.

When it came time for the trek home, all of us, including the banana, made it back to the boat, and the deck hand asked his mate, "Should we charge for the banana as well?" everyone on the boat wanted to see it up close! Now came the real fun stuff. We made it down to the subway with Linda picking up the rear end of the banana and along came our subway. I am sure the people on the train, who, as seasoned New Yorkers, had probably seen everything, had to find this caper funny. The doors opened, and most of the banana made it through the door as people got out of the way to make room for it. The door was closing, leaving the back end of the banana and Linda on the platform. She was finally able to pry the doors open enough to fit herself and the ass end of the banana inside the car. That stupid banana sat in the corner of the girl's room for several years and was the conversation piece of many who came to visit us.

PART 15

Chapter 56

"Yea, though I walk through the valley of
the shadow of death, I will fear no evil:
for thou art with me; thy rod and thy
staff they comfort me." Psalm 23

Grandma spent the better part of spring and summer 1972 down in North Carolina visiting with her Daughter Kay and family. She started not feeling well and was back with us at the end of that summer. Grandma had to have a pacemaker put in, and she was told afterwards that she had to basically cut out all salt. Back in those days, it was difficult to find enough products that had little or no salt in their ingredients, to say nothing about how lousy they tasted without it. Jerry and I decided that Grandma was stressed with all of this and told her to eat the way she wanted. After all, she was around 84 years old and had lived a tough life both back in Calabria, Italy, and here in the United States. Very shortly before her death on November 9, she was hospitalized once more, never to come home again!

Sitting next to Jerry at the funeral for his mother, I whispered, "Isn't it interesting how both of your parents died within two days of each other? Of course in different years!" Sighing, he asked, "What do you mean, Red?" "It said on the little prayer card from Carter's

Funeral Home, 'Guiseppi Marafito died on November 7, 1966.'"
"Goodness, I see what you mean," said Jerry. "You would think that
I would not forget that date, but if you recall, we hadn't owned the
stand for very long and my mind was on all that and losing my
Father. I do remember that Linda came down and relieved me, so
I could go to the funeral." I added, "Oh yes, she was so thrilled to
pitch in, and Linda was only ten years old! But the best part was
that she had to close up shop as well. Our daughter was so proud!"

Apparently, we would not ring in the New Year without once
again crowding around yet another coffin at Carter's. During the last
few years, Nannie's health had been getting worse, and as a result,
her strength was really waning. Back in the days of her childhood,
in Tipperary, Ireland, she worked long hours tending the crops and,
when not in the field, helped raise various members of her family,
some even older than her.

As I sat with my family in church celebrating her funeral mass
on Christmas Eve, 1972, I couldn't believe that my Mother was now
gone from our lives. According to the Catholic religion, at one's
funeral mass you celebrate the person's life and how it specifically
impacted those in attendance. You see, in the fall, she was visiting Helen and her clan down in Flushing Queens and had become
ill and was hospitalized there. Everybody knew that it was just a
matter of time before we would lose her. Helen needed some medical papers from me, and it was agreed that Linda, who at sixteen
knew the subway system inside out, would meet her Son Michael at
a coffee shop in Flushing. They never met on that rainy day, and as
Linda told me later, she was on the No. 7 subway on her way back
to Grand Central, when she felt a hand on her left shoulder. There
was no one sitting next to her, she said, but Linda knew somehow

that Nannie had passed away! Nannie, for years, always had what she called "the touch"; she just knew stuff when there was no reason for her to do so. Apparently, she passed down this gift not only to Linda but to Helen's eldest Son, Dan as well.

Although I was present at my Mother's funeral mass, saying the right prayers with all attendees and singing the appropriate hymns, my mind ran over the past decades with the speed of a fast-moving picture show, and I just couldn't imagine how I would live without her. In these pages, you have been reading all about my Mother (Nannie) and how she was such a pivotal part of my life. She had always been there during the sad times and the happy events, and I knew that the girls would feel the loss of both Grandmothers who they had known literally from birth. How many children today are unable to have this quality time with their grandparents, who in many cases live far away from their grandchildren. Ok, there's skype, but it's a poor substitute for a hug and a kiss.

I recall the times that I was frustrated at not being able to read something, and Nannie was right next to me helping me to make sense of the words on a page. When my Mother first came to America from Ireland, she couldn't read or write English. At that time, she hired out as a parlor maid for the Newbury family in New York City, and it was there that she met Minny, the cook. Because Nannie had worked so hard in Ireland, she could finish her work in half the time of the other maids in service there. Minny taught her to read and crochet and was a Mother to her since she really didn't know her biological one. From that point on, Nannie always had something in her hand to read. We used to laugh because when the local paper arrived, the first place she looked at was the obituaries and then Ann Landers. The kids couldn't go to the library without hauling home a bag full of novels for Nannie to read.

As her funeral service was concluding with the priest saying, "Go in peace" and most of us sobbing at the finality of my Mother's life, I wondered how it would be not to see her every morning at the breakfast table telling me about her plumbing issues. Can you imagine sitting there with teacup in hand and munching on an English muffin when she proclaimed that this morning it was kind of "crusty?" the girls never understood why Nannie didn't like Christmas! But I knew that the main reason was she had buried her mentally ill daughter, Margaret, who had been living in a state hospital for most of her twenty-some odd years, on Christmas Day many years ago.

It was decided in the weeks after we buried Nannie that we would turn her room into a study/office for Jerry. Before this, he had been using a desk in the dining room to do his paperwork for the business and Lions Club. Helen and I were shocked to see that in several places in the room, Nannie had stashed away money, in socks, under the bed, inside the mattress cover, in dress and pants pockets, just to give you an idea. Helen and I realized that Nannie had never forgotten the Great Depression and how she had to scrimp and save to get her family through that tough period that affected most of the country. Jerry's clan had it easier because they lived in the suburbs. His Mom baked her own bread, tilled her own vegetable garden, and meat was more available than in the big cities. Here is a laugh! During that time they ate macaroni and beans (pasta e Faggioli) when meat was scarce, which in today's world can be very expensive in restaurants. The ingredients are so cheap.

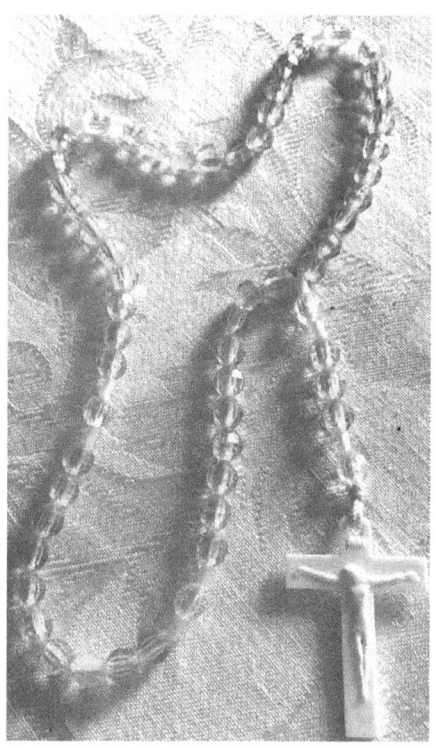

Nannie was a devout Catholic woman and would often
carry with her these shiny-green rosary beads

Chapter 57

"Is There a Place in Westchester Called Greenwich?"

When Nance was attending her junior and senior years in high school, she was working for the local Carvel a block away from our house. I am a lifelong member of the Junk food junkie Club and salivated when she brought home the "mistakes." There were lopsided Flying Saucer Sandwiches, yum! And best of all, a cone filled with chocolate ice cream and dipped in chocolate sauce. She froze the ones that sort of fell in the drink, but to me, it was double yum! It was during these working hours that she met her soon-to-be Husband Gerry Barsamian, who stopped by for ice cream after playing softball games. Croton-Harmon High School had a progressive secretarial program, and Nance dove in with both feet. She excelled to a point where she earned a full scholarship to a prestigious secretarial/administrative studies school, Katherine Gibbs, located in the Pan Am building adjacent to Grand Central Terminal.

Nance was eager to drive a car, so we wanted her to have the best teacher that we could find and we lucked out in a big way! Tommy Carr was a retired police officer and taught her quite well. That is, everything except for having a sense of direction. Jerry and I purchased a used Pontiac Bonneville, which Nance called the "boat." So, one day when Jerry and I were in the car with her after doing some shopping at Sears in White Plains, Nance seemed to be driving far longer than she had to get us back home! I asked, "Nance, can you read a sign so we can get an idea where we are?" Nance, in her cute little voice, asked, "Is there a town in Westchester called Greenwich?" "Greenwich," both Jerry and I bellowed. "There isn't a town with that name!" Jerry said laughing. "Okay," said Nance, "guess we are in Connecticut!" I dare say now, if it wasn't for Linda who had a great sense of direction, Nance may have spent years navigating our county to say nothing of New York City. Even though Linda never could drive, her directions were spot on!

One final word on the driving adventures with Nance. We were at a Broadway theatre and after the show, it appeared that the "boat" had a flat tire. Jerry jumped out of the car and headed for the trunk. After dragging out the spare tire, and looking everywhere for the other essential hardware, he stood up rather puzzled and asked, "Where is the jack and lug wrench?" "The what?" Nance asked sweetly. "The jack holds up the car so that the tire can be changed, and the lug wrench loosens these lug nuts." Putting her hands on her hips, she said disgustedly, "Yuk, those dirty greasy looking pointy things? I threw them out of course!" Jerry just sighed and was heard mumbling as he went in search of a phone booth to call a friend to help us out. Of course, this was long before the invention of a cell phone. Next day, Jerry enrolled her in a plan that would assist her when she had car trouble.

Chapter 58

"Wedding Bell Blues"
5th Dimension

So, it was that Nance and her Husband decided to get married in 1979 and bought a house on Radnor Avenue, right here in Croton. It was hard to believe that a family of seven had lived there. Yes, there was plenty of property for sure. In essence, it was mainly the dining room, kitchen area that needed major remodeling. My Jerry didn't have Cheech to help him this time and turned to Warren Fanelli, another Crotonite, as his construction assistant. He would tell me, "If we needed hardware for our project," Warren would continue saying, "Be back in a few" and would return with just what we needed! He was a pack rat for sure and told me if I needed a barber pole or some really nifty sails, he was the one to turn to!

So, the die was cast. There was the remodeled house, the elaborate wedding reception at the Fountainhead in New Rochelle, the wedding dress that was perfect for Nance's personality, and we were all ready for "Here comes the bride." It seemed to both of us that their marriage was strong in the beginning. Nance's Husband worked for the railroad shop right here in Croton, and Nance embarked on a career helping executives manage their personal and family lives. Nance finally dumped the "boat" and bought a Plymouth Soporro, a car far more suited to her personality. My Son-in-law, on the other hand, was a fan of a Chevy Camaro, and I always felt that I was riding on the pavement whenever I rode in his car. I could imagine myself reaching out the window and feeling the asphalt against my fingers! Then there was also the problem of actually getting out of this sports car. It felt like rolling out of bed with both knees cracking, and I was finally on my feet again.

Only with the passing of time, Jerry and I saw that Nance was unhappy in her marriage, and all we could do as Parents was to be there if she needed us. It was not easy to see her frustration, and only time would tell if this union would endure.

Theresa's younger daughter, Nance weds Gerry Barsamian.
Would their marriage endure?

Chapter 59

"Everything's Coming Up Roses"
Ethel Merman

Jerry built a trellis on one wall of our house, and his roses were the talk of the neighborhood. When the girls were younger, they always wanted to bring a rose to school for their teachers. I think that most of you out there reading this story who are old enough to have been an adult in the 1970s would agree that life was much simpler back then! So it was for our business and the freedom it would give us to get together with our friends. Our part-time employee Manny passed away, and we would always miss him because he gave us more time to be with our family through some tough times that I have described to you so far. At this point, we were lucky to have the taxi dispatcher Joan Chadeayne come to work for us five days a week every afternoon.

My Jerry had been talking to a man named Eldrid who came up to Croton on the last train at night, waiting for 7 A.M. so that he could go to work for the Veterans Hospital in Montrose, New York. He pitched in to help Jerry do the prep work for the rush hour, all those rolls and bagels to butter and donuts and Danish to be displayed. If my name is "Mrs. Clean," then this man was surely "Mr. Clean!" You wouldn't see a stray crumb when he did his thing. Shortly thereafter, he retired from his job and became our setup man in the morning, giving Jerry some extra rest time. What a find he was!

Linda had graduated from high school in 1974, went on to business school and then Pace University. After working for Vision Magazine as a controller, she decided to start her own accounting practice. Her first two clients were legal associations in New York City. So, Linda was available to work at the stand during the rush hour, and then she went on to her clients. This enabled us to go to Vacation Camp for the Blind, the same camp I told you about earlier. Jerry found an Italian resort in the Catskill Mountains, Villa Roma, so this was our destination for another week's worth of rest in the summer months.

Our companions were Fran and Eddie Allen, who continued to be very special friends from back in the days at the Lighthouse and for many years to come. One day, we were parked under a nice tree giving us shade and were engrossed in the card game "Thirty-one" when some other people at the resort happened to be passing by our table. Now, the way we played this game was that after you lost all of your chips, you were on "welfare" until you finally lost a hand and had to drop out of the game.

Eddie asked, "Who's on welfare?" Fran replied, "I'm on welfare." "What about you Jerry?" Eddie asked. "Yup, I'm on welfare also!" All of a sudden, we heard someone say, "Isn't that disgusting, these blind people are on welfare, and who is paying for their trip to this resort, but us tax payers!" and another added, "And they actually are bragging about it no less!" There was nothing that any of us could say that would have swayed the minds of these people; let them think what they would! For sure, it was hard to just sit there and be labeled with misguided branding.

The Marafito family is celebrating Easter today and is eagerly looking forward to chowing down on a sumptuous buffet at a nearby restaurant.

*Linda gave her Mother this flag pin many years ago
and she loved wearing it*

When Theresa was communicating with family or friends, she would most likely be found standing in the dining room with wall phone in hand.

Chapter 60

"Please Sign Our Petition to Help Keep Us in the Station!"

I have been on this planet for some time now and as far as my family is concerned, there was always a storm around the bend when the sky overhead was bright blue. So it was that in April 1982, we were anxiously awaiting our new lease with the Metropolitan Transportation Authority, or MTA, as it was known. We got a letter alright, and it wasn't one congratulating us on our new five-year lease. Quite to the contrary, it stated that our stand location was going out for bid, some difference, huh? What a horror!

As Linda finished reading this letter of doom, she asked, "How can they do that to us?" and Nance who was nearby, said, "Maybe they made a mistake or something!" Jerry let forth a great sigh and added, "Only if that were true!"

Next, I asked my Jerry who was always the optimist, "What can we do, how can we fight this?" after thinking about it for a while, he replied, "Let's tell the customers what's going on and maybe get a petition started!" Linda and Nance added at the same time, "Yeah, also let's get them to slam the switchboard down there in Manhattan with calls from our customers!" we all thought that this was a good plan for now.

Nance, the executive assistant, went to work getting the petition together along with cards with the MTA phone number on them. Two days later, we handed them out and there was much excitement from our customers and I am still blushing over some of the unprintable comments they made about the MTA.

The days passed, and we heard nothing from the MTA. So, we moved on to step 2 and started to gather signatures for our petition. This would be a simple matter in the future when there were computers and the Internet. But then, it meant hoofing it and passing on the details via word of mouth. Some of the commuters took our petitions on the train with them, gathering signatures not only from fellow riders but in their workplaces as well. Everybody wanted to sock it to the MTA, and they signed with glee.

Next, it was the media that weighed in on our behalf. The New York Post, a daily newspaper in the New York City area, showed up for an interview. In the meantime, somebody got Jerry and I tee-shirts that said, "No more Mr. Nice guy!" the Post took a picture of us in our nifty garb and the headline that day, on April 20, 1982, read, "Hey MTA How Many Blind News Dealers Are You Going to Put on Welfare Today?" our media coverage didn't end with the Post article. The following day, NBC television news in New York City sent up a team to Croton-Harmon Station to film a piece for their evening news. Linda had clipboards on the bench next to her with the petitions, and she was holding one out for a commuter to sign saying, "Please sign our petition to help keep us in the station!" When interviewed by Jim Van Sickle, a well-known reporter for NBC, Jerry said very forcefully, "We can't compete with a conglomerate!"

When it was my turn, I said, "We just want enough money to continue helping our family, that's all we ask!"

When Linda was asked how long we had run the stand here at Croton-Harmon Station, her reply was, "Since 1966, my Father took a broken-down looking hunk of junk and turned it into a thriving business and the total cost fell on his shoulders." She went on to say, "In 1972, once again we had to build a new stand because the old station was being relocated to this site. The structure you see now was funded partly by the Commission for the Blind, and, of course, we had to kick in a lot of bucks as well!" Jim Van Sickle's parting words were, as he held up a cup of java, "Who do you want to pour your coffee each day, the MTA?"

It seemed that our campaign was working. We gathered 5000 signatures on our petition and a boatload of letters from the local community and government officials as well. Jerry and I breathed a sigh of relief when we were finally rewarded with a five-year lease that would be renewable, raising our rent in the process, which was par for the course. Despite all of this horror with the MTA, we knew it would only be a matter of time before we would find ourselves fighting the same battle in the future!

Jerry and Theresa are pictured behind their new stand during
their lease fight with the MTA back in 1982

PART 16

Chapter 61

Jerry, My Italian Stallion
Falls Off His Horse

During the early 1980s, I convinced Jerry that he was missing a lot by not reading novels in an audible format on cassette tapes. They were professionally recorded, and the men and women who volunteered their time to produce them for visually impaired people should be highly commended. The recordings were very lifelike in that a single reader could change voices to make each character come alive in our ears. It would be several years later that the general reading public would embrace this new way of consuming novels and literature. Once Jerry got started reading, he realized that there was a whole world that he had been missing having never read books up until then in any format. Many times during a lazy afternoon, we would listen to a novel together. You could change the speed on the machine, and he would say, "How can you read so fast, the voice sounds like Donald Duck!" so, in order to keep the peace, I reluctantly slowed down the speed to a more manageable level for him.

Jerry bought me an organ around the same time, and it was a great addition to my day as I had much more leisure time at that point, thanks to the luxury of having an afternoon part-time employee for our business. It was wonderful having the time to spend doing things that I loved, and I welcomed this organ with great enthusiasm. Eagerly, I summoned up my memory of playing the left-hand chords. Remember, when I was young, my parents bought me a used piano that I really didn't want to play at that time! But now was different; I was blessed with a very sharp ear, enabling me to pick out the melody for tunes that ranged from Broadway to Dixie Land and, let's not forget, old "blue eyes" Sinatra himself. Linda helped me a lot with reading sheet music, I forgot to mention that she took up playing the accordion at a young age. She was also gifted with a very keen ability to hear when a chord or note just didn't sound right to her ears. Laughing to myself, I concluded that all of my family seemed to have a musical ear except for Nance who insisted on playing radio stations that were not tuned in well. When she was younger, Nance almost turned us against Christmas when she decided to sing, "Oh, Holy Night" in the shower. When Jerry got out of high school, he had played in an amateur band as a trumpet player, and one day, after leaving Yankee Stadium, proceeded to take one of those horns that you buy at the park. He opened the window and tried to play the thing as if it were a trumpet. This man of mine always walked through life with a smile affixed to his face. He just enjoyed life to the fullest.

One day, I asked him if he wanted to give the organ a whirl, and of course, he would try anything once. So, we both perched on the bench, and I played the melody with my right hand, and he worked on forming chords with his left. Back when he was a little boy, he remembered that his Mother always carried him around, and later we assumed that Jerry had a touch of Polio. As a result, his left leg was shorter and thinner than the other; necessitating the placement of a lift in his left shoe to compensate for the difference and helped lessen the stress on his right leg and hip. Anyway, it didn't take Jerry long to go solo on the organ. There was a day when he had to cross his left leg over the right to reach the pedals, and he lost his balance and partially fell off the bench. Jerry didn't think much about it until his left side started to bother him a few days later.

I recall, very well, when we visited Fran and Eddie in Yonkers during Halloween weekend, Jerry barely ate anything! Now, he always loved Fran's cooking especially her savory pot roast, mashed potatoes, and spinach, but that night he hardly touched his dinner that was so unusual for him. Jerry always relished food, savoring every bite with a perpetual smile on his face. In my case, I really didn't care much about flavor, unless it was something sweet—then all bets were off. (Maybe it was because I was a long-time cigarette smoker, and they say that can affect one's taste buds.) Fran's Daughter-in-law Maureen, who lived next door, brought Jerry a heating pad so he could sit on the lounge chair with it tucked in next to his left side. Nothing seemed to lessen his pain. Unfortunately, his condition worsened in the next several days.

Jerry bought Theresa this organ that they enjoyed playing together.
This bench was where Jerry took a spill while playing.

Chapter 62

"We'll Fight This Together, Just the Way We Always Did!"

Linda went with Jerry to Kaiser Permanente Medical Center in White Plains and saw Dr. Lask. The two of them shared a mutual affection and great respect for each other, and this doctor always looked forward to seeing Jerry when he was there for his checkups. After examining him, Dr. Lask said, "Jerry, I'm sending you downstairs right away to get an Abdominal Ultrasound. I need to get a better picture of your kidney area!" Jerry asked, "Do you think that I might have kidney stones? I'm sure that I've never had any in my life." With a pat on Jerry's shoulder, he continued, "Let's wait for the test results, okay? After you finish, come back up here, and we'll discuss the situation." Later, when Dr. Lask completed analyzing the films, he sighed and said, "Jerry, it appears that there is a growth or something on your left kidney, but we can't be sure until we do an exploratory operation." "If you think that this is necessary, I have every confidence in you, so let's do it!" Jerry said with great conviction. He continued saying, "I don't know how much longer I can stand this pain!"

So, on November 12, 1986, he was admitted into White Plains Hospital, a half hour from home. I was certainly not a fan of hospitals, with good reason, but the one that Jerry was in then would be okay, especially since Dr. Lask would be overseeing his care. Even now, I can hardly tell this story, because though it is years later, I still feel like my innards are being turned inside out and my brain was then and now trying not to believe what I was hearing and experiencing.

After Jerry had the procedure, Dr. Lask informed us that "Jerry has what they called Germ-Cell Cancer, and it was affecting his ureter. It is understandable why he has so much pain." Dr. Lask said. I could see how difficult it was for this wonderful doctor to deliver such bad news to a patient that he truly admired. "Don't worry, Red, we'll fight this together, just like we always did!" Jerry said confidently. The girls were as dumbfounded as I was to hear this news. I wanted to be the strong shoulder for them to cry on, but I was in a state of shock myself, only hearing every other word.

How could this be happening now after all we have been through? Jerry and I had reached a point in our lives when we could truly appreciate the private time we had together. In some ways, it felt like dating all over again. Jerry and I were not a pair; we were one unit with him being the great optimist and me the timid follower! Unfortunately, this doctor would deliver yet another bombshell. How could the girls and I hear yet anymore horrible news? Dr. Lask summoned up the strength and continued, "Jerry will have to receive some chemotherapy, and we'll try to shrink the affected area. If nothing else, we need to at least lessen his pain." Shuttering, I looked up and asked in a tremulous voice, "With everything that I have heard about that stuff, it poisons the system with chemicals.

Will his body be able to withstand such a treatment?" again, with a great sigh, Dr. Lask continued, "Jerry is in a great deal of pain, so we need to do something, and the best course to follow is chemotherapy. If, on the other hand, he was not in much pain, I might have suggested that he should continue his daily life as before." I'm not sure how Jerry mustered up the courage to ask, "Can this Cancer be cured, doc?" "I am sorry to tell you all, there is no cure at this point for the type of Cancer Jerry has! We can only treat the symptoms as they appear."

After hearing this devastating news, we were all totally flabbergasted. You couldn't hear a pin drop in the hospital room. I'm not sure how I was still on two feet because I felt that my body was collapsing onto itself and being pushed ever so slowly downward through the floor I was standing on. Finally, Jerry asked, "Well, let's get started and see what happens, okay Red?" it was quite ironic that we always made decisions together, and now this was probably the second most important answer I could give him in our life together, after having said, "Yes, I will marry you." I felt like there was a giant golf ball in my throat, but I managed to croak out, "We are all in this together wherever it leads us!" Neither Linda nor Nance could speak without shock and fear taking over their bodies, but I could tell that they were nodding in agreement. The girls needed to go home now and somehow digest this awful paralyzing news, and as for me, I was just in a state of numbness. When we arrived at the elevator, Nance, holding back tears asked, "I don't get it, there is no one in our family that ever had cancer, why did it happen to Daddy, is he going to die?" She asked, finally breaking down in tears. I just couldn't reply because if I said "yes" to her question, it would mean that I really believed that it could be true, and I was not ready yet to mentally accept Jerry's death sentence.

As we drove home that day, there wasn't any way that we could envision the terrible road all of us would travel down over the next month or so. Linda broke the silence saying, "In the next week, I will give notice to my clients that I will no longer be able to serve them!" "I don't want you to do that Lin, you have worked very hard building your Accounting Practice," I told her with great conviction. "It's okay! It really is. This way I'll be able to go down to the station around 1:30 A.M. and prepare for the rush hour. You know that Eldred has been trying to fill in for Daddy, but he is getting on in years, so maybe he can work two days a week and give me some down time. Let's see what happens." Many times in the future I would ask her if she regretted making this decision that would forever change her world. She would always reply that more than once her Father had sacrificed so much for our family. Linda felt that it was her way of giving back.

Nance drove a few more miles before Linda sighed and continued, "I haven't brought this up for obvious reasons, but I have seen some eye specialists, and it seems that I have Glaucoma." "Oh, dear God! Why did you keep this news from us?" I asked not believing what I was hearing! I thought Nance would drive off the highway after hearing this declaration. Linda continued, "How could I bring it up knowing what we have been through as a family over this last month? They gave me drops and only time will tell if they will do the trick of lessening the pressure in my eye!" Linda said hoping for the best. Nance barely seeing the road on which she was driving, said, "How could all of this be happening to us? It's not fair!" I replied, "I know that God only gives us as much as we can handle, so I was taught, but this really shakes one's faith." Linda had compensated very well seeing out of only one eye for decades now, so was she about to go down the same road as I had and become totally blind like me? As the tears welled up in my eyes, I said a silent prayer to God to guide us down this horrible path and give us strength to keep moving forward.

Chapter 63

A Holiday Season We Will Never Forget!

A couple of days before Thanksgiving, Jerry received his first dose of chemo. He told us, "Have your dinner just as we always did, you know that I never liked turkey anyway!" we laughed tremulously at his suggestion. That was the worst Thanksgiving we ever had as a family, well not exactly a whole family for sure. I was the only one of our clan who liked turkey, and the leftovers in other years were sliced or made into salads smothered in mayonnaise, most of which I hungrily devoured with great delight. Well, that certainly wasn't going to happen this year; no way! Just the thought of taking a single bite of our holiday dinner made my stomach start churning, and I am sure that I was not alone in my misgivings as Linda and Nance seemed to be picking at food on their plates as well. Nance made her father some Cavatelli, which he always liked very much. But then again, what macaroni dish didn't Jerry love? After giving up trying to eat at all, we rushed over to the hospital, eager to see how the first chemo treatment went, not knowing what to expect.

Nance reverently served Jerry some Cavatelli, and the poor man could only stomach a few bites. I think that we were all stunned to see what just one dose of that poison did to him. In the few weeks that followed, his general health deteriorated. This was such a shock to us because he had always been a very sturdy, robust guy and had even lettered in high school as a strong wrestler. I knew that chemo could really play havoc with his ability to ward off any ensuing condition because the stuff could destroy Jerry's immune system.

Both family members and friends alike came to see Jerry as often as they could, and he received more chemo. But with each subsequent dose, he progressively became weaker and weaker by the day. Did we make the wrong decision to go down this road, I wondered? But I remembered the advice that Dr. Lask had offered that at best the tumor would have to be shrunk a little to relieve some of his debilitating pain. I guess that I was just numb, but some part of me knew that I was about to lose my life's partner, my soulmate, for sure! Jerry was only sixty-one, so young!

I am not sure how I was able to work down at the stand through all of these weeks, but in retrospect, it was better that way. It gave me something else to occupy my mind if only for a handful of hours a day. It was so difficult to hear all the questions about Jerry's health, and all I could do was tell them that he was in good hands and only time would tell. But the horror was really setting in, and I trembled thinking about what it would be like to come to work each morning and not hear WHUD playing on the radio and Jerry either singing or whistling as he worked.

Jerry had such a beautiful baritone voice, and my mind flew back to the years when he belonged to the Golden Chordsmen, a barbershop chorus in the area. He was so proud of being a part of that group and worked very hard to be able to do his best and not let the other guys down. At that time, Linda helped her Father with his choreography, and he had it all down pat. He was so enthusiastic and wanted to show the rest of the Chordsmen that he could hold his own. I am laughing and tearing up thinking about the regional competition that was held down in Philadelphia several years ago where his chorus was slated against a handful of other groups. I was told later that his chorus leader knew some of the judges and asked them to see if they could identify the guy that was blind in his Golden Chordsmen. At the end of the competition, Jerry's chorus leader showed a picture of his group and asked, "Can you identify the blind man?" the judges in unison pointed to the wrong guy, so perfect was Jerry's performance.

Early one morning, and for the life of me, I don't remember which day it was, it must have been around 2 A.M., Linda woke me up saying that Dr. Lask called. "What happened?" I asked Linda not really sure if I wanted to know more. "Daddy went into Septic Shock, and he is now in Intensive Care!" I could tell that she barely got the words out. Linda went on to say, "He suggested that the family come down to the hospital because it was impossible to predict what the next 48 hours would bring. I already called Nance and we'll pick you up." Gathering herself, Linda went on to say that she would contact Father Jack to give Daddy last rights. I nearly choked on the water I was drinking at hearing this and knew that this Septic Shock must be very serious, even more devastating at the moment than Jerry's Cancer.

All of us camped out in the Intensive Care Unit (ICU) waiting room for two days and nights. Nance's Husband didn't know what to do with himself and volunteered to canvas the area for food that could be brought back for us. I realized that this was his way of handling this horrible situation. Another thing, the chemo had burned the inside of Jerry's mouth, making it impossible for him to eat or drink. Nance fed him chips of ice, being careful not to touch another part of his mouth as she gently, ever so gently, placed them on his swollen tongue. At this point, he was getting fluid in his lungs, and several times when one or another of us was visiting Jerry, we helped to hold his arms down while they siphoned off the fluid via his mouth. It killed us to see him suffer so, but he was drowning in his own fluid and the procedure was necessary. Finally, they made a port somewhere in his neck and continued the process moving forward using this opening.

Jerry's older Sister Rose came to the hospital and planted herself at the foot of Jerry's bed, refusing to get up, so quiet and devastated was she. Finally, one of her nine children persuaded her to go home and rest for a while, promising that they would bring her back later in the day. The next order of business was alerting Jerry's younger Sister Kay, who lived in Austin, Texas. Over the past few weeks I called her and tried to impress on her the seriousness of Jerry's illness. Whether she couldn't handle the reality or something, I don't know. Linda grabbed the phone in the waiting room and called her Aunt. After the usual pleasantries, she said, "Here's the story, Aunt Kay, if you don't get here in the next day or so, you won't see your Brother alive!"

The entire room went silent in disbelief about what they were hearing, but sometimes it takes shocking people to get them to realize the seriousness of a situation. In an hour, Kay called back to tell us that her plane would arrive at Newark the next evening, and Nance and her Husband said that they would pick her up. Throughout our stay in the ICU lounge, there was another issue that totally unnerved us. Can you imagine how terrified we were when the loud speaker in the Unit would call out, "Code blue, ICU?" we knew full well that was the hue and cry for help needed for a patient who had arrested, and it would be their job to try and get that patient's heart to start beating again. It was just too much to bear any more. Every time we heard this announcement, our collective hearts skipped a beat thinking that maybe this time it was our beloved Jerry who had stopped breathing.

That Saturday night, December 13th, we went home to get some real rest. The stress was really getting to us, and a break was badly needed. It was agreed that we would return the next afternoon after attempting to get some sleep and nibbling on some food. Jerry was out of Septic Shock, and Dr. Lask felt that there would not be any change overnight, plus he saw how totally distraught we all were.

On Sunday morning, Linda was helping me sort out some papers in our home office when she suddenly stopped reading. "What is wrong, Linda, can't you see the words okay?" quickly she answered in a tremulous voice, "No, it's not that, I just felt a freezing cold knife run down the length of my body. What a horrible feeling, I think that Daddy just died!" I knew from past incidents that Linda had Nannie's touch and seemed to know stuff whether it was good or bad. Ten minutes later, Dr. Lask called to tell us that Jerry had passed away but was not in any pain.

Chapter 64

"On my own, pretending he's beside me,
all alone, I walk with him till morning"
"Les Misérables"

With my family and friends around me, I couldn't believe that we are once again going to celebrate a funeral mass and for a man who was only days away from his sixty-second birthday. Over the past few days, I had put one foot in front of the other, speaking to countless people, but what I said, I couldn't remember. It felt like I was floating on a dark cloud, semi-alert but not bodily aware of much. Our visually impaired friends came from New York City to Jerry's wake and were joined by our family, the Lions Club, the Knights of Columbus, friends and customers from the stand, along with railroad workers. They came to the funeral home by the hundreds.

The final tribute to Jerry's life came the next day when it was standing room only at Holy Name of Mary Church. I vaguely heard Lil McGrand play "Ave Maria" on the organ from the choir loft. She had a beautiful voice and was joined by her counterpart, Marie Michaelson, as she stood on the altar blending in her own harmony that made everyone present gasp at the sheer beauty of this duet. How would I go on after all of these nice people went home at the end of this day? I knew that I had Nance to lean on and Linda who promised to show me how to do all the bookwork for the stand, but the nights, how would I get through those long hours?

In the past when I came home from the stand, Jerry used to take a nap and when he got up, sometimes the both of us would read together, listen to some talk radio shows until the baseball season started, and then it was the Yankees, "let's go Yankees!" I recalled that during summer, I would whip up a lemonade surprise drink filled with whatever fruit I had on hand and lest not forget the vodka. I added ice and then blended it all up. Jerry, who couldn't swim a lick, spent more time in our semi-below-ground pool built back in 1976 than anyone else in the family. He would lean on a float in anticipation of the drink that I was going to bring him. Ah memories, there were so many. Would I be able to laugh at some of the funny stuff we did in time? Would I see him in my dreams and walk with him through the night till morning?

The mass was now ending and oh, my God! They were playing, "Let there be peace on earth, and let it begin today!" this was Jerry's favorite song from his barbershop chorus days. The congregation seemed to be waiting for this last piece of music to be played because, as we walked back up the aisle following Jerry's coffin, people were openly weeping, all those wonderful men, women, and children who were here for my Jerry! Dear God, I thought, will I be able to remain on my feet through the rest of this day?

There is a tradition that once the funeral is over and everyone is back in their cars, the hearse passes by the family home. This was particularly awful as Jerry never came home after he went into the hospital for what was supposed to be just an exploratory operation, gosh was it only a month ago. I can still remember to this day, as we passed the house, Nance half in tears saying, "Poor Daddy!" and the rest of us once again were in tears. Jerry's grave service was attended by people that emptied out of over 200 cars that had followed us, making a loop around Croton! When we arrived at the cemetery, the last car was leaving the church, what an outpouring for someone who was everybody's friend!

CROTON LIONS CLUB BULLETIN
*** JANUARY, 1987 ***
MARTY AMSEL, PRESIDENT   941-1052
GEORGE SMALLS, SECRETARY   271-8446

January meetings of the Croton Lions will be held on the 8th and the 22nd at Watch Hill Inn at 8:00 PM. THE MEETING ON THE 8TH WILL BE AN OFFICIAL VISIT BY DISTRICT GOVERNOR ED CARTER. A NEW MEMBER, GERALD LEVINE, SPONSORED BY MARTY AMSEL, WILL BE INSTALLED BY DISTRICT GOVERNOR ED. LET'S HAVE A LARGE TURNOUT FOR THIS IMPORTANT EVENING.

The Croton Lions suffered a very painful loss this month: Lion Jerry Marafito died on December 14th. Jerry was a long-time member and past Lion President, and as faithful and hard-working a Lion as could be imagined. In this short space it is impossible to even begin to say anything which would do justice to Jerry, but for all of us who know him, the pleasure of having had his friendship will keep our memory of him alive and cherished. He was a great Lion, a great friend, and an inspiration to all who knew him. We all extend our sympathy to Terry, Linda and Nancy, and Lion Jerry Barsamian, for their loss.

To honor Jerry's memory, the Croton Lions have started a Jerry Marafito Memorial Campership for the Vacation Camp for the Blind. Donations may be sent to the Croton Lions Club, PO Box 296, Croton, NY, 10520. Also, the Club's annual scholarship to a Croton HS graduate is being named the Jerry Marafito Memorial Scholarship.

Croton Lions Club Bulletin announces the death of Jerry Marafito.

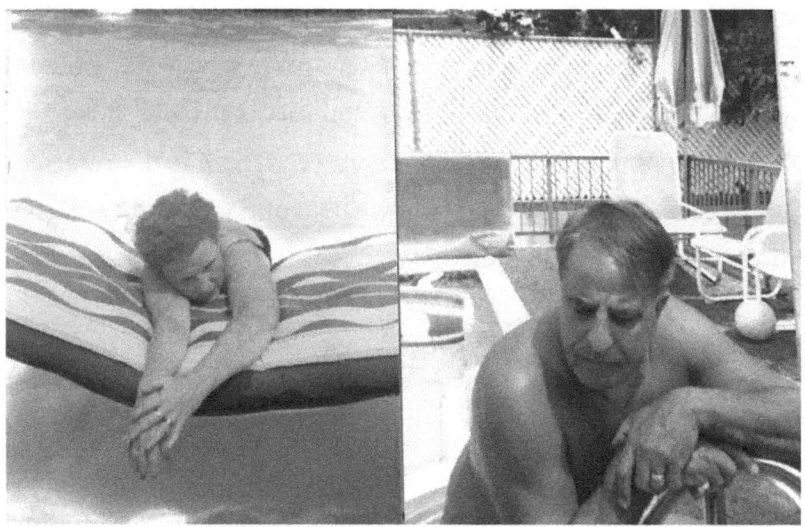

Theresa remembers all the good times spent with friends and family out by the pool. She weeps remembering all the drinks she mixed up for all of them. Jerry spent more time in this pool than anyone else. Jerry couldn't swim!

Jerry always loved Christmas and here is how he usually decorated his "b-a-r," but not this year for sure.

PART 17

Look! There's a Ray of Sunshine Peeking Through
the Storm Clouds! 1987—2002

Chapter 65

Taking Drastic Measures!

Someway, somehow, the girls and I made it through the holidays. Jerry always loved this season, and I guess you could have
called him Mr. Christmas! Linda had it really tough as she was
living near Holy Name of Mary Church and was subjected to one
Christmas Carol after another. She often said that this was a nice
touch for the village, but not this Christmas. It just led to more tears
and painful memories!

At some point in the past, and I can't recollect when it was,
Linda and Jerry sang together from the choir loft during the weekly
Saturday evening mass for quite some time. Linda told me that
her Father always put his Brailed music on the ledge; one night he
sneezed and went to wipe his nose, and his papers floated downward
toward the seats below. Can you imagine what people were thinking
when the sheets were collected, wondering what they were looking
at? How many of your friends or family members have ever seen a
sheet of thick paper with a bunch of raised dots on it? The priest
saw what was going on and commented, "See what happens when

you pray, things just float down to earth from heaven!" Of course everyone laughed, and Jerry was screwed because the hymn Linda and her Father were singing was new to him. Somehow they made it through without Jerry's Brailed notes with Linda thankfully taking the lead. They were happy when the priest said, "Go now in peace." Jerry said rather loudly, "Thanks be to God, Amen!"

Every year between Christmas and New Year, Jerry's Nieces and Nephews would always come down for an afternoon to eat, drink, and be merry; but not this year, the bar was not open for business. Linda and Nance really felt odd visiting their childhood home without seeing their Father. I know that they had tears in their eyes whenever they came over. It would be a matter of time before my girls would see their childhood home as their main anchor on this earth. But certainly not now when the loss of their Father was so fresh in their hearts.

Shortly after ringing in the New Year 1987, I set up a little shrine on the desk in our bedroom. Originally Jerry was a cigar smoker, but in recent years, he developed a liking to a pipe, which I personally felt was easier for me to bear, not so darn stinky. So, I set up his pipes and chanced to open the humidor where he stored his last supply of tobacco and was immediately overcome with tears. Some way, I would make it through and I prayed to Jerry to help me to move one foot in front of the other. Just one day at a time, I told myself, just one day at a time! Hell, it was more like, one hour at a time!

Starting on January 10, which was my 54th birthday, and for a couple of months thereafter, I went through the process of donating Jerry's clothes to St. Vincent DePaul Society, an organization that my Sister Helen was involved with down in Queens. She visited me as much as possible, and each time, I had a load of stuff to send back with her. I know what you are thinking, and you wouldn't be alone in saying, what was wrong with this woman that she could rid herself of her Husband's personal belongings so soon? What sort of woman could she be? After all, you would continue saying, Terry you were married for thirty-two years, and how could you so easily just throw your Husband's effects out the window? Well, here is my answer to these questions. I believe anyone who is grieving tends to do things like this when it feels right to do so. Forcing the issue just makes the whole sordid deal far worse for the loved ones left behind. Weekdays were easier to manage because I was down at the stand. All of my customers were equally distraught about Jerry and knew that I was really suffering. They made me feel more at ease than I thought I could be.

Once home after work was when the loneliness would set in. To keep myself busy, I read and listened to preseason Yankee games, but that too brought tears to my eyes because Jerry had been an avid fan. With great effort, I remembered an incident many years ago when Jerry was working out in the backyard while listening to Phil Rizzuto call a Yankee game. All of a sudden, I heard things being thrown around out back and went to investigate. There was Jerry tossing around chairs yelling, "You stupid fool, how could you just stand there with the bat on your shoulder without swinging?" "People will think that you are beating me up and will call the police!" I said laughing. "But that jerk," he continued mumbling as he set the chairs back in place.

Meanwhile, back to the present, the drops Linda was taking for her Glaucoma were not working at all, and she was advised to go up to Boston to the Massachusetts Eye institute for a thorough workup. It was the opinion of those in New York that Boston was the place where the most up-to-date eye research was taking place at the moment. Eddie Allen went up with Linda to Boston on her birthday, January 3, 1987 and wouldn't you know, the previous night, over a foot and a half of snow fell, making their trek quite an experience. Over the space of one day, she was subjected to every eye test known to mankind. Eddie and Linda returned back home via Amtrak, and now it would be a waiting game until she heard back from Dr. Latina, the head of the research group in Boston. It didn't take long to get word from him that the team felt that some laser surgery was in order to try and stop the progression of Linda's Glaucoma. I was very nervous about the use of a laser because, in those days, the procedure was very new and no one could be sure of whether there could be complications down the road from its use. Still something had to be done because the pressure in her eye was climbing every day, and the drops she was taking were useless. I certainly know what Glaucoma pain is like after suffering with it for so many years myself.

This time, my Sister Helen, Linda's Godmother, made the trip up to Boston with her. Again, it was a wait, watch, and see deal, and Dr. Latina told them it wouldn't take long for the doctors on his team to analyze the case and issue their final determination. Dr. Latina returned a judgment that Linda had to have a filter put into her eye that would help drain fluid more readily. He went on to say, those up there in the know reasoned that in six months, if she didn't have the surgery, she would lose all of her vision. Good God, how could all this be happening now? Linda's vision had been very useful for decades up until now. She only used glasses to read small print and traveled very well. The only thing Linda couldn't do was drive a car. It is one thing when you are faced with a decision where you are given clear choices, but when you are told that there is only a one-way path, the decision-making process is out of your hands and the rest is left up to God! This is pretty similar to what happened with Jerry's Cancer. Without the chemo, he would have had no relief from the severe pain that was increasingly growing worse by the day.

So, the die was cast, and the cards were dealt; the third and final trip was made to Boston for the procedure in early February 1987. All Nance and I could do was pray that those renowned doctors knew what they were doing! With a great sigh of relief, after the surgery, the injection of an anti-scarring medication, which was still at the time in research trials and only available at that facility, she returned back home with her vision only slightly blurred. The surgery was a success and after several weeks, her vision cleared, and she no longer had to use eye drops!

Following her recuperation, Linda was eager to get down to the station to work with me once again and received a warm welcome from commuters and railroad workers alike. Unfortunately, in the mid to late '90s, Glaucoma would yet again intrude on Linda's eye health, and within the next several years she would go under more surgery to deal with this disease. This time she would not be so lucky, and her vision would slowly deteriorate. Insult to injury came when her retina detached from that recent surgery and with it the independent life she had led for almost fifty years. At each point in these events, I just couldn't believe that Linda was navigating down the same path I had been walking on for the better part of my life. Again, my faith in God was wavering because I just couldn't understand why my family was being put through one heartache after another. I often wondered how much upset I could stomach without slowly losing my grip on life.

Now, for my Nance, as I explained earlier, both Jerry and I were aware that her marriage was not all hearts and flowers. We knew that if things didn't work out between her and her Husband, all we could do as parents was stand by and let them make the decision to stay together or part ways. Maybe it was her Father's death that finally made Nance decide to leave her Husband and try to make a new life with someone new! She was still young, and Linda and I knew our blue-eyed Nance with the laughing face would have no trouble finding happiness, that was for sure! It seemed that maybe it was high time that the black cloud that hung over this family these past few years would start to dissipate, giving us a glimpse of the blue sky that we knew was up there somewhere. Only time would tell!

Chapter 66

"I Only Have Eyes for You"
Art Garfunkel

While Linda was in Boston having her eye surgery in February 1987, there was a chance meeting on the train one day when Nance was commuting to New York City. She met a man named Stewart. Was she thinking from the start that maybe this guy was her key to happiness? Nance knew that her marriage was over before she met Stewart, and both Linda and I would certainly help her through the painful ordeal of dividing up the stuff they had amassed through their marriage, not to mention the mental stress of the whole ordeal. Nance told me one day after a heated argument with her Husband, "It seems so ridiculous to bicker over who gets the vacuum cleaner and what about the other stuff we collected!" I asked her, "Do you want to stay in your house?" Nance replied emphatically, "Yes I do, I remember how many countless hours Daddy put in making my house a real home!" so, I am sure that there was a great debate among their lawyers, trying to come up with a buyout agreement that would leave Nance owning her house on Radnor Avenue in Croton.

It seemed to me that Nance's relationship was becoming more serious as the months passed during 1987. She made many trips up to Kerhonkson in the Catskills where Stewart's family lived. By that summer, Nance and Stewart came to me and expressed their intention to marry some time later in 1988, and honestly, I was very happy for them both. With tears threatening to trickle down my cheeks, I knew that Jerry would have been so, so happy for his youngest Daughter.

Since they were commuting to their respective jobs in New York City and would be traveling down there by train together, Nance and Stewart asked me if they could move in with me during the interim until her divorce was final and the house was totally hers after that. It took me awhile to get used to the idea, but I came from a different generation where such a plan would be looked down upon by the families involved, to say nothing of the neighbors. But alas, the times were changing! Secretly, I was aware that Nance and Stewart were attuned to the fact that I was seemingly very lonely, but, oh yes, this living arrangement did make sense for their commuting ease as well.

One day at dinner, I asked them, "Do you plan to have children?" together they both replied, "Yes!" I continued, "What religion will you introduce to your kids, since Nance is Catholic and Stewart, you are Jewish? Will the children learn about both religions?" Nance cleared her throat, and I wondered what she was thinking. I didn't have to wait long to hear her say, "I am converting to the Jewish religion!" after nearly choking on some macaroni, I asked, "Are you sure that is what you really want to do, Nance?" right away she answered, "Both Stewart and I talked it over and made the decision together." At the time, I was not sure about this proclamation, but I have to say in years to come that Nance made a better Jew than she ever did as a Catholic. She really immersed herself in the traditions of the Jewish religion and followed the Judaic laws as if she grew up with this teaching.

So, it was that in November 1988, to be exact, it was Thanksgiving weekend, Nance and Stewart said their vows to each other as we stood having our fannies nearly catching on fire as the ceremony took place in front of a roaring fire! I said a prayer that I was sure my Jerry heard from on high. We always wanted Nance to be happy and I felt sure that finally she had found her soulmate. I didn't have to wait long for my first grandchild to be born, and they blessed me with a bouncing baby boy they named Joshua Lee Cohen, who arrived in May 1989. Guess he got cooked a little early, because he wasn't due until June! Jerry would have been in his glory to see this little baby. He loved children so much, and in private I shed more tears just thinking about what he had missed since he left this world before his time. What a Grandfather he would have made; well I guess that I will just have to be both Grandma and Grandpa, all wrapped up in one bundle.

Theresa's younger daughter Nance marries Stewart Cohen on November 27, 1988.

Chapter 67

"I'd Really Love to See You Tonight"
England Dan/Tom Ford Coley

Fran Allen had been my best friend for decades, and now she must have noticed that beneath the surface, I was truly lonely and needed an outlet to just have a little fun. Yes, we talked on the phone everyday about the books we were reading, what happened recently when little Joshua came to visit me, a new recipe that Fran had tried making spinach balls and so forth. But still when I hung up from speaking with her, there was the empty void that I couldn't fill. One day, Fran and Eddie came to the rescue and asked if I would like to try a camp down in Barnegat, New Jersey, sponsored by the Lighthouse. "Who will I bunk with?" I asked Fran one day as we were discussing this camp. Right away she answered, "There is a woman around your age who recently lost her Husband and was hesitant also to go to camp, so I thought you would have something in common with her!" I hesitated for a moment and thought, well maybe it would be good to see our old friends from years ago!

So it was that I packed up to go to camp in July of 1989, and who would have ever thought that I was about to meet my second

Husband! This fellow named Joe Fiorentino, who was of Italian heritage, one night asked me to dance to the tune, "I'd Really Love to See You Tonight." Would this be our wedding song, perhaps? In months to come, only time would tell. From there on, our friendship started to grow stronger. He lived in Mt. Vernon, which is on the South east side of our county. There was a van service for disabled people that Jerry and Linda used to get around the county, so this was how I could go down to his apartment and he could come up to Croton via the same transport.

Linda and Nance were aware of my friendship with Joe and, of course, asked me a ton of questions. I could understand their concern since I was very vulnerable at that time, and they didn't want me to get hurt. When in early 1990 we announced that we were getting married on Valentine's Day that was when Linda and Nance attacked with both barrels. Nance said, "Not Valentine's Day! Okay, I get it that you care for Joe, but Linda and I remember too many times when Daddy did something special for you on that day!" no sooner did Nance finish when Linda tossed in her two cents, "Remember that your anniversary with Daddy was on April 18, so that date is out of the question as well!" a new date was agreed on, and in the meantime, Nance had to have a gynecological procedure but was told that she would be strong enough to attend my wedding. Unfortunately, that did not come to pass. Nance always had issues with anesthesia and was too weak to share my wedding day with us. The big day was bitterly cold, and the church had no heat. Helen walked me down the aisle as Linda's vision was not cooperating that day. So, when we said, "I do!" It was with trembling lips and chattering teeth.

Theresa weds Joe Fiorentino

*This is a rare photo of Theresa, her beloved Sister Helen
and Brother-in-law Dan*

Theresa is celebrating Christmas at home sitting in her living room with Son-in-law Stewart

Chapter 68

As Our Concession Turns

Before my Jerry passed away in December 1986, it was known by us, that once again the MTA in its divine wisdom, decided to move the Croton-Harmon Station yet again. This time it would be on bridge level so that people would walk down the staircases to board their trains. I tried to get Jerry interested in our new project but he knew deep down that he would never live long enough to see our new concession stand. Eddie Allen, Linda, and I worked on a design that would fit the footprint required by the MTA. Nance was still working down in the city and taking care of her toddler, Joshua, and it would be a few years more before she would come to work with us at the stand on a permanent basis. Of course, our new folly would cost over forty thousand dollars to build, so once again I had to take out a business loan. Even though my Jerry was gone from me forever, I still considered this business to be ours, not mine alone. It was ironic that all the loans, including our house mortgage, had been paid in full years ago, thanks to that coffee urn spouting out liquid gold down at the station. Jerry and I had sworn that once the loans were paid off, we would stay debt-free for the rest of our lives. Well, so much for that wish!

As I opened the doors for business in April 1990, my tears were not far behind as I thought that Jerry had missed seeing the largest, most efficient working area that we had since the beginning back in 1966. There was room for two beverage vending machines and a snack machine that we filled with all sorts of sweets and chips. Linda developed a way to whip up a bowl of scrambled eggs that would be placed on rolls and kept warm in a heated cart. This was a nice addition to our breakfast fare on a cold winter day. She also made chicken soup and chili at home to serve to our afternoon customers who were also looking for something hot to eat. How far we had come from the limited space we had for our first location back in 1966. At that point, who would have ever dreamed of seeing all of the cabinets that we now had above our heads, making it easy to grab coffee cups, their lids, and a whole storage room that allowed us to take advantage of sales on soda and other assorted goodies for our snack machine.

There was no way that I could know then that on November 30, 2017, the Marafito dynasty would pour their last cup of coffee after serving their commuters for over fifty-one years. Unfortunately, the location would go out to bid, and as my Jerry had said back in 1982, "We can't compete with a conglomerate." Money meant more to the MTA than the value my family brought to thousands of their train customers.

Chapter 69

The Stork Makes another Delivery at Nance's House

In July 1993, I was blessed again by another Grandchild, who decided to make his appearance two months early. Sean Joseph Cohen would remain in the Neonatal Intensive Care Unit (NICU) for several weeks because his lungs were not fully cooked when he was born. As a result, Sean would have a lifelong battle with asthma and allergies. Whenever Nance's family went on vacation, it was a toss-up whether Sean would land up in one emergency room or another because he had so much trouble acclimating to different climatic conditions. Before Sean's birth, it seemed for months and months that a second child was not in the cards for Nance and Stewart because they went through every possible fertilization program known at the time, but no dice! It was when they finally gave up and decided that Joshua would not have a sister or a brother that Nance got pregnant with Sean! He had to take various steroids, which made the poor little baby difficult to handle, howling so loud and carrying on, but my Joe seemed to have the right touch with him. It was at this point that Nance decided to be a full-time mom and work with us down at the station.

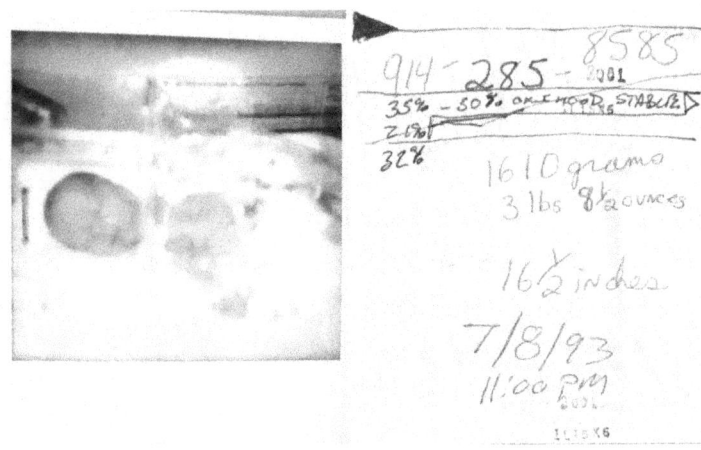

Theresa's second grandson Sean is born prematurely on July 8 1993, and will spend two months in the hospital neonatal intensive care unit (NICU).

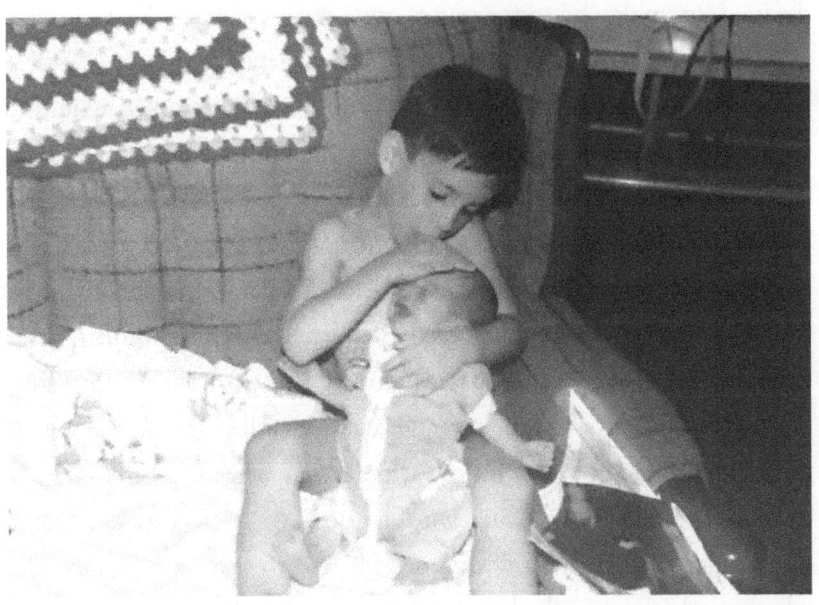

Joshua is holding his baby brother Sean, who was now two months old.

Chapter 70

My Organ Goes on the Road

During the past decades when Jerry was in the Lions Club, I became involved with many of their fund-raising projects. With my connections running our business, I ordered oodles of food and equipment for yearly events including the Clearwater Sloop Revival, the crab fest, and pancake breakfasts. Several years ago, the Croton Caring Committee was started by Anne Kennedy to assist disabled and older folks to get to doctors and other appointments. At one point, the Committee held a monthly lunch for seniors and the disabled. When it was the Lions Club's turn to host the lunch, Joe DiMarzo who owned the local appliance store, took my organ, plopped it on a dolly, and off it went to the Masonic Hall and I would play for the crowd. Jerry would tell me later that there were several elderly people dancing while holding onto the poles in the hall. I was so thrilled to have brought happiness to those people who were living through their last years on God's earth. One year when it was time for the annual Lions Club Christmas party, there was music on wheels, and Joe DiMarzo was once again the method of transport for my organ. Let me say at this point that for a few years after Jerry's death, I just couldn't summon up the interest to play my organ. Every time I sat on the bench, memories of Jerry and I playing together when he first learned to form chords, resulted in the tears flowing once again.

*Theresa clad in her apron is seen here at home
with her husband Joe at her side.*

Chapter 71

Suburban Girl Meets City Slicker!

Linda went through the usual attempts to find her soulmate, attending singles dances, blind dates with men that her friends thought would be a good match for her, and let's not forget about the bars that were nothing more than pickup joints. Linda had a few men in her life down through the years, but all of them just had too much baggage to deal with. One day in the late 1990s, Linda found out about a new dating service started by radio station WHUD that a lot of us listened to in the Lower Hudson Valley. She was naturally skeptical about what results it would bear but decided to sign up and give it a whirl. After having a few dates, she just thought the whole process was mentally tiring to say the least. However, she decided that she would try one more contact and had to choose from Anthony from "da Bronx" or Larry from Queens. The latter was chosen, and in late 2000 they were married. I couldn't have been happier for them. Linda liked to travel, and in the next seven years, they could be found at National Parks in both the United States and Canada as well as riding gondolas up the mountains of Switzerland,

Germany, and France. Both of them loved country music and attended concerts and festivals from sea to shining sea. Their beautiful life came to a grinding halt when in mid-2008, Larry was diagnosed with Multiple Myeloma Cancer and passed away nine months later in late April 2009.

Theresa's oldest daughter Linda marries Lawrence (Larry Kramer)
November 5th, 2000.

Linda and husband Larry are visiting Lake Tahoe. This is one stop on their many adventures that would find them all over the United States, Canada and Europe.

Chapter 72

Who or What is a Kabuki?

Around 2000 when Sean was about seven years old, he had been pestering my Joe to get him a dog. He really wanted one so badly. Nance had always been a cat fan but took time to search out a dog breed with human-like hair, since any other type would have made Sean's asthma and allergies worse. So, enter a Shih Tzu named Kabuki, and even though this little pup was Sean's buddy, it would come to be very important to me in a few years to come, you will see why moving forward.

Chapter 73

Good Grief, Could It Really Be Happening, Yet Again?

Joe was very good to me through our marriage that lasted twelve years, and we went to the same summer camps with Fran and Eddie as we did before when Jerry was alive. It is not right in my opinion to draw a comparison of my love for Jerry and that of Joe. In my case, Jerry would always be my soulmate, we just had so much more history together, the good times and the awful ones when he was my strength going through the eye operations. Jerry was so care-free, whereas Joe had quirks of his own, having lived alone for quite a while since his divorce.

For instance, he really didn't enjoy company, and this was a radical change from my social life with Jerry. How many times did I hear him call Fran and Eddie and ask them to come up for the weekend? No such invitation was presented to them from Joe. I truly missed all the pool parties Jerry and I shared, not to mention the card games and countless barbecues. Joe was a good companion, and I supposed that I should be thankful that I would not spend days and nights alone. We had twelve years together, well that is because Cancer would enter my life yet, again!

Joe had some sort of blood cancer that required transfusions and also did not have a cure. This odyssey started in the late 1990s, and I just couldn't go through losing another Husband. The only way that I knew to get through those three years of hell was to put myself in a sort of bubble, where I could retreat from reality and be safe from anymore heartache. Instinctively, I knew that it had to be this way because I was really scared of losing my mind totally and the will to live, I had just been through too much upset in my life! Thank God my precious Nance came to the rescue, somehow seeing that I was surviving and not really capable of much more. She went back and forth to the hospital countless times when Joe went in for blood transfusions. It's not that I didn't see Joe in the hospital because I did. But the mere thought of being in that house of sickness just made me tremble and brought back memories of my vigil when Jerry was dying. Joe went into a coma, and one day I took my recorder to the hospital and played some Italian music for him, but there was no reaction at all. His heart and soul had left this earth never to enjoy life again!

So, once again, in early 2002, we sat in Holy Name of Mary Church, but this time the man I chose to do the singing was none other than John, the son of my lifelong friend Josephine who had such a beautiful voice. Through the years I heard him sing and play the guitar at Vacation Camp for the Blind. Some of the CDs that he recorded were part of my vast music collection. Somehow, I drifted through Joe's funeral, still feeling detached in some way. There was no grave service as he had wanted to be cremated.

Well, here I go again, dealing with the miserable task of gathering Joe's belongings and contacting his relatives and offered them whatever items they wanted to help them remember him. This is when Kabuki became my pal. He would visit from time to time and sensing there was something wrong with me, was careful not to step in my way when walking from room to room. When I took my afternoon nap, there he would be, under the covers cuddled up right next to me. When I had my gallbladder removed, and again I am not sure when it was exactly, but Nance would come to my house to check on things while I was in the hospital. She didn't see Kabuki for a while, went to investigate, and there he was sitting in front of my closed bedroom door. Surrounding him were his toys that he had gathered from various places in the house. It was just so sweet!

Several years earlier, Kabuki had an accident and lost one eye, so I thought that he was now keeping the right company and wondered if Nance should file for doggie disability. Kabuki lived until he was 18 years old and would lose the sight in his second eye as well as having hearing problems. Toward the end of his life, he used his nose to help him navigate around Nance's house, what a smart little dog!

*Even though little Kabuki was purchased for Sean, he became very
important to Theresa and would spend many hours cuddled
up against her for an afternoon nap.*

PART 18

Ashes to Ashes, Dust to Dust
March 18, 2008

Chapter 74

I Know My Way!

The morning of March 18, 2008, is starting much the same way as other workdays. Well, except last night I might have stayed up too late listening to the Yankee preseason game. After all, they were playing the Red Sox! Getting dressed, I remembered to put on the flag pin that Linda gave me several years ago, and it was the source of many nice compliments from our women commuters. Yesterday, being of an Irish descent, I was wearing my shamrock earrings and pendant. Oh, how I always loved my costume jewelry! Another St. Paddy's Day had gone by!

As usual, my breakfast consists of a cup of tea with milk and Sweet' N Low and oh, best of all a handful of cookies! Yeah, Linda and Nance keep me well stocked with all varieties, but my favorites are sugar wafers and chocolate chip with walnuts, yum, yum! Ok, I told you that I was a junk food junkie, but relax, they are sugar-free, so they can't be all that bad, right?

Opening the porch door, I think that I hear my taxi waiting outside. Now let's see, I have my cane, which I call my "stick," and let's not forget a handful of Russell Stover individually wrapped dark chocolate pieces to fortify me through the rush hour. The last thing I grab are my cigarettes and lighter, now it's off I go to work!

The rush hour is similar to that of any other day, the customers really get a thrill when I remember what they usually buy. Who knows what problems they might have left back at home, so a little TLC on my part hopefully can make the difference in their day? Checking my Braille watch I think, Oh, goody! Time for my cigarette. Thanks to the ruling that had been in place for a number of years now, there is no more smoking allowed inside the station proper. So, I have to take the elevator right outside the stand door, which takes me down to the platform where I can lean against the wall next to it and light up.

As I walk out of the stand, open my cane, and prepare to summon the elevator, Nance tells me, "Ma, the elevator you are used to doesn't work you'll have to use the one on the other side. Do you need help?" making a right turn, I say very confidently, "I know my way!" As I walk toward the working elevator. I press the button and the doors open, and I am pretty sure that the button panel is the same as in the elevator that I know, so I push the "1" button and the doors closed. The elevator arrives on the platform level, I am stepping out and moving to the right so that I can lean against the wall. Lighting up, I am enjoying my first puff. Lately, I am satisfied with about a half a cigarette and today is no exception. So I put the butt on the ground and make sure to extinguish it properly. Okay, I am ready now, let's push the button to call the elevator. Ah, here it is and stepping in, I push 2 and away we go on my way upstairs! I am thinking to myself, I forgot to defrost the chicken breasts to make salad for the stand. Oh well, it will have to wait until tomorrow.

Also, I forgot yesterday to check on my pills to see if I need refills, I'll call Save Mor later.

. . . .

When security tape was analyzed later, it showed that after Terry entered the elevator, the doors had closed, but a commuter must have pushed the button on the platform level so that the elevator doors would open again to allow him to enter.

. . . .

We must be back upstairs, I can hardly feel the elevator rising upward. I need to pay more attention to stuff going on around me and not get so distracted. I am 75 years old now, and this behavior is probably normal. Oh, well let's get a move on so that I can return to work and prepare the deposit for the bank.

Confidently, I move to get off and there's a person that I have to walk around. Not sure where he came from, don't remember anyone getting on the elevator when I walked in downstairs. This is really weird! No problem. I am not bothering to use my stick. I know where I am. So with purpose I turn left, and move quickly toward the door to the stand. What in God's name...I am walking but where is the floor? All of a sudden, my mind is asking, "How is this possible? Where is the station floor, it's not here! Sweet Jesus, how can I be flying through the air? What in the name of God is going on?" I feel my body spin, twist, and crash down on a hard, metallic surface. I damn near lose consciousness. The realization of where I am hits me when I feel the track bed under me. Dear God in heaven, how did I get down on the tracks? I remember pushing the correct "2" button when entering the elevator, so, Jesus, what did I do wrong? The fact that I am lying on the tracks isn't possible.

The elevator has taken me back upstairs, hasn't it? Oh my God, what will I do? People are shouting and is that Nance screaming? To my horror, the ground that I am lying on begins to vibrate. Dear merciful God that must be a train coming down this track! I have to move, or I'll be killed. But when I try to lift my body, I realize that when I fell, I must have broken something in my back. Is it too late for anyone to save me? Why can't people hear me, am I really screaming or is it just in my mind?

They say that when you are about to die your entire life flashes in front of you, but there is no time for that to happen. The train must be near now; the vibration under me is becoming more forceful and I can hear what sounds like screeching brakes. Did someone alert the engineer that I have fallen down on the tracks? Will it stop in time?

The next morning after Theresa's tragic death, many of her commuters brought bouquets of flowers to the stand expressing their grief at her loss.

Theresa's favorite baseball team was the New York Yankees, and this uniform shirt was signed by so many of her customers to express their condolences.

One commuter writes a note accompanying three dollars for his normal everyday purchase at the stand. Never again would he place the money into Theresa's outstretched hand.

*Some commuters decided to write personal notes to show
their grief at Theresa's passing.*

Chapter 75

On the Wings of an Angel

Just as the train is about to crush my mortal body, I feel a presence lifting my heart, soul, and brain, all the stuff that makes me who I am. My carrier is soft and fluffy. I am thinking… Can it be the angel I have always been taught is saving the best part of me? Will my angel be my transport to heaven, and will St. Peter be greeting me at the pearly gates the way that I learned in catechism classes? I can get glimpses of what is going on below, but I don't know what lies ahead for me in heaven. How is it possible that my eyes can see everything? I am totally blind! It feels like my tears should be flowing but my broken body is down on earth; oh, this is quite confusing! I was totally blind ten minutes ago, but now I can see everything in great detail! Is this a miracle? Is this God's gift to me as I leave this world?

. . . .

While all this was taking place at the train station, Linda had been bombarded with nightmares all night and was quite jittery. She knew that something bad had occurred or was about to happen. At times like this, having "Nannie's touch" just made things worse for Linda.

. . . .

What else am I able to see…My sweet Nance is totally distraught and is calling her Sister on the phone, but she can't seem to tell Linda what had happened. All Linda hears from Nance was "I can't" in a long drawn-out wail. A railroad cop is instructing Linda to come down to the station because her Sister needs her!

Nance is now sitting in the ambulance, sipping water and trying to grasp what has just happened mere minutes before. As Linda arrives with Larry at the station, she still doesn't know what is going on. They are going upstairs, and Mary Ellen who had been working with me and Nance this morning, fills them in. Poor Linda. I have never heard such a keening wail like that in my life. What horror have I inflicted on both my girls? Will they be scarred forever losing their Mother in this tragic way? Isn't it bad enough that their Father died from cancer so young?

It seems that only a few minutes have gone by when next I see Linda and Larry at Carter's Funeral Home picking out my casket. As if Linda is in a trance, she moves toward a pretty blue and very shiny selection. I am thinking…"Thata girl," I was always Mrs. Clean with a can of Pledge in one hand and paper towels in the other! And you remember that I always wanted to "color the sky blue."

. . . .

You see, I died on the Tuesday before Easter and by church law, I couldn't be buried until the following week. It must have seemed like an eternity for all those I loved to wait so long to give me a proper sendoff.

. . . .

Now I am looking down on the loads of people at my wake. It is amazing to see our customers, railroad workers, and even the two officers who were on the platforms that horrible day, coming to pay their respects. I am laughing because the funeral director is having problems keeping the cascades of flowers perched on my shiny coffin from falling off.

Goodness! Now I am at my funeral mass and there is John Luland preparing to sing my favorite version of "Ave Maria!"

As he begins, you can't hear a pin drop, so enchanted are the congregation with this man's beautiful, cultured voice. It seems like only yesterday that he sang at Joe's funeral. There's Father Mike on the altar, who I have always admired and with whom I have had many conversations over the past few years.

Earlier that week, when Linda and Father Mike were picking out the readings for my funeral mass, he told her that he had been nearby at a doctor's office when he heard that someone had been killed at the train station and went down to pray for the deceased and was shocked to see that it was me when he unzipped the bag and my head was revealed to him. Father Mike told her that when he pulled down the zipper on the bag holding my crumpled body that he gasped and couldn't believe that it was me lying there. And went on to say that somehow my head was fully intact with some scratches on my cheeks, but the rest of me that was another story.

. . . .

Good! He is reading the Twenty-third psalm, the King James Version. I always kidded the girls, saying that if the newer, far less poetic and lyrical version is read at my grave I will haunt you both forever!

As my view of life on earth starts to fade, I know that both my girls will be there for each other now that they have lost their parents. I wonder how my Sister Helen will be able to live with the loss of her baby Sister. She will be 81 years in August. Why has this horrible accident happened? This is the second time that addiction to cigarettes has touched my family. It is worse, this time; those damn cigarettes have shortened my life and have forever changed the world my two beloved and precious girls will live through for years to come. Will they forgive me for leaving them in such a tragic way? Time will tell, and they have each other to lean on.

My view of the world that I loved and cherished has completely faded now, but, in my ears, I hear a chorus of voices, family and friends that had passed on before me. They are as white and ethereal as I thought that they would be. St. Peter is leading me through the heavenly gates and I wonder if I will be reunited with my Jerry, my true soulmate, and be allowed to "walk with him" not only until morning, but for eternity!

Theresa's casket is being carried out of Holy Name of Mary Church.
She will never again attend mass and share conversations with her
favorite priest Father Mike.

Theresa's big Sister Helen and her Son-in-law Stewart are accompanying Nance holding the program from her mother's mass.

CHAPTER 15

Afterword

By Co-Author Linda Odubayo Thompson

This Memoir was first conceived after Jerry's death. Theresa (Terry) felt an overwhelming drive to put down in words all the memories, both happy and sad, from her childhood, as a young woman getting married, sharing a business with her beloved Jerry that would survive for five decades, blessed with children, and her oldest being visually impaired as well. Doing this exercise helped Terry to put one foot in front of the other as she tried to face each day after the loss of her husband, the center of her world.

Out of these ramblings, came her mission, wanting sighted people to see firsthand through the use of dialogue how visually impaired members of a typical household conduct their daily business. Looking at your family and that of others around you, would you conclude that Terry's world was not so very different?

She wanted you, her reader…, "always remember to color the sky blue" so that when storm clouds hang over your life and threaten to totally overwhelm you, what you should do is just remember the beauty of a bright blue sky.

Terry's mental strength came from those closest to her, and she would be quick to point out, "Jerry was the optimist, and I was the timid follower."

It felt really surreal sitting at the closing for the sale of our family home. The Village of Croton-On-Hudson bought it for their Ambulance Corps. Nance and I nearly had a heart attack when they initially wanted to tear down the house and make a parking lot out of the property. Thank God that plan never saw the light of day!

Believe It or Not, You Be the Judge!

Several incidents took place before and after the burial of Theresa Marafito…

When Nance left the train station after witnessing the horrible death of her Mother, she gravitated toward her family home and took a walk out into the backyard, envisioning the beautiful flowers and the tomato plants that her Mother would have soon planted, but not this year for sure! With tears sliding down her face, she looked toward the screened-in patio and almost fainted on the spot. A few years earlier, a heavy pretty blue statue of a girl was placed next to the entrance, and Nance couldn't believe her eyes now because the little girl was lying down on her side. Considering its weight, Nance knew, it would be nearly impossible for it to fall on its own without some divine intervention. She transported the little blue girl statue up to her house in Newburgh, New York, and it found its home watching over her garden. Now here is the really strange thing, in the past ten years, with all the rain and high winds, the statue never fell over again! Nance also transplanted flowers and other plants from her Mom's garden, and they have continued to yield quite a crop over the past ten years.

As the Ambulance Corps moved into our former family home, strange things began to occur. Since this house was conceived out of love and perhaps due to the tragic death of its final family member living there, the happenings I am going to share with you are not at all violent. Keep in mind that those Corps members occupying the house were young and didn't know our family at all. Here is what happened. These incidents along with others were covered in an article published in the local newspaper:

- Young girls were heard laughing and playing down in the basement

- The sound of an organ was heard playing and people were singing

- Two guys in the Corps were sitting in the kitchen, and one of them spilled something on the table. All of a sudden, the roll of paper towels sailed over to the table from the countertop.

- An electrician was doing some wiring up in the attic on a hot afternoon, and the exhaust fan was very near where he was working. He became dizzy, started falling straight down into the spinning sharp metal blades, woke up near the fan, but somehow was lifted out of harm's way.

- One evening at a Corps meeting, all cell phones were to be silenced for the duration of the proceedings. When one guy returned home, his wife asked, "Why did you call me and hang up on me?" becoming flustered, he declared that his phone was on silent, and showed her. It indicated that no phone calls or texts had been sent that night. At this point, she pointed to the record of his incoming call on her cell. There was no logical answer for this to have happened.

- The master bedroom was fitted with two beds that could be occupied by members of the Corps who would sleep there overnight to answer ambulance calls more rapidly. The guy sleeping nearest to the clothes closet, woke up to see a woman perched on the end of his bed, just sitting there. She scared the wits out of him! When informed, we noted that it was the side of the double bed where our Mother slept.

- In the room where Nance and I slept as children, was also where our Mom had her computer set up. One day when one of the Corps members was working on their computer, she felt two hands lightly placed on her shoulders. She was so scared and ran out of the house.

Now finally, but certainly not the least, is what happened when my Sister was gathering photos for our Mother's memoir. Thinking that she had found all the good stuff, Nance unearthed the 25th Anniversary photo album from a big party we gave our parents to celebrate this timely event. An index card was found in the album which was clearly not part of the original content.

Nance and I would like to share with you the message Brailled on this card so many years ago. The inspiration she put forth is appropriate for those who read it. Just send an email to the following address: linda@ghostbookwritergoldilocks.com

The only time that this heavy little blue girl statue fell over was on the morning of Theresa's death 03/18/2008.

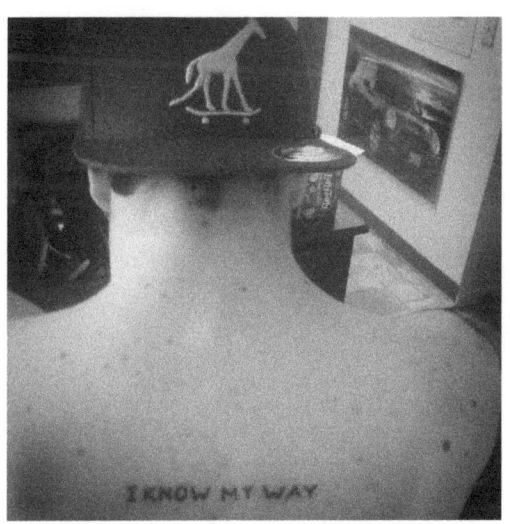

Theresa's youngest Grandson, Sean, was so devastated by the death of his Grandmother, whom he referred to as (Nannie) and he wanted to find someway to keep her close to him. He decided to have a tattoo "I Know My Way" placed on his upper back. This way, she will always be with him as he travels through life.

Recognitions

Westchester County Board of Legislators March 25, 2008 meeting of the Legislators dedication In Honor and Memory of Theresa Marafito Fiorentino

Woman of Valor Plaque, presented by family and friends to Theresa in honor of her 75th Birthday

Newsstand Dealer of the Year recognized by USA Today

Croton Historical Society Interview with Historian, 52-year Resident of Croton on Hudson, New York

Park Bench dedicated in Memory of Theresa, by VISIONS located at Vacation Camp for the Blind, Spring Valley, New York

Park Bench dedicated in Memory of Theresa by Croton Lions Club Located at Holy Name of Mary Church Croton on Hudson, New York

Temple Sinai Sisterhood Award to Theresa, Volunteer of the Year, For her Community Service

Croton Jewish Center Humanitarian Award, In recognition of Theresa's services and contributions to the Jewish community

Acknowledgements

Thank you to my sister Nance Cohen, who took on this project with me. We shared laughter, shed tears, recalled memories, and the pure joy of knowing that we saw it through together; fulfilling our mother's lifelong dream.

Edelweiss, Edelweiss
Every morning you greet me
Small and white, clean and bright
You look happy to meet me
Blossom of snow may you bloom and grow
Bloom and grow forever
Edelweiss, Edelweiss
Bless my homeland forever…

(Lyrics from Edelweiss, song written for the 1959 production of "The Sound of Music" the last movie our mother saw as a sighted person)

About the Co-Author

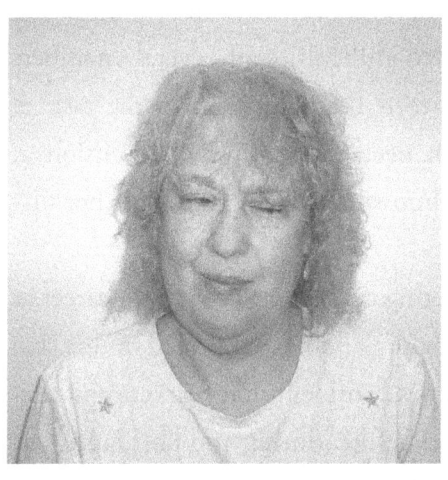

Linda Odubayo Thompson, the co-author of her mother's memoir I Know My Way, subtitled Always Remember to Color the Sky Blue! Has been a professional writer for over ten years. She developed her own version of a "business conversational tone" to help companies better engage with their potential/ tried- and- true customers. Linda is now turning her attention to individuals who have a story to share with the world in the form of a memoir or life story. She has adapted her writing style to marry narration with a considerable amount of dialogue; all to help her readers feel a part of the conversation rather than just looking in the window watching the action unfolding before them.

I Know My Way is a memoir about Linda's Mother who was born visually handicapped, and would spend a lifetime struggling with operation after operation in a futile attempt not to become totally blind.

In late 1986, Theresa's perfect world came to a crashing halt when her soul mate Jerry lost his life to cancer. Theresa was so devastated that she poured her heart out on an old manual typewriter trying to capture all of her precious memories. It was after her very tragic death in 2008 that the ream of notes were found and became the starting point of her memoir.

Linda knew it would be a great pleasure to capture the essence of her mother's life in this memoir, and help the sighted world to have a better understanding about the everyday existence of a normal suburban family with the added difficulties of several members being visually impaired. Linda feels that she is up to the task of explaining the level of emotion needed to convey the tension at every turn because she is now almost blind herself and lost her first husband to cancer as well.

Linda has also been a marketing consultant in her first career as an Accountant and Financial Advisor, and has continued in this vein with her copywriting clients. She is confident that marketing strategies that are being put into place before, during and post launch of this memoir I Know My Way, will help make Linda a sought- after indie author/book marketer.

Contact Linda Odubayo Thompson

E-Mail: linda@ghostbookwritergoldilocks.com
Telephone: 914-944-1474
Website: http://www.ghostbookwritergoldilocks.com

Co-Author Associations and Memberships

Alliance of Independent Authors

American Writers and Artists

Association of Ghost Writers

Author Marketing Club

National Association of Memoir Writers

Online Book Club

Professional Writers' Alliance

Story Circle Network

Women Only Connected

This photo was taken in 1981 of Theresa and her oldest daughter Linda.

Lightning Source UK Ltd.
Milton Keynes UK
UKHW04f2045081018
330212UK00001B/145/P

9 781732 209602